Terms Introduced with PSP0.1 (continued)

Total Size (T)—Actual	The actual total size of the program, generally $T = B + A - D + R$
New Reused Size—Actual	The actual size of the added code that is to be used on other projects after development

Terms Introduced with PSP1

PSP1 Project Plan Summary	
Size/Hour	The total added an ... divided by the hours required ... Hour = 60*(A&M, To Date)
Base Size (B)—Plan	When you plan to modify a previously developed program, the estimated or measured total size of that unmodified program is the base size.
Deleted Size (D)—Plan	The estimated size of the deletions from the base. It is estimated during planning.
Modified Size (M)—Plan	The estimated size of the changes to be made to the base program. It is estimated during planning.
Added Size (A)—Plan	The estimated size of the program additions. It is estimated as $A = A\&M - M$
Reused Size (R)—Plan	The estimated size of the previously developed programs that will be reused without change
Added and Modified Size (A&M)—Plan	When using PROBE, Projected Added and Modified Size (P) from the Size Estimating Template is entered here.
Total Size (T)—Plan	The planned total size of the program: $T = P + B - M - D + R$
New Reusable Size—Plan	The portion of the added code planned for addition to the reuse library
Estimated Proxy Size (E)	The estimated size (E) from the Size Estimating Template

Size Estimating Template	
Base Parts	The estimated and actual values of the Base, Deleted, and Modified size
Base Additions (BA)	The total estimated size of the code to be added to the base program(s)
Parts Additions (PA)	The total estimated size of the new program parts to be developed
Estimated Proxy Size (E)	The estimated size of the base additions plus the parts additions plus the size of the modifications to the base code: $E = BA + PA + M$
Projected Added and Modified Size (P)	The projected size of the added and modified code. Calculated on the Size Estimating Template as $P = \beta_0 + \beta_1*E$
β_0, β_1	Linear regression parameters for projecting size and development time. There are separate β values for the size and time estimates.
Correlation (R^2)	The correlation between the estimated proxy and actual sizes or between the estimated proxy size and actual development times for a set of programs.
Prediction Range	The 70% or 90% range within which an estimate is likely to fall. The size and time ranges are calculated on the Size Estimating Template.
LPI	The lower prediction interval, calculated separately for the size and the time estimates: $LPI = P - Range$ or $Time - Range$
UPI	The upper prediction interval, calculated separately for the size and the time estimates: $UPI = P + Range$ or $Time + Range$ *(continued)*

(PSP1 terms continued inside back cover)

PSP^{SM}

PSP^{SM}

A Self-Improvement Process for Software Engineers

Watts S. Humphrey

♦♦ Addison-Wesley

Upper Saddle River, NJ • Boston • Indianapolis • San Francisco
New York • Toronto • Montreal • London • Munich • Paris • Madrid
Capetown • Sydney • Tokyo • Singapore • Mexico City

Carnegie Mellon
Software Engineering Institute

The SEI Series in Software Engineering

U. S. Corporate and Government Sales
(800) 382-3419
corpsales@pearsontechgroup.com

For sales outside the U. S., please contact:

International Sales
international@pearsoned.com

Visit us on the Web: www.awprofessional.com

Library of Congress Cataloging-in-Publication Data:

Humphrey, Watts S., 1927–
 PSP : a self-improvement process for software engineers / Watts S. Humphrey.
   p. cm. — (The SEI series in software engineering)
  Includes bibliographical references and index.
  1. Software engineering. 2. Computer software—Management. I. Title. II. Series.
 QA76.758.H8624 2005
 005.1—dc22   2004030348

ISBN 0-321-30549-3
Text printed in the United States on recycled paper at Courier in Westford, Massachusetts.
Third printing, July 2007

CONTENTS

PREFACE

The record of most development groups is poor, but the record of software groups is particularly bad. The Standish Group reports that more than half of all software projects are seriously late and over budget, and that nearly one-quarter of them are cancelled without being finished.[1] Under 30% of the projects were considered successful. Most of the software developers I know are well aware of these problems and can even explain their causes: unrealistic schedules, inadequate resources, and unstable requirements. Although these problems are common and not hard to solve, few developers know how.

It is tempting to blame others for our difficulties, but a victimlike attitude doesn't solve problems. When you approach these software management problems in the proper way, you can generally solve them. However, this requires skills and practices that you may not have learned. It also requires dealing with management on management's terms. You can gain the required practices with the Personal Software Process (PSP).[2] This book describes the PSP and explains the practices and methods you will need to deliver quality products on predictable schedules. After learning these skills, you will be qualified to participate on a team

---

[1]The Standish Group International, Inc., 586 Olde King's Highway, Dennis, MA 02638; www. standishgroup.com.
[2]Personal Software Process, PSP, Team Software Process, and TSP are service marks of Carnegie Mellon University.

that uses the Team Software Process (TSP). Such teams are called **self-directed** because they define their own working practices and negotiate their plans and schedules with management. The final chapter of the book describes the TSP and how it helps to put you in charge of your own work.

Being a Software Engineer

An engineer is someone who knows how to consistently and predictably do quality work. Many of the states in the United States have regulations governing the practice of engineering and they do not allow people to call themselves engineers unless they have demonstrated competence in their professional specialty. Most engineering fields were originally established because the public demanded protection from unqualified work, particularly in building construction, steam power plants, and the like. Without such licensing, steam boilers frequently exploded and bridges collapsed. Although licensing did not magically solve all of these problems, it has been a big help.

Licensed engineers use known and proven methods, they are tested to ensure that they consistently do quality work, and they are required to demonstrate their competence at producing safe products. The difference between a licensed engineer and any other technical worker is that the engineer knows the proper ways to do his or her job and is required by law to work that way regardless of management, customer, or other pressures.

If we are to call ourselves engineers, we must learn to produce quality products on predictable schedules. This requires that we learn how to consistently meet our commitments and that we know how to handle the normal challenges of creative development work. Software development is the most challenging professional occupation I know of and we must all consistently use the best available methods to meet our management's and our customers' needs.

Quality Problems

Poor quality management causes many of today's software problems. Most software professionals spend nearly half of their time testing and fixing their products during development and final testing. Poor quality also leads to schedule problems, with defective products delivered long after they were committed. Although fixing a few defects may seem inconvenient, even fairly small programs can have hundreds of defects, and finding and fixing them can take many weeks or even months. Software quality starts with the individual developer. If any of the program modules that we develop have numerous defects, they will be hard to test, take time to integrate into larger systems, and be troublesome for our users.

Most of us can be highly productive when writing very small programs. However, our productivity falls off sharply when we develop larger programs. Although developing bigger systems involves some added architectural and design work, most of the added effort is caused by defects. The average amount of time it takes to find and fix each defect increases exponentially as programs become larger. However, if you can consistently write high-quality module-size programs, you will produce better products and improve your and your organization's productivity.

A disciplined software engineering process includes effective defect management, comprehensive planning, and precise project tracking and reporting. This book shows you how to use these disciplines to do better development work as an individual and as a TSP team member. It also shows why these practices are essential if you want to manage your own work.

The Benefits of Being a Software Engineer

As our lives increasingly depend on software, the demands for safety, security, and quality will only increase. This means that the demand for capable software professionals will also increase. Unfortunately, few software developers have any way to distinguish themselves from the many programmers who bang out poor-quality code. With PSP training, you can apply to the Software Engineering Institute to become a PSP-certified software professional. This will distinguish you from the many developers who have no unique qualifications. PSP training will also qualify you to participate on a TSP team, and PSP certification will assure potential employers that you are a professional who is capable of producing high-quality software for predictable costs and on committed schedules. Other personal benefits of PSP certification are the added recognition of being a skilled software professional and easier access to more responsible and higher-paying positions. Developers with such qualifications are now widely sought and will be increasingly needed in the future.

Who Should Learn the PSP?

Modern technical work involves many specialties, and the people who participate in developing modern products and systems now come from a wide range of disciplines. To produce quality products on predictable schedules, all of the work that these people do must be planned, managed, and quality-controlled. This means that just about everyone associated with system development must know how to do disciplined engineering work. It also means that just about anyone doing such work would benefit from learning the PSP.

Although the examples and exercises in this book concern developing small programs, this is only because, even for small programs, software development is a marvelously rich process that can be measured and analyzed. This makes the software process particularly suitable for teaching disciplined engineering practices. Most modern professionals in almost any technical field now learn to write programs during their education, so the PSP course is appropriate for almost anyone planning an engineering or technical career, and it is particularly appropriate for anyone planning to work in product or system development.

The Approach Taken by This Book

With the growing importance of software and software products, organizations will increasingly need software engineers who consistently use disciplined personal practices. To meet this need, we must learn and consistently practice these disciplines with every program we write. If we don't use sound development practices when writing module-size programs, there is little chance that we will use them when writing large programs.

When students start to program, they generally begin by learning a programming language. They practice on toy problems and develop the personal skills to deal with issues at this toy level. As they take more courses, they build their personal skills and can soon develop fairly large programs relatively quickly. These programming-in-the-small skills, however, are inherently limited. Although they may suffice on small-scale individual tasks, they do not provide an adequate foundation for solving the problems of large-scale, multiperson, distributed project teams.

This book follows a fundamentally different strategy. It scales down industrial software practices to fit the needs of module-size program development. It then walks you through a progressive sequence of software processes that provide a sound foundation for large-scale software development. By doing the exercises and using the methods described in this book, you will learn how to use the methods for yourself. Once you have learned and used these practices on module-size programs, you will have the skills to use them on larger projects. Although some additional requirements, design, implementation, and testing methods are needed for developing large programs, the basic software engineering disciplines taught by this book apply directly to large-scale system development. The reason, of course, is that large systems are built from collections of program modules that are much like the programs you develop in the PSP course.

The principal goal of this book is to guide you in developing the personal software engineering skills that you need to perform at your very best. Consider the challenge of improving personal performance. In sports, for example, runners know the length of the track, their personal time, their fastest time, and the record time for each event. With proper coaching and guidance, they learn their personal strengths and weaknesses and see how to improve. In software, without clear performance measures, few of us can understand our personal strengths and weaknesses or see how to improve. The methods in this book will help you to assess your own performance, to identify ways to improve, and to guide your improvement efforts.

In addition to helping you improve your personal performance, this book will also help you build the engineering skills needed for large-scale software work. You will learn how to make accurate plans, how to estimate the accuracy of these plans, and how to track your performance against them. You will use defect management, design and code reviews, design templates, and process analysis. You will do this with a defined and measured personal software process. These measurement and analysis disciplines will help you to evaluate your performance, to understand your strengths, and to see where you should try to improve. From all of this you will develop the tools you need to continue personal improvement throughout your professional career.

What's Involved in Learning the PSP

In learning the PSP, the benefits you get will depend on the effort you invest. Although there are many ways to organize a PSP course, the basic requirements are reading the 14 chapters of this book and completing the programming and report exercises provided on the SEI Web site (**www.sei.cmu.edu/tsp/**). This web site also includes various course plans. The original PSP course called for a total of ten exercise programs and five report exercises. Other strategies have used various numbers of program exercises, but the basic requirement is to write a program at each of the six PSP process levels plus an additional two to four programs to master the methods and build the data to support your continuing work.

Reading the chapters should not take too long; the time it takes to write the programs can vary widely. These PSP exercise programs have now been written many thousands of times, and I use a sample of 8,100 sets of PSP program data for many examples in this book. In writing these programs, half of the developers spent less than four hours each, and one-third averaged under three hours. To minimize your time, use the programming language and environment that you know best, and keep your designs simple and straightforward.

Because the PSP course involves writing programs, people often think it is a programming course. It is not. Even after writing all of the assigned programs, if you did not follow the prescribed PSP processes and gather, analyze, and use all of the specified data, you would not learn the PSP. This is a process course, and to avoid wasting your time, follow the prescribed process to write each program. If you have problems doing this, ask your instructor for help.

The following two suggestions will ensure that you get the most from the PSP course. First, do not substitute programs from your work for those called for by the text. Of the thousands of developers who have completed PSP training, no one has done this successfully. Taking this course involves learning new and unfamiliar methods. The exercises in this course are like experiments, and working programmers are universally reluctant to experiment with unfamiliar methods when they work on a project. Second, do not merely read the book and then try to apply the methods without doing the exercises. Until you have completed the course and the exercises, you will not be able to apply the methods on the job. At least, nobody has done so thus far.

Book Overview

The 14 chapters of this book introduce the PSP methods in steps. Chapter 1 describes the overall principles of the PSP and the introduction strategy. Chapters 2 and 3 explain how to follow a defined process and how to gather and use the data required to manage a programming development job. Chapters 4, 5, 6, and 7 cover estimating and planning, and Chapters 8 through 12 cover quality management and design. Chapter 13 describes how to use the PSP for various kinds of work, and Chapter 14 describes how the PSP methods are used in the TSP process and how the TSP guides PSP-trained software engineers in using these methods on a project. It also discusses the personal issues involved in learning and using the PSP.

Support Materials

This book has extensive support materials, which are available at **www.sei.cmu. edu/tsp/**. The support items are a data-gathering and planning tool, the PSP exercise assignment kits, and reference materials. Also included are pointers to PSP course descriptions and the addresses of SEI-authorized organizations that can help you to introduce and use the PSP and TSP in your organization. The PSP can also be taught as a university course. For this purpose, the online support materials include an instructor's guide, suggested slides for PSP course lectures, and class exercises. These items are also publicly available on the Web site.

Book Background and History

This is the fourth book I have written on the PSP. I wrote *A Discipline for Software Engineering* in 1995[3] and I published *Introduction to the Personal Software Process* in 1997.[4] *Introduction to the Team Software Process* followed in 2000.[5] The *Discipline* book was for a graduate course in computer science, and the introductory books were texts for undergraduate courses. In the intervening years, thousands of software developers have taken the PSP course and hundreds of TSP teams have used the PSP methods on their projects. The results have been far better than I had hoped.

This experience demonstrated that a PSP textbook was needed for industrial software developers. Although *Discipline for Software Engineering* covers all of the required materials, it also includes a number of topics that are of more academic interest and are not essential for teaching industrial software developers. Because course duration is a principal concern for industrial organizations, these more academic topics have been omitted from this book.

Acknowledgments

Working with software developers and teams to originally develop the PSP and to later introduce the TSP has been the most rewarding experience of my life. None of this work would have been possible without some daring people who were willing to try these ideas on their jobs. They had the vision and imagination to see new possibilities and the nerve to try these ideas in practice. To them, I owe a debt of gratitude.

My group at the Software Engineering Institute (SEI) is a joy to work with. They are all PSP trained and we all use the TSP for planning and managing our work. The members of this marvelously supportive group are Dan Burton, Anita Carleton, Noopur Davis, Caroline Graettinger, Jim McHale, Julia Mullaney, Jim Over, Marsha Pomeroy-Huff, Dan Wall, and Alan Willett. They are a great team to work with and I never lack for advice and assistance when I need it. In addition, Kim Campbell, Marlene MacDonald, and Jodie Spielvogle provide us with truly great support. I am also much indebted to SEI management for the encouragement and guidance they have provided for my work. This has been a great place to work.

[3]Watts Humphrey, *A Discipline for Software Engineering*, Addison-Wesley, 1995.
[4]Watts Humphrey, *Introduction to the Personal Software Process*, Addison-Wesley, 1997.
[5]Watts Humphrey, *Introduction to the Team Software Process*, Addison-Wesley, 2000.

In writing this book I have also had the help and support of many people. Several thousand software engineers have now taken the PSP course and provided the data I have used to refine and explain the methods. I greatly appreciate their efforts as well as the commitment and dedication of the many people who have now become PSP instructors. Their support has been essential in getting this material more widely understood and used. I also thank those who supported my original PSP work and participated in reviewing and teaching courses with early drafts of the original *Discipline for Software Engineering* text. That earlier work provided the foundation and experience needed for this book. In addition, I particularly thank the people who have helped me by reviewing early drafts of this book. They are Jim Alsted, Dan Burton, Anita Carleton, David Carrington, Rod Chapman, Noopur Davis, Caroline Graettinger, Carol Grojean, Capers Jones, Jim McHale, Julia Mullaney, Bob Musson, Paul Newson, Jim Over, Marsha Pomeroy-Huff, Ron Radice, Mark Sebern, Victor Shtern, Yeun-Chung Tan, Dan Wall, and Alan Willett.

Finally, when *Discipline for Software Engineering* was published, I dedicated it to Dr. John E. Yarnelle. He was my first mathematics teacher and the joy he imparted to the subject has been a lifelong inspiration. He had a remarkable ability to make mathematics and science both enjoyable and interesting. I was fortunate to have had such an inspiring teacher at an early age. Although it was many years before I had the opportunity to dedicate a book to him, he made an enormous contribution to my life. After publishing the *Discipline* book, I was able to find him and reestablish what had been a marvelous early relationship. I therefore dedicate this book to the memory of Dr. John E. Yarnelle.

—Watts S. Humphrey
Sarasota, Florida

1

The Personal Process Strategy

"This is an absolutely critical project and it must be completed in nine months."
The division general manager was concluding his opening remarks at the kickoff
for a project launch. As the Software Engineering Institute (SEI) coach, I had
asked him to start the meeting by explaining why the business needed this product and how important it was to the company. As he told the development team, the
company faced serious competition, and marketing could not hold the line for
more than nine months. He then thanked me and the SEI for helping them launch
this project and turned the meeting over to me.

After describing what the team would do during the next four days, I asked
the marketing manager to speak. He described the new features needed for this
product and how they compared with the current product and the leading com-
petitor's new product. He explained that this new competitive machine had just hit
the market and was attracting a lot of customer interest. He said that if this team
did not develop a better product within nine months, they would lose all of their
major customers. He didn't know how to hold the line.

On that happy note, we ended the meeting. The nine developers, the team
leader, and I went to another room where we were to work. The team was scheduled to present its project plan to management in four days.

The developers were very upset. They had just finished one "death march"
project and didn't look forward to another. After they calmed down a bit, Greg,

the team leader, asked me, "Why make a plan? After all, we know the deadline is in nine months. Why waste the next four days planning when we could start to work right now?"

"Do you think you can finish in nine months?" I asked.

"Not a chance," he said.

"Well, how long will it take?"

"I don't know," he answered, "but probably about two years—like the last project."

So I asked him, "Who owns the nine-month schedule now?"

"The general manager," he said.

"OK," I said, "Now suppose you go back and tell him that nine months is way too little time. The last project took two years and this is an even bigger job. What will happen?"

"Well," Greg said, "he will insist that nine months is firm. Then I will tell him that we will do our very best."

"Right," I said, "that's what normally happens. Now who would own the nine-month schedule?"

"Oh," he answered, "I would."

"Suppose you promise a nine-month schedule and then take two or more years. Would that cause problems?"

"It sure would," Greg said. "Nobody would believe us again and our best customers would almost certainly jump ship."

"Listen," I explained, "management doesn't know how long this project will take, and neither do you. As long as you are both guessing, the manager will always win. The only way out of this bind is for you to make a plan and do your utmost to accomplish what management wants. Then, if you can't meet his deadline, you will understand why and be able to defend your schedule."

Then Ahmed, one of the development team members, jumped in. "OK, so we need a plan, but how can we make one if we don't even know the requirements?"

"Very good question," I answered, "but do you have to commit to a date?"

"Well, yes."

"So," I asked, "you know enough to commit to a date but not enough to make a plan?"

He agreed that this didn't make much sense. If they knew enough to make a commitment, they certainly ought to know enough to make a plan. "OK," he said, "but without the requirements, the plan won't be very accurate."

"So," I asked, "when could you make the most accurate plan?"

"Well, I suppose that would be after we have done most of the work, right?"

"That's right," I replied, "and that's when you least need a plan. Right now, your plan will be least accurate but now is when you most need a schedule that you can defend. To do this, you must have a detailed plan." With that, the team agreed to make a plan.

This was one of our early Team Software Process (TSP) teams and the members had all been trained in the Personal Software Process (PSP). They then used the PSP methods described in this book to make a plan that they believed was workable, and they then negotiated that plan with management. Throughout the project, they continued to use the PSP methods and, in the end, they delivered a high-quality product six weeks ahead of the 18-month schedule management had reluctantly accepted.

While this book is about the PSP, most PSP-trained software engineers end up working on TSP teams. This chapter describes how the PSP develops the personal disciplines you will later need. Then, after you are familiar with the PSP methods, Chapter 14 explains how you will apply these disciplines when you work on a TSP team. It also shows some of the results that TSP teams have achieved and describes how the PSP helped them accomplish such impressive work.

1.1   The PSP's Purpose

The PSP is a self-improvement process that helps you to control, manage, and improve the way you work. It is a structured framework of forms, guidelines, and procedures for developing software. Properly used, the PSP provides the data you need to make and meet commitments, and it makes the routine elements of your job more predictable and efficient.

The PSP's sole purpose is to help you improve your software engineering skills. It is a powerful tool that you can use in many ways. For example, it will help you manage your work, assess your talents, and build your skills. It can help you to make better plans, to precisely track your performance, and to measure the quality of your products. Whether you design programs, develop requirements, write documentation, or maintain existing software, the PSP can help you to do better work.

Rather than using one approach for every job, you need an array of tools and methods and the practiced skills to use them properly. The PSP provides the data and analysis techniques you need to determine which technologies and methods work best for you.

The PSP also provides a framework for understanding why you make errors and how best to find, fix, and prevent them. You can determine the quality of your reviews, the defect types you typically miss, and the quality methods that are most effective for you.

After you have practiced the exercises in this book, you will be able to decide what methods to use and when to use them. You will also know how to define, measure, and analyze your own process. Then, as you gain experience, you can enhance your process to take advantage of any newly developed tools and methods.

The PSP is not a magical answer to all of your software engineering problems, but it can help you identify where and how you can improve. However, you must make the improvements yourself.

1.2   The Logic for a Software Engineering Discipline

Software has become a critical part of many of the systems on which modern society depends. Everyone seems to need more and better software faster and cheaper. Many development projects are now so large and complex that a few brilliant specialists can no longer handle them. Unfortunately, there is no sign of a magical new technology to solve these problems. We must improve the quality and predictability of our work or society will have to either forgo these more sophisticated systems or suffer the damages caused by unsafe, unreliable, and insecure software-intensive systems.

The intuitive software development methods generally used today are acceptable only because there are no alternatives. Most software professionals are outstandingly creative but a few do really poor work. And, not surprisingly, poor practices produce poor products. Most software products can be made to work, but only after extensive testing and repair. From a scientific viewpoint, the process is distressingly unpredictable. It is much like the Brownian motion of particles in a gas. Here, physicists cannot predict what any individual particle will do, but they can statistically characterize the behavior of an entire volume of particles. This analogy suggests that large-scale software development should be treated as a problem of crowd control: don't worry about what each individual does as long as the crowd behaves predictably.

This approach, while generally tolerated, has been expensive. An intuitive software process leaves the quality of each individual's work a matter of blind luck. Professionals generally develop their own private methods and techniques. There are no disciplined frameworks, no sets of acceptable standards, no coaching systems, and no conducted rehearsals. Even agreement on what would characterize "good" professional performance is lacking. Software developers are left to figure out their own working methods and standards without the guidance and support that professionals find essential in sports, the performing arts, and medicine.

This situation becomes critical when each individual's contribution is uniquely important. A symphony orchestra best illustrates this idea. Although the orchestra's overall performance is a careful blend of many instruments, each musician is a highly competent and disciplined contributor. Individual performers occasionally stand out, but their combined effect is far more than the sum of these parts. What is more, any single sour note by any individual could damage the entire performance.

Unlike the musician, the software engineer must be part composer as well as performer. Like an orchestral performance, however, the performance of a software system can be damaged by almost any defective part. Because computers today possess extraordinary computational power, one badly handled interrupt or pointer could eventually cause an entire system to crash.

As our products become larger and more complex and as they are used for increasingly critical applications, the potential for damaging errors increases. The software industry has responded to this threat with increasingly rigorous and time-consuming tests. However, this testing strategy has not produced either safe or secure products. New large-scale software systems commonly have many security vulnerabilities. The suppliers have reacted by quickly producing and distributing fixes for the identified problems. Although this strategy has worked in the past, the hacker community has learned to launch attacks between the fix notice and user installation. In addition, because the fixes are themselves often defective and because it is very expensive to make systemwide updates, many organizations cannot afford to keep their systems current.

The only practical answer is to produce higher-quality products. Because the current test-and-fix strategy is incapable of producing products of suitable quality, this is now a problem for the software profession. The only responsible solution is to improve the working disciplines of each software professional.

In most professions, competency requires demonstrated proficiency with established methods. It is not a question of creativity versus skill. In many fields, creative work simply is not possible until one has mastered the basic techniques. Well-founded disciplines encapsulate years of knowledge and experience. Beginning professionals in the performing arts, high-energy physics, and brain surgery, for example, must demonstrate proficiency with many techniques before they are allowed to perform even the most routine procedures. Flawless skill, once acquired, enhances creativity. A skilled professional in such fields can outperform even the most brilliant but untrained layperson.

The PSP strategy is to improve the performance of practicing software engineers. A disciplined software engineering organization has well-defined practices. Its professionals use those practices, monitor and strive to improve their personal performance, and hold themselves responsible for the quality of the products they produce. And most important, they have the data and self-confidence required to resist unreasonable commitment demands.

Practiced disciplines have the further benefit of making software engineering more fun. Developing programs can be highly rewarding. Getting some clever routine to work is an achievement, and it is enormously satisfying to see a sophisticated program do what you intended. This satisfaction, however, is often diluted by the treadmill of debugging and the constant embarrassment of missed commitments. It is not fun to repeatedly make the same mistakes or to produce poor-quality results. Regardless of how hard you worked, nobody appreciates a late, over-budget, or poorly performing product.

Although developers are initially nervous about the structure and discipline of the PSP, they soon find it helpful. They quickly learn to make better plans and to achieve them. They find that the PSP discipline accelerates routine planning and project management while giving them more time for requirements and design. They also find that they can do things they never thought possible. Their reaction is like one developer who wrote on his PSP exercise, "Wow, I never did this before!" He had just written a program containing several hundred lines of code that compiled and tested without a single defect. The PSP can help to make software engineering the fun it should be.

1.3   Using Disciplined Development Practices

To consistently follow disciplined software engineering practices, we need the guidance of a defined and measured process that fits our project's needs and is convenient and easy to use. We also need the motivation to consistently use this process in our personal work.

A defined process specifies precisely how to do something. If we have not done such work before and we don't have a defined process readily available, we will not know the proper way to proceed. For example, if management gives us an aggressive deadline and we want to do the job in the best possible way, we need to understand the basic requirements before starting on the design or coding work. Unfortunately, without prior experience or a lot of guidance, few of us would know precisely how to do the requirements work. It would probably take us several days or weeks to figure it out.

While we are learning how to do this requirements work, the project clock is ticking and we have made no headway with the requirements, design, or implementation. Therefore, when faced with a tight schedule, what can we do? Like most developers, we would do what we know how to do: design and code. We would also hope that somebody else would clear up the requirements problems before we got too far along with development. Unfortunately, that rarely happens and we often end up building the wrong product. That is one reason why nearly 25% of all software projects are cancelled before development is completed.

1.4   Operational Processes

When people talk about processes, they usually talk in general terms about things such as prototyping, the spiral model, or configuration management. We all know what they mean in general terms, but to actually use one of these processes we need to know precisely what to do and the order in which to do it. To do this, we must have what is called an **operational process** (Deming 1982).

Most developers object to the idea of using an operational process. They think of a process as something that is imposed on them. We all object to being told how to do our job, particularly by someone who doesn't know as much about the work as we do. Although following an operational process sounds fine in theory, the real question is "Whose process is it?" That is what this book is all about—learning how to define and follow the operational processes you select to do your work. That is what turns an operational process into a convenient and useful personal process. In fact, it is the process that you *want* to use to do your *own* work.

1.5 Defining and Using a Personal Process

This book shows you how to define and use an operational personal process. However, the examples use my processes and not yours. When first experimenting with the PSP, I did not know what such a process should look like or how it would feel to actually use one. Over several years, I developed and scrapped many processes because they didn't work, were too complex, or they just didn't feel comfortable. After doing this for nearly three years, and after writing 72 programs in Pascal and C++, I finally got the hang of it. Process design and development is not all that hard if you approach it properly and if you have actually used such a process yourself.

This book shortcuts this entire process learning cycle by having you use my processes so you can see what it feels like to follow a defined, measured, planned, and quality-controlled personal process. It is surprisingly easy and the results are truly amazing.

Take the example of Maurice Greene, who broke the world record for the 100-meter race in Athens on June 16, 1999. Although he had always been a fast runner, he had not been winning races and was becoming discouraged. Then he went to see coach John Smith in Los Angeles. Smith videotaped Greene doing a sprint, and then broke Greene's ten-second run into 11 phases. He analyzed each phase and showed Greene how to maximize his performance in every one. This became Greene's defined and measured personal running process. After several months of coaching, Greene started winning world records, and for several years he was known as the fastest man alive.

How would you like to be the fastest software developer alive, or the best by any other measure you choose? Today, we have no way to even talk about this subject. Our work is essentially unmeasured. Like Greene, we are all trying harder but we don't know whether we are improving, or even what improvement would look like. That is what a defined, measured, planned, and quality-controlled personal process can do for you. Although you may not want to put in the months of rigorous training needed to become a world champion, we all want to do our jobs in the best way we can. With a defined and measured process, not only will you know how well you are doing your job today, you will see how to improve, and to keep improving as long as you keep developing software.

So there it is. Like coach John Smith with Maurice Greene, I am asking you to use my process, at least until you see how such a process works. Although this process may not be the one you would design for yourself, once you have finished the PSP course, you will understand how these processes work and can design some of your own. For now, try to live with my processes and use them as well as you can. So far, thousands of developers have used them and many have continued to use them after finishing the PSP course.

1.6   Learning to Use a Personal Process

When you use this book in a PSP course, you will write several programs using the evolving process shown in Figure 1.1. The first process, PSP0, is a simple generic process that starts you writing programs much as you do today. The only addition

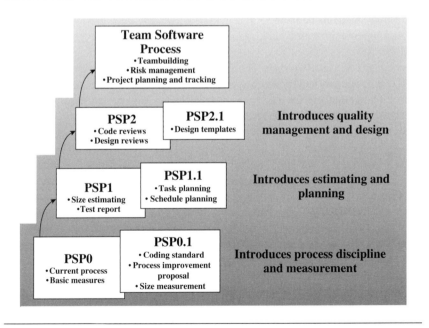

FIGURE 1.1 PSP PROCESS EVOLUTION

is time and defect measures. The PSP0 process is described in Chapter 2 and is used to write at least one program. Then, in Chapter 3, size measures are added to produce the PSP0.1 process that you use to write one or more additional programs. As you will see, size measures are essential for understanding how well you work. For Maurice Greene, for example, the size measure was the length of the track. Without that measure, he would not have known how fast he ran or if his times were improving.

Next, Chapters 4, 5, 6, and 7 show you how to use historical size and time data to estimate program size and development time. These chapters introduce the PSP1 and PSP1.1 processes that you use to write more programs. Chapter 8 covers quality, and Chapter 9 describes the PSP design and code reviews. With PSP2, you then write one or two more programs. Finally, in Chapters 10, 11, and 12, you write several more programs using the PSP2.1 process and the PSP design and quality methods. These methods show you how to develop essentially defect-free programs that you can test in a tenth of the time required for programs developed with prior methods.

1.7   Preparing for the Team Software Process

Once you finish this book and work through the program and report exercises, you will be prepared to work with other PSP-qualified professionals on a TSP team. The PSP shows you how to do quality work for predictable costs on committed schedules. This is software engineering. Once software developers have taken the PSP course and learned how to be software engineers, most of them end up working on teams that use the TSP. The rest of this book describes the PSP. Finally, Chapter 14 describes the TSP and shows how the PSP prepares you to be a TSP team member.

1.8   Summary

A personal process is something that you use to guide your work. With the PSP concepts and methods in this book, you can determine how well your current process works for you and learn where and how to improve. With the PSP, you will make accurate plans, consistently meet commitments, and deliver high-quality products. Although the exercises in this book concentrate on writing module-sized programs, that is only to help you learn PSP principles and methods. After completing this book, you should define and use your own personal processes for every aspect of your work, from requirements through test and product maintenance. Thousands of engineers have now been trained in the PSP and they have almost universally found that these methods help them to do much better work. They have also found that using these methods on a TSP team is a truly enjoyable and rewarding way to work. It will, in fact, change your life.

Reference

Deming, W. E. *Out of the Crisis.* Cambridge, MA: MIT Press, 1982.

2

The Baseline
Personal Process

If you are an experienced software developer, you probably wonder why you need a process. After all, you have written many programs and know what to do. How can a process help? A process can help in several ways.

First, most of us would like to improve the way we do our jobs. To do this, however, we must know how we work and where we could do better. Just like Maurice Greene, the runner described in Chapter 1, there is a big difference between generally knowing what you do and having a precisely defined and measured process. With a defined process, you can easily determine where you are having problems and identify ways to improve.

Second, even if you don't plan to improve the way you work, you will almost certainly have to commit to dates for completing your assigned tasks. To responsibly do this, however, you will need a plan. As you will see in the next few chapters, if you don't have data on your prior performance, it is almost impossible to make an accurate plan. And, as you will also see, to get the data you must have a precise definition of how you work. That is a process.

Finally, even if you don't need data, you will likely work at one time or another on large or complex jobs. Here, where the job steps are not obvious and where you must coordinate your work with others, you must agree with your coworkers on how to do the work. Regardless of what you choose to call it, the definition of how you plan to work is a process.

11

Therefore, whatever the name or format, you need a process. What you may not yet appreciate is that a defined, measured, and planned process will help you to make accurate plans, work predictably, and produce high-quality products. This book shows you how.

2.1   What Is a Process?

A process is the sequence of steps required to do a job, whether that process guides a medical procedure, a military operation, or the development or maintenance of software. The process definition is the description of the process. When properly designed, a software process definition will guide you in doing your work. When team members all follow different processes, or more commonly, where they use no defined processes at all, it is like a ball team with some members playing soccer, some baseball, and others football. On such teams, even the best individual players make a losing team. In contrast, when all team members follow a well-structured and properly defined process, they can better plan their work, coordinate their activities, and support each other.

The software process establishes the technical and management framework for applying methods, tools, and people to the software task. The process definition identifies roles, specifies tasks, establishes measures, and provides exit and entry criteria for the major steps. When properly used, a defined process also helps to ensure that every work item is properly assigned and that its status is consistently tracked. In addition, defined processes provide orderly mechanisms for learning. As better methods are found, they can be incorporated into the process definition. This helps all teams learn and it shows new teams how to take advantage of the experiences of their predecessors.

In summary, a defined process identifies a job's principal steps:

- ☐ It helps you separate routine from complex activities.
- ☐ It establishes the criteria for starting and finishing each process step.
- ☐ It enhances process understanding and provides a sound basis for process automation.

A defined process also includes measures:

- ☐ These measures can help you to understand your performance.
- ☐ They help you and your team manage your work.
- ☐ The process measures also help you to plan and manage the quality of the products you produce.

A defined process provides a sound basis for project management:

- ☐ You can make detailed plans and precisely measure and report your status.
- ☐ You can judge the accuracy of your estimates and plans.
- ☐ You can communicate precisely with users, other developers, managers, and customers about the work.

A defined process provides a solid foundation for process management and improvement:

- ☐ The process data help you identify the process steps that cause the most trouble.
- ☐ This will help you improve your personal performance.
- ☐ The process will simplify training and facilitate personnel mobility.
- ☐ Well-designed process definitions can be reused or modified to make new and improved processes.

2.2   Defining Your Own Process

Because every project and every team is different, when you work on a TSP team you will define your own processes. Rather than starting from scratch, however, you will have a family of proven TSP processes to build on. You will also have the experience gained from using the PSP processes in this book. The first step in preparing you to be on a TSP team is learning how to use an efficient personal process like the PSP. This chapter defines the initial process you will use for the first exercise in this book. In subsequent chapters, this process will be enhanced with new techniques and methods.

When you define your personal process, abstract tasks become structured and subject to analysis. Until you define the tasks in sufficient detail, however, you will not be able to improve. For example, it is hard to reason about a vaguely defined design process. Once you separate the design work into defined steps, however, you can understand the various elements of design work and see how they relate. To use a sports analogy, when people start weight lifting they think about building their arm, leg, or torso muscles. However, more experienced bodybuilders work on specific muscles: the deltoids, pecs, and abs. The clearer the focus, the better they can improve in each area. A precise process will help you to focus on the most promising areas for personal improvement.

2.3   Baseline Process Contents

The principal objective of PSP0, the baseline process, is to provide a framework for writing your first PSP program and for gathering data on your work. The data from the first PSP programs provide a comparative baseline for determining the impact of the PSP methods on your work. The PSP0 process is shown in simplified form in Figure 2.1. The scripts guide you through the process steps, the logs help you to record process data, and the plan summary provides a convenient way to record and report your results.

The PSP0 process provides the following benefits:

☐ A convenient structure for performing small-scale tasks

☐ A framework for measuring these tasks

☐ A foundation for process improvement

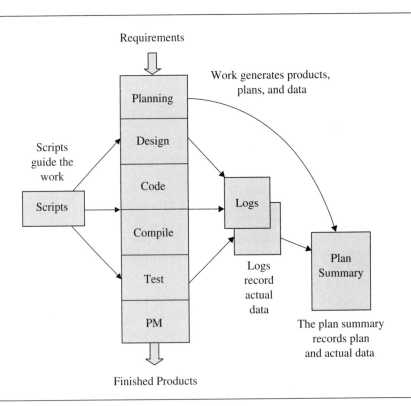

FIGURE 2.1 PSP0 PROCESS FLOW

Convenient Working Structure

When you perform any but the most trivial task, you always face the question of how to attack it. What do you do first, second, and so on? Even when you do this task planning properly, it takes time. With a defined process like PSP0, you can save task-planning time because you already determined how to do the tasks when you developed the process. When you do similar tasks many times, it is more efficient to develop and document the process once, rather than stop to devise a new process each time you start a job.

The PSP has been tested with many users, so there is no question that it works. In this book, you will use these predefined processes as a way to gain the knowledge and experience needed to later define the processes that best fit your needs. Although a defined process may sound restrictive, it is not. In fact, if you find your personal process inconvenient, uncomfortable, or not helpful, change it. Don't try to change the process until you have finished the PSP course, but after that it is yours and yours alone to manage. Then, when your process doesn't work for you, change it until it does.

Measurement Framework

A defined process establishes the process measures. This enables you to gather data on the time you spend on each task, the sizes of the products you produce, and the numbers of defects you inject and remove in each process step. These data help you to analyze your process, to understand its strengths and weaknesses, and to improve it. A defined process also gives measurements explicit meaning. When you define the coding phase, for example, the time spent in coding or the number of defects injected during coding are clear and specific values with precise definitions. This precision, however, requires that each process phase have explicit entry and exit criteria. With the baseline PSP0 process, some of the entry and exit criteria are not very precise. This is because PSP0 is a simple process. In later chapters, with progressively refined processes, these process steps are better defined.

Foundation for Improvement

If you don't know what you are doing, it is hard to improve the way you do it. Most software professionals would argue that they know what they do when developing software. However, they can rarely describe their actions in detail. When you follow a defined process, you are more aware of how you work. You observe your own behavior and can often see how to break each larger step into smaller elements. PSP0 is a first step in building this more refined understanding.

2.4   Why Forms Are Helpful

The PSP uses several forms. Although you might initially view this as a disadvantage, you will find the forms to be an enormous help. Consider, for example, how forms could help in planning your work. Any reasonably challenging job generally involves the following series of steps:

1. Determine what is to be done.
2. Decide how to do it.
3. Do it.
4. Check to make sure it is correct.
5. Fix any problems.
6. Deliver the final result.

Even for relatively simple tasks, the preparation and checking steps can take a significant amount of time. Suppose, for example, you were asked to produce a plan for your next development job. If you had never made such a plan, it would take some time to figure out what the plan should contain and how to produce it. Then you would have to decide on the plan format. Finally, you would make the plan. When you finished, you would still have to make several checks. First, did you leave out anything important? Second, was the information correct? Finally, are the format and content appropriate?

Suppose, instead, that you have a planning form. Now you don't need to decide what data to provide; the form tells you. All you do is fill in the blanks. The form may even provide guidance on how to do the required calculations. Then, when you are through, you should check to ensure you did the work properly. With a form, this is easy. You just ensure that all of the spaces contain data. Properly designed forms improve your efficiency and help you produce complete and correct results.

Just like a process, however, good forms are hard to develop and they must be periodically reviewed and revised to ensure that they still meet your needs. It is also important to ensure that all the process forms are designed as a coherent whole and supported by a well-designed tool. When forms are not carefully designed, they may call for duplicate information, terminology may be inconsistent, or formats may have confusing variations. This can cause inefficiency and error.

2.5   The PSP Process Elements

The overall PSP0 process is shown in Figure 2.1 (page 14). In the planning step, you produce a plan to do the work. Next are the four development steps: design, code, compile, and test. At the end, in the postmortem step, you compare your actual performance with the plan and produce a summary report. Although these planning and postmortem steps may not seem necessary when you are writing small programs, they are needed to gather the data to manage and improve your personal process. If the program is so simple that planning seems pointless, then making the plan should be a trivial task. However, these "trivial" programming jobs often hold surprises that a plan could have helped you anticipate. Also, as you gain experience, you will find that the postmortem is an ideal time to think about your data and to see where and how to improve.

A process may be simple or complex. Large defined processes, for example, will have many elements or phases, each of which can also be viewed as a defined process. At the lowest level, the process phases are composed of steps that have no further defined substructure. In a large process, for example, each step in the overall script would be a phase. At the next level, each phase would itself have a process definition with the steps being lower-level tasks. In the case of PSP0, the planning, development, and postmortem phases have process definitions, but design, code, compile, and test are named as unrefined steps. When a process element has a definition and a structure, I call it a phase. When it has no defined structure, I call it a step or a task.

The Planning Phase

A planning form guides you in producing and documenting your plan, and it provides a consistent format for the results. Although your initial PSP0 plans will not be very complex, they will provide some initial planning experience and data.

The Postmortem Phase

The postmortem phase is an important part of every process. When you have completed even a small project, you have a large amount of potentially useful data. Unless you promptly record and analyze the data, you probably will not remember precisely what you did or be able to correct any data-gathering errors. Even if you wait only a week to produce the summary report, you probably will waste time checking the data and trying to remember what you did and why. By learning and practicing the planning, reporting, analysis, and postmortem steps with these PSP exercises, you will build project planning and management skills. Experience with these small exercises will help you to develop the habits you will need to plan, track, and manage the larger-scale work you will do later on a TSP team.

2.6   The PSP0 Process

The PSP scripts guide you through the process steps. The principal script elements are its purpose, the entry criteria, the phases (or steps) to be performed, and the exit criteria. The PSP0 Process Script is shown in Table 2.1. It describes in words the simple process structure shown in Figure 2.1. A second PSP0 script, the Planning Script, is shown in Table 2.2. It briefly summarizes the planning steps for PSP0. With a simple process like PSP0, you may not need to look at the script very often, but with a more complex process, it is a good idea to use the script much like a checklist. Then, at the beginning and end of every process phase, you can verify that you didn't overlook anything important.

   The planning and postmortem phases are quite clear from the scripts in Tables 2.1, 2.2, and 2.4, but the development phase in Table 2.3 has four steps: design, code, compile, and test. Until these steps have been explicitly described,

TABLE 2.1 PSP0 PROCESS SCRIPT

Purpose		To guide the development of module-level programs
Entry Criteria		• Problem description • PSP0 Project Plan Summary form • Time and Defect Recording logs • Defect Type standard • Stopwatch (optional)
Step	Activities	Description
1	Planning	• Produce or obtain a requirements statement. • Estimate the required development time. • Enter the plan data in the Project Plan Summary form. • Complete the Time Recording log.
2	Development	• Design the program. • Implement the design. • Compile the program, and fix and log all defects found. • Test the program, and fix and log all defects found. • Complete the Time Recording log.
3	Postmortem	Complete the Project Plan Summary form with actual time, defect, and size data.
Exit Criteria		• A thoroughly tested program • Completed Project Plan Summary form with estimated and actual data • Completed Time and Defect Recording logs

TABLE 2.2 PSP0 PLANNING SCRIPT

Purpose	To guide the PSP planning process	
Entry Criteria	• Problem description • Project Plan Summary form • Time Recording log	
Step	**Activities**	**Description**
1	Program Requirements	• Produce or obtain a requirements statement for the program. • Ensure that the requirements statement is clear and unambiguous. • Resolve any questions.
2	Resource Estimate	Make your best estimate of the time required to develop this program.
Exit Criteria	• Documented requirements statement • Completed Project Plan Summary form with estimated development time data • Completed Time Recording log	

TABLE 2.3 PSP0 DEVELOPMENT SCRIPT

Purpose	To guide the development of small programs	
Entry Criteria	• Requirements statement • Project Plan Summary form with estimated program development time • Time and Defect Recording logs • Defect Type standard	
Step	**Activities**	**Description**
1	Design	• Review the requirements and produce a design to meet them. • Record in the Defect Recording log any requirements defects found. • Record time in the Time Recording log.
2	Code	• Implement the design. • Record in the Defect Recording log any requirements or design defects found. • Record time in the Time Recording log.
3	Compile	• Compile the program until there are no compile errors. • Fix all defects found. • Record defects in the Defect Recording log. • Record time in the Time Recording log.
4	Test	• Test until all tests run without error. • Fix all defects found. • Record defects in the Defect Recording log. • Record time in the Time Recording log.
Exit Criteria	• A thoroughly tested program • Completed Time and Defect Recording logs	

TABLE 2.4 PSP0 POSTMORTEM SCRIPT

Purpose	To guide the PSP postmortem process
Entry Criteria	• Problem description and requirements statement • Project Plan Summary form with development time data • Completed Time and Defect Recording logs • A tested and running program

Step	Activities	Description
1	Defect Recording	• Review the Project Plan Summary to verify that all of the defects found in each phase were recorded. • Using your best recollection, record any omitted defects.
2	Defect Data Consistency	• Check that the data on every defect in the Defect Recording log are accurate and complete. • Verify that the numbers of defects injected and removed per phase are reasonable and correct. • Using your best recollection, correct any missing or incorrect defect data.
3	Time	• Review the completed Time Recording log for errors or omissions. • Using your best recollection, correct any missing or incomplete time data.

Exit Criteria	• A thoroughly tested program • Completed Project Plan Summary form • Completed Time and Defect Recording logs

there is no way to tell when each step starts or ends. One common confusion, for example, concerns the distinction between coding and compiling. While the compiler is first run, that is clearly compile time, but how do you classify the time spent making the necessary coding changes to fix the defects found during compilation? In this book, I suggest that you classify the time spent correcting compile defects as compile time, and the time spent correcting and compiling test defects as test time. Similarly, the exit criteria call for a thoroughly tested program. Thorough testing should be defined for each program during planning, requirements, or design. Until all of the entry and exit criteria are precisely defined, however, the measurements for these steps are imprecise. To learn how to define and measure a process, I have found it most effective to start with imprecise measurements and then use the resulting data to make the process and its measures more precise.

2.7   PSP0 Measures

PSP0 has two measures:

1. The time spent per phase
2. The defects found per phase

The time spent per phase is a simple record of the clock time spent in each part of the PSP process. Although recording time and defect data can take a little time, several PSP support tools are available. When using one of these support tools, time recording is simple and takes little time. Time recording is discussed in Section 2.8, and PSP support tools are covered at the end of the chapter.

Recording defect data is a little trickier. For PSP0, record the specified data for every defect you find during compiling and testing. A defect is counted every time you change a program to fix a problem. The change could be one character, or it could be multiple statements. As long as the changes pertain to the same compile or test problem, they constitute one defect. Note that you determine the defect count by what you change in the program. Some compilers, for example, generate multiple error messages for a single defect. If these were all connected to one problem, then you would count it as one defect.

Also count defects in the test cases and other materials but treat each test case as a separate program and record defects against it. Defect recording is discussed in Section 2.9. Record all the defects found and fixed in a program against the new code written for that program. When you work on a team, you will often be enhancing larger programs, so you should separately record the defects found in the older base program against that program and not against the new code you are developing. In general, don't record any defects from any other programs, test procedures, or support systems against your new code. Doing so would make it difficult to assess the quality of your work.

The reason for gathering both time and defect data is to help you plan and manage your projects. These data will show where you spend your time and where you inject and fix the most defects. The data will also help you to see how your performance changes as you modify your process. You can then decide for yourself how each process change affects your productivity and the quality of your work products.

2.8   Time Recording

Table 2.5 shows the PSP Time Recording Log and Table 2.6 shows the Time Recording Log Instructions. Even though the time logs in various PSP support tools may look somewhat different, they all record the same basic data:

☐ The project or program being worked on

☐ The process phase for the task

☐ The date and time you started and finished working on the task

☐ Any interruption time

☐ The net or delta time worked on the task

☐ Comments

Before using any PSP support tool, you must enter your name, the project, and any other information required by the tool. When you start an activity, such as planning your first PSP program, enter the date and the time you start. Then, when you finish planning, enter the time you finished. The tool will automatically calculate the difference between the start and stop times in the *Delta Time* column. If you were interrupted during this phase, record the interruption time in the *Interruption Time* column.

With activities that take several hours or more, you will often be interrupted by phone calls, questions, or other things. If you consistently ignore the time such interruptions take, you will not know how much time you actually spent on any activity. Though you might think that the interruption times are so small that you could ignore them, they often turn out to be as long or longer than the actual time spent on the task itself. Unfortunately, with most interruptions, it is impossible to tell at the outset how long they will take. You could note in the *Comments* column when the interruption started and then calculate the lost time when the interruption was over. For an 18-minute interruption, for example, you would enter 18 in the *Interruption Time* column. Then the PSP support tool would subtract 18 minutes from the elapsed time at the end of the task.

Often, you will forget to record the start or stop times of a phase or an interruption. When you realize this, make your best estimate of the time involved. If you do this promptly, it is likely to be fairly accurate. I handle interruptions by keeping a stopwatch at hand and starting it when I am interrupted. I often work at home and my wife initially objected to being "on the clock." She has gotten used

TABLE 2.5 THE PSP TIME RECORDING LOG

Student _____   Date _____

Program _____   Program # _____

Instructor _____   Language _____

Project	Phase	Start Date and Time	Int. Time	Stop Date and Time	Delta Time	Comments

TABLE 2.6 TIME RECORDING LOG INSTRUCTIONS

Purpose	Use this form to record the time you spend on each project activity. For the PSP, phases often have only one activity; larger projects usually have multiple activities in a single process phase. These data are used to complete the Project Plan Summary. Keep separate logs for each program.
General	Record all of the time you spend on the project. Record the time in minutes. Be as accurate as possible. If you need additional space, use another copy of the form. If you forget to record the starting, stopping, or interruption time for an activity, promptly enter your best estimate.
Header	Enter your name and the date. Enter the program name and number. Enter the instructor's name and the programming language you are using.
Project	Enter the program name or number.
Phase	Enter the name of the phase for the activity you worked on, e.g., Planning, Design, Test.
Start Date and Time	Enter the date and time when you start working on a process activity.
Interruption Time	Record any interruption time that was not spent on the process activity. If you have several interruptions, enter their total time. You may enter the reason for the interrupt in comments.
Stop Date and Time	Enter the date and time when you stop working on that process activity.
Delta Time	Enter the clock time you actually spent working on the process activity, less the interruption time.
Comments	Enter any other pertinent comments that might later remind you of any unusual circumstances regarding this activity.

to it, however, and I have found it very convenient. It is actually easier to start and stop a stopwatch than to make notations in the Time Log. Some support tools have a built-in "stopwatch" function for this purpose. Again, when you occasionally forget to start or stop the stopwatch, make your best estimate as soon as you remember.

By keeping an accurate Time Log, you will discover that you are frequently interrupted. Because each interruption breaks your train of thought and is a potential source of error, reducing interruption frequency and duration can pay big dividends. Having such data helps you understand the interruption problem and figure out ways to address it. In one case, a TSP team member who used the PSP had a cubicle right beside the copy center and people would stop to chat with her when they were waiting for an available machine. Her interruption time records helped her justify a request to move to a different cubicle.

A common time-recording problem is deciding when a process phase starts or ends. With compile, for example, the time you enter for compile is the time you spend getting the first clean compile. As you find and fix defects in test, however, you will recompile each fix. Enter this time as part of the test phase and not as part of compile. Compile ends with the first clean compile. Even if you are designing as part of fixing a defect or you are struggling with an implementation problem, record your time in the phase in which you found and fixed the problem.

Although you must use judgment in deciding the phase you are in, the basic rule is to enter what seems most appropriate to you. With some interpretative and fourth-generation systems, this can be confusing, particularly when there is no compile step. With these systems, skip the compile phase and go directly from code to test. I discuss compile more completely in Section 2.11, and cover incremental development issues in Section 2.12.

2.9 Defect Recording

An example Defect Recording Log and its instructions are shown in Tables 2.7 and 2.8. When you first encounter a defect and decide to fix it, start counting the fix time. Once you have fixed the defect, enter all of the data for that defect. Most tools will automatically enter a unique defect number, but you will have to enter the defect type, the phase in which the defect was injected, the phase in which it was removed, the fix time, and a brief description of the defect. If you don't know any of these time or phase data, enter your best estimate. The *Remove* phase is the one in which you found the defect. If, for some reason, you fix a defect in a phase other than the one in which you found it, enter the phase in which it was *found* and note in the *Description* section where it was *fixed*. Also, if you make a mistake fixing one defect and later find and fix that new defect, note the number of the defective fix in the *Fix Ref.* column. With a little practice, you will usually be able to enter the data for one defect in a minute or less. The example data in Table 2.7 show how one developer completed his Defect Log for PSP exercise Program 1.

For defect type, use the number from the Defect Type Standard shown in Table 2.9. Although this standard is quite simple, it should be sufficient to cover most of your needs. If you prefer to use a different standard, you can develop your own, but wait until after you have completed PSP training and have enough data

TABLE 2.7 A DEFECT RECORDING LOG EXAMPLE

Defect Types

10 Documentation	60 Checking
20 Syntax	70 Data
30 Build, Package	80 Function
40 Assignment	90 System
50 Interface	100 Environment

Student Student 3   Date 1/19

Program Standard Deviation   Program # 1

Instructor Humphrey   Language C

Project	Date	Number	Type	Inject	Remove	Fix Time	Fix Ref.
1	1/19	1	20	Code	Comp.	1	

Description: Missing semicolon.

Project	Date	Number	Type	Inject	Remove	Fix Time	Fix Ref.
		2	20	Code	Comp.	1	

Description: Missing semicolon.

Project	Date	Number	Type	Inject	Remove	Fix Time	Fix Ref.
		3	40	Des.	Comp.	1	

Description: Wrong type on RHS of binary operator, must cast integers as float.

Project	Date	Number	Type	Inject	Remove	Fix Time	Fix Ref.
		4	40	Code	Comp.	1	

Description: Wrong type on RHS, constant should be 0.0.

Project	Date	Number	Type	Inject	Remove	Fix Time	Fix Ref.
		5	40	Code	Comp.	1	

Description: Wrong type on RHS, had to cast an integer as float.

Project	Date	Number	Type	Inject	Remove	Fix Time	Fix Ref.
		6	40	Des.	Comp.	7	

Description: Exponent must be integer, sqrt. Integral not correct.

Project	Date	Number	Type	Inject	Remove	Fix Time	Fix Ref.
		7	80	Code	Test	1	

Description: Std. dev. incorrect, subtract when should divide.

TABLE 2.8 PSP DEFECT RECORDING LOG INSTRUCTIONS

Purpose	Use this form to hold data on the defects you find and correct. These data are used to complete the project plan summary.
General	Record each defect separately and completely. If you need additional space, use another copy of the form.
Header	Enter your name and the date. Enter the program name and number. Enter the instructor's name and the programming language you are using.
Project	Give each program a different name or number. For example, record test program defects against the test program.
Date	Enter the date you found the defect.
Number	Enter the defect number. For each program or module, use a sequential number starting with 1 (or 001, etc.).
Type	Enter the defect type from the defect type list summarized in the top left corner of the form. Use your best judgment in selecting which type applies.
Inject	Enter the phase when this defect was injected. Use your best judgment.
Remove	Enter the phase during which you fixed the defect. This will generally be the phase when you found the defect.
Fix Time	Enter the time you took to find and fix the defect. This time can be determined by stopwatch or by judgment.
Fix Ref.	If you or someone else injected this defect while fixing another defect, record the number of the improperly fixed defect. If you cannot identify the defect number, enter an X.
Description	Write a succinct description of the defect that is clear enough to later remind you about the error and help you to remember why you made it.

to do a competent job. In addition, keep the number of defect types small until you understand your personal defect data and can be explicit about the types that most concern you. When you make a new standard, do it with care because changing the defect standard can invalidate your historical data.

TABLE 2.9 PSP DEFECT TYPE STANDARD

Type Number	Type Name	Description
10	Documentation	Comments, messages
20	Syntax	Spelling, punctuation, typos, instruction formats
30	Build, Package	Change management, library, version control
40	Assignment	Declaration, duplicate names, scope, limits
50	Interface	Procedure calls and references, I/O, user formats
60	Checking	Error messages, inadequate checks
70	Data	Structure, content
80	Function	Logic, pointers, loops, recursion, computation, function defects
90	System	Configuration, timing, memory
100	Environment	Design, compile, test, or other support system problems

Fix Time

Recording fix time can be a bit more of a problem. You will likely fix most compile defects in about a minute, so you can generally enter 1 under *Fix Time*. In some cases, however, you may think you can fix a problem in a minute but find that it takes a lot longer. If you do not use a stopwatch to track fix time, enter your best estimate. In test, however, it is easy to lose track of the time spent fixing each defect. In this case, it is generally wise to use a stopwatch or to record the clock time when you start and stop working on each fix. Some PSP support tools provide a timer for this purpose.

The Multiple-Defect Problem

One common problem concerns multiple defects: While fixing one defect, you encounter and fix another. In this case, separately record each defect and its fix time. For example, if you spent a few minutes fixing defect 18 while working on a more complex defect (defect 17), deduct the fix time for defect 18 from the total fix time for defect 17. Figure 2.2 illustrates this example for the data shown in Table 2.10. These defects were fixed in the test phase so they are all test defects:

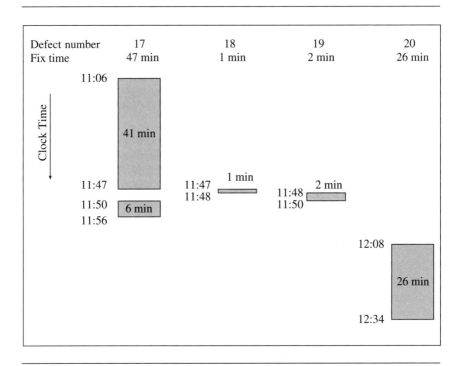

Defect number	17	18	19	20
Fix time	47 min	1 min	2 min	26 min

FIGURE 2.2 A DEFECT FIX TIME EXAMPLE

- □ Defect 17 is a logic defect you encountered in testing at 11:06. After 41 minutes, you had a fix ready to compile.
- □ While compiling the fix for defect 17, you encountered defect 18—a typographical error you made while fixing defect 17. You found it at 11:47 and fixed it in 1 minute.
- □ While fixing defect 18, you noticed defect 19 and started to fix it at 11:48. It was a wrong name that had been introduced in coding. It took 2 minutes to fix.
- □ After fixing defect 19, you spent 6 more minutes compiling and testing the fix to defect 17 before you were convinced you had fixed it. Your total elapsed time was 50 minutes but the actual fix time for defect 17 was only 47 minutes.
- □ A little later in testing, you found defect 20. It is a logic error that you injected while fixing defect 17. It took 26 minutes to fix.

The total elapsed time for all of this fix activity was 76 minutes, with 12 minutes of intervening test time between the end of defect 17 at 11:56 and the start of defect 20 at 12:08. You presumably stopped the clock on defect 17 at 50 minutes

TABLE 2.10 A MULTIPLE-DEFECT EXAMPLE

Project	Date	Number	Type	Inject	Remove	Fix Time	Fix Ref.
1	1/10	17	80	Des.	Test	47	

Description: StepPointer advanced extra step when CycleCount loop exceeded limit

Project	Date	Number	Type	Inject	Remove	Fix Time	Fix Ref.
		18	20	Test	Test	1	17

Description: Misspelled Step-counter when fixing 17

Project	Date	Number	Type	Inject	Remove	Fix Time	Fix Ref.
		19	50	Code	Test	2	

Description: Noticed SummaryFile improperly referenced

Project	Date	Number	Type	Inject	Remove	Fix Time	Fix Ref.
		20	80	Test	Test	26	17

Description: Forgot to adjust SyncPointer when fixing 17

when you thought you had it fixed. However, subsequent testing showed that you introduced defect 20 while fixing defect 17. This defect took another 26 minutes to fix. Here, defects 18 and 20 are both noted in the Defect Recording Log in Table 2.10 as injected during testing. The fact that these were fix errors is noted with an entry in the *Fix Ref.* space. You will find this information helpful when you later analyze your data. Only the times for defects 18 and 19 are deducted from the elapsed time of 50 minutes to arrive at the fix time of 47 minutes for defect 17. Your Defect Recording Log now has four new defects, as shown in Table 2.10.

These defect data are only used by you (and later by your TSP team) to decide where and how to improve your process. Although numerical precision is not critical, the fix times help identify the time saved by your process changes. Fix times for identical defect types are generally five to ten or more times longer in the test phases than earlier in the process. These fix time data will demonstrate the value of removing defects early in the process. They will also help you evaluate the cost and schedule consequences of your personal process improvements.

In the *Description* spaces, describe each defect in enough detail so you can figure out how to prevent similar defects in the future or how to find them earlier in the process. A simple description, usually just a few words, is generally adequate. For a more complex defect, however, you may have to write a more complete description. Make this description clear enough that, even weeks later, you can decide how that defect could have been prevented or found earlier. Because you will use the data to help improve your process, you need good records.

Record the data on each defect when you fix it. If you don't, you probably won't remember it later. In any but the smallest programs, there are generally so many defects that they are easily confused. Once you join a TSP team, your defect data will help you and your teammates to consistently produce products that have few if any defects left after customer delivery. You will also save many hours, weeks, or even months of test time. To get these test-time savings, however, you must have formed good defect-recording habits during PSP training and you must continue recording and analyzing your defects when you subsequently work on a TSP team.

2.10   The PSP0 Project Plan Summary

The PSP0 Project Plan Summary form is shown in Table 2.11, and its instructions are provided in Table 2.12. If you properly log all of your time and defect data, most PSP support tools will automatically enter the actual values in the Project Plan Summary form. You will, of course, have to enter the plan data yourself.

In planning Program 1, use whatever method you can to estimate how much total time you think it will take to write the program. If you don't have a better way, you will have to guess. Enter this number in the support tool as the total planned time for Program 1. Because you don't yet have data on the distribution of your development time by phase, you cannot allocate your total time among the PSP phases for the first program.

During the postmortem, examine the data in the completed Project Plan Summary form. Although the support tool will have entered the actual time and defect data for you, you must ensure that these data are correct. For example, if the Plan Summary showed that you injected more defects than you removed, check the Defect Log to find and fix the problem. Similarly, if the times for any phases look wrong, check the Time Log to find the mistake and fix it. Example data for a completed Project Plan Summary form are shown in Table 2.11.

The *To Date* column in the Project Plan Summary form holds the actual time and defect data for the programs you have written for the PSP course. For example, Student 3 spent 30 minutes in designing Program 1. Because this was his first program, he also entered 30 in the *To Date* column for design. With Program 2, if he spent 25 minutes in design, the actual design entry would be 25, but the *To Date* design entry would be 55 (30 + 25). The defect *To Date* entries are made in the same way.

The *To Date %* column shows the distribution of the *To Date* data among the phases. For example, Student 3 injected 2 defects in design and 5 during coding for a total of 7. Because 2 is 28.6% of 7, he entered 28.6 in the *To Date %* column for actual defects injected in design. The other *To Date %* entries are calculated in the same way.

TABLE 2.11 EXAMPLE OF THE PSP0 PROJECT PLAN SUMMARY

Student	Student 3	Date	1/19
Program	Standard Deviation	Program #	1
Instructor	Humphrey	Language	C

Time in Phase (min.)	Plan	Actual	To Date	To Date %
Planning		5	5	4.3
Design		30	30	25.6
Code		32	32	27.4
Compile		15	15	12.8
Test		5	5	4.3
Postmortem		30	30	25.6
Total	180	117	117	100.0

Defects Injected		Actual	To Date	To Date %
Planning		0	0	0.0
Design		2	2	28.6
Code		5	5	71.4
Compile		0	0	0.0
Test		0	0	0.0
Total Development		7	7	100.0

Defects Removed		Actual	To Date	To Date %
Planning		0	0	0.0
Design		0	0	0.0
Code		0	0	0.0
Compile		6	6	85.7
Test		1	1	14.3
Total Development		7	7	100.0
After Development		0	0	

2.11   The Compile Phase

The compile phase generally causes a lot of debate. First, if you are using a development environment that does not compile, then you should merely skip the compile step. If, as is usual, you have a build step, however, you can record the build time and any build errors under the compile phase. However, in my experience, the build activity is generally so short and contains so few build defects that the resulting data are not very useful. As a result, at least with VB.NET, I recorded my build time as well as my build defects under test. If you would like a separate record of these data, you could record them under compile.

For those environments that have a compile step, the compile data are extremely useful and I urge you to gather complete compile time and defect data.

TABLE 2.12 PSP0 PLAN SUMMARY INSTRUCTIONS

Purpose	To hold the plan and actual data for programs or program parts
General	"To-Date" is the total actual to-date values for all products developed.
Header	Enter your name and the date. Enter the program name and number. Enter the instructor's name and the programming language you are using.
Time in Phase	Enter the estimated total time. Enter the actual time by phase and the total time. To Date: Enter the sum of the actual times for this program plus the To-Date times from the most recently developed program. To Date %: Enter the percentage of To-Date time in each phase.
Defects Injected	Enter the actual defects by phase and the total actual defects. To Date: Enter the sum of the actual defects injected by phase and the To-Date values for the most recent previously developed program. To Date %: Enter the percentage of the To-Date defects injected by phase.
Defects Removed	To Date: Enter the actual defects removed by phase plus the To-Date values for the most recent previously developed program. To Date %: Enter the percentage of the To-Date defects removed by phase. After development, record any defects subsequently found during program testing, use, reuse, or modification.

Some developers feel that the compile defects are unimportant and not worth recording. We now have data on thousands of programs written with the PSP and it is clear that those developers who gathered and analyzed all of their defect data were more productive and produced much higher quality products than those who did not. Therefore, do your best to gather complete defect data during PSP training. It will not take much time and the results will be worth the effort.

2.12   Incremental Development

There are many styles and methods for writing programs. Although some people will argue that one method is better than another, you are the only person who can make that determination. Unfortunately, most developers make such decisions

based solely on their intuition and what other people tell them. With the PSP, however, you will have the data to determine which methods most help you to efficiently produce quality programs for predictable costs and on committed schedules.

Some developers, when they take the PSP course, argue that the only way
they can develop programs is to write a few lines of code and then compile and
test them to make sure that they run. Then they write another couple of lines
and compile the combined old and new code and run it. They follow this incremental approach until they have a complete running program. Although there are
many potential problems with this approach, no development approach is entirely
problem-free.

Unfortunately, this particular method of developing programs requires a different process than the one presented with the PSP. Although there are many ways
you could define a process to work this way, these processes are generally difficult
to teach. The problem is not that the processes are inefficient or bad, but they are
hard to measure and the resulting process data are difficult to interpret.

You could use whatever method you prefer for writing the PSP programs and
merely record the small increments of time for each step. For example, if you
spent three minutes writing two lines of code, a minute compiling the code, and
another three minutes testing it, you could record your time that way. Then, with
the next few lines, another four minutes of coding would bring your coding time
up to seven minutes, and so forth. You could then accumulate your time in this
way until you completed the program. However, doing this has two disadvantages.
First, some of the PSP methods introduced a little later will be more difficult to
handle with this type of process. Second, your data will not be comparable to that
of the many thousands of developers who have already taken the PSP course. This
will make it more difficult for your instructor to assess your work and to advise
you on how best to improve.

In Chapter 13, I discuss various example processes you might want to try out
after you complete the PSP course. One of these is the PSP3 process, which follows
an iterative development strategy. However, PSP3 presumes that your iterations are
each somewhat larger than a few lines of code. I also discuss the process I used in
learning VB.NET. Here, I was using a very large and complex environment with
many canned functions that I did not know. I found it most convenient to use a prototyping process that first produced running code. I then produced and reviewed the
program's design. This process enabled me to experiment with the various functions to find the ones that best fit my needs without worrying about recording all the
defects normally associated with learning. Once I found something that seemed to
work properly, however, I did record all the subsequent defects I found.

During the PSP course, try to follow the process given in the scripts. Then,
after you have learned the PSP, feel free to modify the process in whatever way
suits you. However, as you do, gather data on your work and use that data to guide
you in deciding on the best processes and methods to use.

2.13   PSP Tool Support

When I originally developed and taught the PSP, no support tools were available, so we had to manually gather the data with paper forms, make the required analysis calculations by hand or on a spreadsheet, and store the data on paper records or a personal data repository. Although this manual process was inconvenient and error prone, it took surprisingly little time. Now, with the available PSP support tools, data recording is relatively painless and the required process calculations are done automatically. For information on the available PSP support tools, see **www.sei.cmu.edu/tsp/**.

2.14   Summary

A defined process can help you to understand your performance as a software developer and to see where and how to improve. This chapter introduces the PSP0 process, which you will use to complete the initial programming assignment in the text.

With the PSP0 process, you measure the time spent in each development phase and the defects you inject, find, and fix. You will also use a support tool for defect and time recording. Then you will use these data in later chapters to make better plans and to improve the quality and productivity of your work.

2.15   Exercises

The standard assignment for this chapter uses PSP0 to write one or more programs. The assignment kits for these programs can be obtained from your instructor or at **www.sei.cmu.edu/tsp/**. The PSP assignment kits contain the specifications for the exercise programs and the PSP process scripts. In completing the assignments, faithfully follow the specified PSP process, record all required data, and produce a program report according to the specification given in the assignment kit.

3

Measuring Software Size

To make a software development plan, first produce a conceptual design and then estimate the size of the product to be built to that design. With the size estimate, you can then estimate how long it will take to develop the product. Before you can estimate a program's size, however, you must have a way to measure size. This chapter describes the principal ways to measure the sizes of various products and how to use these measures for project planning and quality management. Later chapters show how to estimate program size and development time. They also describe how to produce a schedule and how to measure, track, and report development status. The planning process, however, starts with size estimates, which require size measures.

3.1   Size Measures

The first question to address in selecting a software size measure is whether that measure will be useful for estimating development time. For a size measure to be useful, it must be precise, specific, and automatically countable. For example, although *number of pages* might seem to be a very precise and simple measure, even it must be properly specified. Are these single-spaced or double-spaced pages and are they in single or multiple columns? How will you count empty or partially filled pages? And what size font should you use? These are the kinds of questions you must answer for every size measure you plan to use.

Using Size Measures in Planning

Not surprisingly, more resources are required to develop large programs than small ones. If the size of a program is approximately proportional to the time required to develop it, the size and time data are said to be correlated. **Correlation** is the degree to which two sets of data are related. The correlation value, r, varies from -1.0 to 1.0. When r is close to one, then the two sets of data, say x and y, are highly correlated. That means that increases in the value of x imply proportionate increases in the value of y. When r is close to -1.0, increases in x would imply proportionate decreases in y. For the PSP, we are principally interested in positive correlations. To be useful for estimating and planning purposes, the value of r should be greater than 0.7. Although many PSP tools calculate the correlation, the mathematical formula for the calculation is shown in Box 3.1.

BOX 3.1 CALCULATING THE CORRELATION COEFFICIENT

1. To determine if two sets of data, x and y, are sufficiently related for planning purposes, calculate their correlation coefficient and significance.

2. Start with n pairs of numbers x_i and y_i where x is the set of estimates and y is the actual data for those estimates.

3. The correlation r of the two sets of data is given by the following equation:

$$r(x,y) = \frac{n \sum_{i=1}^{n} x_i y_i - \sum_{i=1}^{n} x_i \sum_{i=1}^{n} y_i}{\sqrt{\left[n \sum_{i=1}^{n} x_i^2 - \left(\sum_{i=1}^{n} x_i \right)^2 \right]\left[n \sum_{i=1}^{n} y_i^2 - \left(\sum_{i=1}^{n} y_i \right)^2 \right]}}$$

4. The values of r vary from -1.0 to $+1.0$. If $|r| >= 0.7$, the relationship is considered good enough for estimation purposes.

5. The closer $|r|$ is to 1.0, the better the predictive value of the relationship. However, because small values of n can result in high correlations, the significance of the correlation should also be considered. The significance calculation is shown in Box 3.2.

The degree to which a correlation measure is meaningful is also important. It is indicated by what is called **significance**. The significance measures the probability that this relationship could have occurred by chance. Thus, a significance of 0.25 indicates that one-quarter of the time, this result could have occurred as the result of random fluctuations in the data. Conversely, a significance of 0.005 indicates that this result would likely occur at random only about once in 200 times. That is a very high significance. A significance of 0.05 is generally considered good; one of 0.20 is considered poor. The significance calculation is described in Box 3.2. By finding the correlation and significance for the size and time data for a number of programs, you can determine whether that size measure would be a useful predictor of development time.

For database work, for example, a count of database elements is a potentially useful size measure. Figure 3.1 shows how the count of database elements (fields, GUI controls, etc.) compares with the development time for several database development jobs. In this case, the correlation value is $r = 0.84$ with a significance of 0.01. Because r is greater than 0.7, this relationship is good enough for estimating purposes. In addition, with a 0.01 significance, the chance that this relationship occurred by chance is less than 1%.

BOX 3.2 CALCULATING SIGNIFICANCE

1. The significance value indicates whether the correlation of two sets of data, x and y, is sufficiently strong that the data can be used for estimating purposes or the relationship likely occurred by chance.

2. Start with n pairs of numbers x_i and y_i where x is the set of estimates and y is the actual measured values for the estimated items.

3. If the correlation $|r|$ of these data is greater than 0.7, calculate its significance.

4. Calculate the t value for this relationship as follows:

$$t = \frac{|r(x, y)|\sqrt{n-2}}{\sqrt{1 - r(x, y)^2}}$$

5. Since r can be plus or minus, the absolute value, $|r(x, y)|$, is used.

6. Look up the value of the t-distribution in Table 3.1. Use the 95% column and, for $n = 5$, use 3 degrees of freedom ($d = 3$).

7. A t value of 3.182 or greater indicates a significance of less than (better than) 0.05, or less than a 5% chance of having occurred by coincidence. Values less than 0.05 are considered adequate.

TABLE 3.1 VALUES OF THE *t*-DISTRIBUTION FOR VARIOUS
AMOUNTS OF DATA

Degrees of Freedom *d*	70% Prediction Interval	90% Predication Interval	95% Prediction Interval
1	1.963	6.314	12.706
2	1.386	2.920	4.303
3	1.250	2.353	3.182
4	1.190	2.132	2.776
5	1.156	2.015	2.571
6	1.134	1.943	2.447
7	1.119	1.895	2.385
8	1.108	1.860	2.306
9	1.100	1.833	2.262
10	1.093	1.812	2.228
15	1.074	1.753	2.131
20	1.064	1.725	2.086
30	1.055	1.697	2.042
∞	1.036	1.645	1.960

Figure 3.2 shows a counterexample for which size and time are not highly correlated. These data are for the time it took me to write 25 chapters of a book. Although the times were relatively balanced around the average of 27.5 hours, they varied from 8.8 to 42 hours and the correlation was a very low 0.26. With an *r* of less than 0.7, these page counts were not very useful as a size measure for estimating the writing time for these chapters. You would think that writing time would be closely related to the number of pages written, but the content of these chapters was so different that page count did not accurately predict writing time. However, because page count is generally a useful measure for predicting the average writing time of large documents, I use it, particularly as I haven't found anything that works better.

On large projects, developers usually produce many kinds of products. In addition to code, there may be manuals, databases, support packages, or other items. Because these products all require development effort, you should plan their development. Some of the size measures that development projects typically use are document pages, test scenarios, requirements pages, and database fields or records. Again, to be useful, these measures must meet the planning criteria for usefulness: the size values must correlate with the time needed to develop the products, and

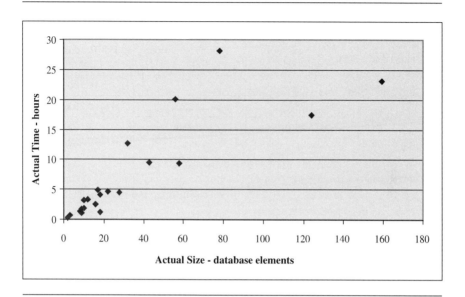

FIGURE 3.1 DATABASE ELEMENTS VERSUS DEVELOPMENT TIME

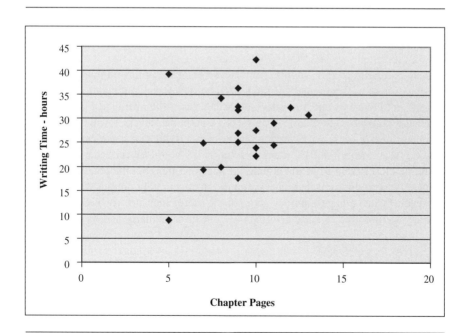

FIGURE 3.2 BOOK CHAPTER PAGES VERSUS WRITING TIME

the measures must be precise, specific, and automatically (or otherwise easily) countable:

- □ **Precise Size Measures:** A precise size measure gives an exact value for the size of a product. To be precise, the measure must be exactly defined by the product's content. Then, every time the size is measured, the result must be the same, with no room for judgment or opinion.

- □ **Specific Measures:** A specific measure is one that is based on defined product properties. For example, a C++ size measure would be defined differently from one for VB, SQL, Pascal, and so forth.

- □ **Countable Measures:** Once you have selected a precise and specific size measure, you need an automated means to count it. Manually counting almost any size measure is tedious, time-consuming, and inaccurate. For large products, it is practically impossible.

3.2   Establishing a Database Counting Standard

For database work, there are many ways to count product elements. For example, if you were producing a database, you might count fields or tables. When developing programs to use a database, you might count queries, GUI elements, tables, or code lines. In addition, when using a GUI tool, you could count the buttons, boxes, labels, and so on. The key, however, is to determine which of these elements is likely to be most significant in determining your development effort. In the example shown in Figure 3.1 (see p. 39), the developer counted all of the database tables and forms and all of the buttons and controls in the GUI interface. Because the correlation had an r of 0.84 with a significance greater than 0.01, this was a useful size measure. However, the developer found that some large database queries also required a significant amount of VB code. Because he had not included a line-of-code (LOC) measure to cover the code development work, his estimates for a couple of larger jobs were too low.

3.3   Establishing a Line-of-Code Counting Standard

A measure of the number of source lines of code (sometimes called **SLOC**) meets all the criteria for a useful size measure for many kinds of programming. Because LOC correlates well with development effort for the exercise programs in this book, this measure is used in many of the examples in this and later chapters.

However, the PSP estimating methods are equally usable with other size measures such as database elements, document pages, forms, or any other measure that meets the size-measurement criteria and correlates with development effort.

The first step in defining a LOC counting standard is to establish a counting strategy. You could take a large-scale view of logic statements and treat each construct as a single countable line. Then, using a simple Pascal-like language, for example, the statement

    if A>B
        then begin A := A–B end
        else begin A := A+B end;

would be one statement. Similarly, it would still be one statement if you wrote it as

    if A>B
        then
            begin
                A := A–B
            end
        else
            begin
                A := A+B
            end;

On the other hand, you could count selected keywords and functions such as **if**, **then**, **else**, **begin**, **end**, and **assignment** (:=). Your count in this case would be nine. Although the choice is arbitrary, you must be explicit and consistent.

For my work, I have adopted the following simple guideline:

☐ Count logical statements such as, for example, every semicolon and selected keywords.

☐ Write every countable statement on a separate line.

☐ Count all statements except blank and comment lines.

☐ Count each language separately.

These guidelines produce open and clean-looking code that looks like the preceding nine-line example. It also simplifies automatic LOC counting. Blanks and comment lines are not counted because the number of logical program statements generally determines the development effort. If, however, you find that the time required to write comments is significant, then you could decide to count them. The way to decide this would be to measure size with and without counting comment lines to determine which provides a higher correlation with development time.

3.4   Size Accounting

Even after selecting the size-measurement definition, there are many ways to use the measures. This is particularly true when you work on a development team that produces multiple versions of large legacy products. To track all of the program changes and additions and to gather the data you need for estimating, you must use a size accounting system.

Although size seems like a simple concept, size measures can be hard to track if they are not properly defined and used. For example, if you started with a 1,000-LOC program and added 100 LOC, the result would be 1,100 LOC. If you merely wrote a new 100-LOC program, however, the result would be a 100-LOC program. Although this result seems obvious and the development effort would probably be roughly comparable, the sizes of the resulting products are vastly different. Size accounting will help you to understand and properly use size data. The basic program elements in the size accounting system are as follows:

- **Base:** This is the measure of the initial unmodified base program to which subsequent enhancements are added. For a new program, the base size would be zero.

- **Added:** This is the new code that is added to the base. Again, for a new program, the base size would be zero and the added code would be all the code.

- **Modified:** The modified code is that part of the base code that is changed.

- **Deleted:** The deleted code is that part of the base code that is removed and not used in the next program or program version.

- **Reused:** When an existing program or program routine is copied from some library or otherwise included in a new program, it is counted as reused code only if it is unmodified. If it is even slightly modified, the size of this included program is included in the base size and the changes are counted as modifications.

- **Added and Modified:** For many kinds of software development work, the effort required to write a new LOC is roughly comparable to the effort required to modify an existing LOC. In these cases, it is convenient to combine the Added size measures and Modified size measures into an "Added and Modified" size measure. This is the measure generally used in the PSP exercises for estimating development effort and for measuring and managing quality.

□ **New Reusable:** A common development strategy is to build a library of commonly used functions and to reuse them whenever they are subsequently needed. Because this strategy can save a great deal of effort, the PSP includes a New Reusable size measure for the newly developed code that is planned for inclusion in the reuse library. If you rework base code to be reusable, also mark it with an asterisk.

□ **Total:** Total program size measures the entire program, regardless of how its parts were produced.

The reason to track program additions, deletions, and modifications is illustrated in Figure 3.3. Starting with version 0, which has a counted size of 350 LOC, you add or modify 125 LOC. Thus, you expect to have a finished version 1 of 475 LOC. When you measure version 1, however, its total size is only 450 LOC. Where did the 25 LOC go?

This can best be explained by using the size accounting format shown in Table 3.2. Here, starting with a new program base of zero LOC, you develop 350 new LOC, for a total of 350 LOC in version 0. This 350 LOC is the base on which you develop version 1. In developing version 1, you add 100 LOC and modify 25 LOC of the V1 base. The 125 LOC is thus made up of 100 LOC new and 25 LOC modified. Notice, however, that the 100 LOC are shown only in the *Added* column on the left of Table 3.2, but the 25 LOC are shown in both the *Added* and *Subtracted* columns. The reason is that a modified LOC must be counted as a one-line addition and a one-line deletion. This is because that line is already counted in the base. If you don't subtract the 25, you will double-count it. Version 1 (or version 2 base) now is shown to contain 450 LOC, just as the counter indicated.

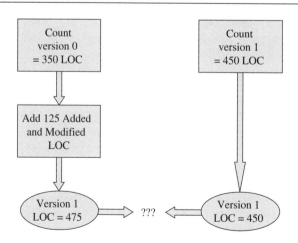

FIGURE 3.3 THE SIZE ACCOUNTING PROBLEM

TABLE 3.2 SIZE ACCOUNTING EXAMPLE

	Added	Subtracted	Net Change	Base
Base V0				0
Added	350			
Deleted		0		
Modified	0	0		
Reused	0			
Totals V0	350 –	0 =	350 +	= 350
Base V1				350
Added	100			
Deleted		0		
Modified	25	25		
Reused	0			
Totals V1	125 –	25 =	100 +	= 450
Base V2				450
Added	60			
Deleted		200		
Modified	75	75		
Reused	600			
Totals V2	735 –	275 =	460 +	= 910
Final Product				910

Another way to describe the relationship of these various size measures is shown in Figure 3.4. Here, the base for version 2 is shown as the 450 LOC from version 1. In developing version 2, we delete 200 LOC from the base, modify 75 LOC, and leave 175 LOC unmodified. Of the original 450-LOC circle, 200 LOC is outside the version 2 circle and both the 75 modified and 175 unmodified LOC are within the version 2 circle. To this we add the 60 lines of added code and the 600 lines of reused code to arrive at a final version 2 total size of 910 LOC (175 + 75 + 60 + 600).

All of the items in Table 3.2 must be counted for every version or the totals will not likely be correct. One nice feature of the LOC accounting structure is that it is additive. This is particularly important when many groups contribute code to a large system. Then, after developing several versions, you can add the numbers of added, deleted, modified, and reused code to get the combined effect of the total development effort for all of the versions. For example, in the case shown in Table 3.2, the initial base code is 0, the added code is 350 + 100 + 60 = 510 LOC, the deleted code is 0 + 0 + 200 LOC, and the modified code is 0 + 25 + 75 = 100 LOC. If we

Version 1
Base program
450 LOC

Version 2
New program
910 LOC

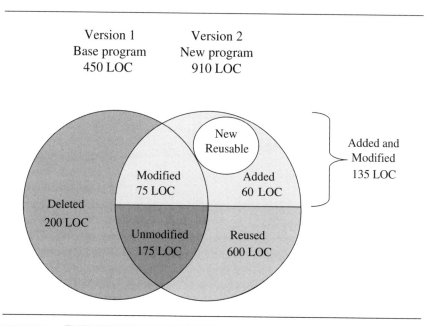

FIGURE 3.4 THE VERSION 2 SIZE ACCOUNTING EXAMPLE

count the modifications as additions and deletions, the total is the additions (510 + 100 = 610) minus the deletions (200 + 100 = 300) plus the reused code (600), giving 610 – 300 + 600 = 910 LOC as the correct final total LOC.

Although size accounting may seem unnecessarily complex, after several releases of a large program you may need to know where all of the code came from and the effort required to develop it. This accounting scheme permits you to find this out. It also gives you a way to precisely account for all of the size changes in a large number of releases. This exact approach can be used to track the sizes of documents, databases, or any other product for which you have defined size measures.

3.5 Using Size Data

The principal ways to use size data are in planning, quality management, and process analysis. The following paragraphs describe how to use size measures in planning, their value in assessing program quality, and how they help in evaluating your personal work.

Using Size Measures for Planning

In planning a development job, if you have a defined size measure and historical size and time data, you can use these data to accurately estimate the size of the new product. With these same data, you can also accurately estimate the development effort. For the PSP exercises in this book, I suggest that you use the added and modified code (or database elements) and not the deletions or other unmodified inclusions in estimating development effort. The effort to add or modify code in these exercise programs will probably be roughly the same, while the effort required to delete or include a previously developed line will generally be much less. For other kinds of work, however, you might make different choices. In maintenance work, for example, the effort required to delete a line could take as much or more time than the effort required to add or modify a line. Examine each situation and be guided by your data. Some methods for making such choices are discussed in Chapter 5.

Assessing Program Quality

In evaluating program quality, it is often helpful to make cross-product comparisons. For example, dividing the number of defects found in a phase by that program's size gives the program's **defect density** for that phase. This is important in planning projects because testing, maintenance, and service costs are generally closely related to a program's defect content at various points in the process. With data on similar programs, you can use estimates of defect density and size to estimate testing, maintenance, and service costs. The defect-density measure can partially compensate for size differences among programs and take advantage of the historical data for a larger number of prior projects.

In calculating defect density, count only the code added and modified during development. When considering the relative quality of several finished programs, however, consider their total size. Although I know of no published data on this point, my experiences at IBM suggest that total program size correlates most closely with product service costs. Although this may seem strange, it is logical when you realize that, for all but very poor-quality products, defect-related costs are only a small part of total service costs. At IBM, we found that the total number of support calls was more closely related to total program size than to the added and modified size of each release. Once you have sufficient data, you can decide what method works best for you and your products.

For program quality, defect density is generally measured in defects per 1,000 LOC, or KLOC. For finished products, however, the most suitable measure is defects per 1,000,000 LOC, or defects per MLOC. For measures of database work, document writing, or other product development, defects are generally counted per 100 or 1,000 elements, depending on which measure gives numbers between about 10 and 100.

Every counting choice has advantages and disadvantages. Using total program size as a quality measure is most appropriate when small modifications are not significant. However, an unpublished IBM study found that small code modifications were 39 times as error-prone as new development when measured in defects per modified LOC (Humphrey 1989). Conversely, counting only added and modified code would ignore any quality problems with the large inventory of existing code. If this existing code had any significant defect content, maintenance cost estimates would then likely be too low. In determining the relative quality of several releases of a single program, one is generally interested in both the defect density for the added and modified code and the defect density of the total product. Again, when in doubt, gather the data and see what works best in your particular situation.

Evaluating Your Personal Work

For the PSP, the principal focus is on the quality of your *personal* process. Here, you should probably use data on added and modified database objects, lines of code, or other suitable measures to make the quality analyses in this book. However, you should also keep track of the size of the reused, added, deleted, and modified code. The PSP process shows you how to do this.

3.6 Calculating Productivity

Productivity is generally measured as the labor hours required to do a unit of work. It is such a simple concept that people tend to think of productivity as a simple calculation. Although the calculation is simple, using the right data and properly interpreting these data is not so easy. Proper productivity calculations must consider, for example, the unique conditions of each job and the quality of the resulting product. If you estimate the size of a new job and then use some global productivity factor to determine the total hours required, you will generally get a misleading result. It would be analogous to always allowing for the average driving time when you go to the airport. With that method, you will miss a lot of flights around rush hour and do a lot of waiting the rest of the time.

When calculating productivity, divide the size of the product produced by the hours spent producing it. This gives the volume of product produced per hour. For programming, for example, if you developed a 600-LOC program in 60 hours, your productivity would be 10 LOC per hour. Although this may seem simple enough, you face many choices for picking these size and hours measures. For example, various combinations of the numbers used in the LOC accounting example in Table 3.2 (see p. 44) are shown in Table 3.3. There is some basis for

TABLE 3.3 VARIATIONS IN LOC PRODUCTIVITY

Productivity Option	Size LOC	Productivity LOC/Hour
Added (350+100+50)	500	8.33
Added + Modified (500+100)	600	10.00
Added + Modified + Deleted (600+200)	800	13.33
Added + Modified + Reused (600+600)	1200	20.00
Added + Modified + Deleted + Reused (1,200+200)	1400	23.33
Total Finished Product	900	15.00

arguing that any one of these six numbers should be used to measure development productivity. Assuming that you spent a total of 60 hours developing this program, the various productivity options could differ by factors of two or more times. This variation is caused solely by the choice you make for using the size measures. That is why comparisons of productivity numbers between organizations or even among individuals are rarely useful and why each developer must choose his or her own method and use it consistently.

For most new or major enhancement projects, added plus modified product is probably most appropriate for calculating productivity. For small modifications to large programs, however, the issue is much more complex. The reason is that the productivity for software modification is often much lower than for new development (Flaherty 1985). By gathering data on the time spent, the sizes of the changes, the size of the base program, and the fraction of the base program modified, you will likely find that small changes in large programs take much more time than either new development or large-percentage modifications of existing programs. Study your own data and see what categories provide the best correlation with development effort. Again, the methods discussed in this book will help you to arrive at appropriate productivity figures.

3.7 Size Counters

Although it is relatively easy to count the sizes of small programs, manually counting even small programs can be time-consuming and error-prone. For large programs, however, manual counting is impractical, making automated size counters essential.

Counters can be designed to count the number of almost any product element as long as the definition for that element is precise and specific. For example, a

LOC counter could count physical lines or logical lines. Although automatically counting database elements can be a bit more complex, if the object model is accessible, you can usually count selected sets of database elements.

Physical LOC Counters

The simplest type of size counter counts physical LOC. Here, you count all text lines except comments and blank lines. A text line that has both comments and source code is counted as one LOC.

Logical LOC Counters

Logical LOC counters work much like physical counters except that line-counter stepping is more complex. My Object Pascal logical line counter had 939 LOC and took me about 50 hours to develop. Don't try to develop a logical line counter unless you have plenty of time to do it. Although people can endlessly debate the best way to count LOC, the details are not that important. The key is to be precise and consistent. In my Object Pascal and C++ programs, I counted every logical program statement. Although some may argue that counting **begin** and **end** statements is not a good idea, this is a matter of personal preference. If you could show, however, that the time required to develop a program had a higher correlation with LOC when **begin-end** pairs were counted than when they were not, that would be a good reason to use them. This would also be the proper way to resolve almost any size counting question.

Presently, there is no compelling evidence to support any one counting method over any other. With good data, however, a study of the various alternatives could quickly show which, if any, would be best for your work. It may show, as is likely, that many different approaches produce roughly equivalent results. In that case, the selection is arbitrary. The fact that it is arbitrary, however, does not mean that everyone should do it differently. If all of the projects in an organization used the same counting standard, they could afford to develop a single high-quality automated counter for everyone to use. They would also have a much larger volume of data to use in planning and quality analysis.

Counting Program Elements

It is often desirable to measure the sizes of various parts of large programs. For example, if you intended to reuse some newly developed classes or procedures, you would like to know how large each one is. As you will see in Chapter 5, such counts can also help with size estimating.

To maintain separate counts for each class or procedure, you must determine where each one starts and ends. Because the way to do this depends on the programming language, there is no general guideline. The counter I built for Object Pascal recognized the keywords **procedure**, **function**, **constructor**, and **destructor** as the beginning of procedures. I found the endpoints by counting **begin-end** pairs. With a little study, you can determine the indicators for the beginning and ending points of the methods, procedures, classes, functions, or other elements for the language you use. You can then use this definition to scan the program text and start and stop the size counter at the appropriate points.

Using Coding Standards and Physical LOC Counters

One simple way to count logical LOC is to use a coding standard and count physical LOC, omitting comments and blanks. The idea is to write the source code with a separate physical text line for every countable line. Then, when you count physical lines, you are also counting logical lines. To use this method, you must carefully follow a coding standard like the example shown in Table 3.4. If, at the same

TABLE 3.4 EXAMPLE C++ CODING STANDARD

Purpose:	To guide the development of C++ programs
Program Headers	Begin all programs with a descriptive header.
| Header Format | ```
/************************************************************/
/* Program Assignment:  the program number                 */
/* Name:                your name                          */
/* Date:                the date program development started */
/* Description:         a short description of the program  */
/*                      function                            */
/************************************************************/
``` |
| Listing Contents | Provide a summary of the listing contents. |
| Contents Example | ```
/************************************************************/
/* Listing Contents:                                       */
/*      Reuse instructions                                 */
/*      Modification instructions                          */
/*      Compilation instructions                           */
/*      Includes                                           */
/*      Class declarations:                                */
/*          CData                                          */
/*          ASet                                           */
/*      Source code in c:\classes\CData.cpp:               */
/*          CData                                          */
/*          CData()                                        */
/*          Empty()                                        */
/************************************************************/
``` |

TABLE 3.4 (continued)

Reuse Instructions	• Describe how the program is used. Provide the declaration format, parameter values and types, and parameter limits. • Provide warnings of illegal values, overflow conditions, or other conditions that could potentially result in improper operation.
| Reuse Example | ```
/**************************************************************/
/*  Reuse Instructions                                        */
/*      int PrintLine(char *line_of_character)                */
/*      Purpose: to print string, 'line_of_character', on one print line */
/*      Limitations: the maximum line length is LINE_LENGTH   */
/*      Return: 0 if printer not ready to print, else 1       */
/**************************************************************/
``` |
| Identifiers | Use descriptive names for all variables, function names, constants, and other identifiers. Avoid abbreviations or single letter variables. |
| Identifier Example | ```
int  number_of_students;                /* This is GOOD   */
float x4, j, ftave;                      /* These are BAD  */
``` |
Comments	• Document the code so that the reader can understand its operation. • Comments should explain both the purpose and behavior of the code. • Comment variable declarations to indicate their purpose.
Good Comment	`If (record_count > limit)   /* have all the records been processed?  */`
Bad Comment	`if(record_count > limit)   /* check if record_count is greater than limit */`
Major Sections	Precede major program sections by a block comment that describes the processing that is done in the next section.
| Example | ```
/**************************************************************/
/* This program section will examine the contents of the array */
/* "grades" and will calculate the average grade for the class. */
/**************************************************************/
``` |
| Blank Spaces | • Write programs with sufficient spacing so that they do not appear crowded.
• Separate every program construct with at least one space. |
| Indenting | • Indent every level of brace from the previous one.
• Open and close braces should be on lines by themselves and aligned with each other. |
| Indenting Example | ```
while (miss_distance > threshold)
{
    success_code = move_robot (target_location);
    if (success_code == MOVE_FAILED)
    {
        printf("The robot move has failed.\n");
    }
}
``` |

(continued)

TABLE 3.4 (continued)

Capitalization	• Capitalized all defines. • Lowercase all other identifiers and reserved words. • Messages being output to the user can be mixed-case so as to make a clean user presentation.
Capitalization Example	#define DEFAULT-NUMBER-OF-STUDENTS 15 int class-size = DEFAULT-NUMBER-OF-STUDENTS;

time, you also follow consistent formatting standards, you will get highly readable code. Note, however, that when you count LOC this way, you cannot reformat the code without changing the LOC count.

One problem with this approach is caused by instructions that span multiple text lines. Because the LOC counter will count each line, you will get too large a count. In these cases, either modify the counter to recognize multi-line instructions, write a true logical LOC counting program, or count these cases by hand. If multi-line instructions are rare in your programs, the easiest approach is to ignore the problem and trust your estimating method to allow for those cases. If such instructions are common, however, you should either count the cases by hand or adjust your counter to properly count multi-line instructions.

Counting Deletions and Modifications

One of the more difficult counting problems is keeping track of the additions, deletions, and changes in multiversion programs. For small programs, you can manually count the added and modified elements, but for large programs this is impractical. Even for small programs, such manual counts are almost impossible unless you do the counting immediately after completing each modification.

One approach is to flag each program line separately with a special comment. A special counter could then recognize these flags and count the added and deleted product elements. Although nice in theory, this approach is impractical. While modifying a program, you will find it almost impossible to remember to comment every addition and deletion. It is even more difficult to remember to do it when you are fixing defects in testing. A second alternative is both practical and convenient, but it involves a bit of programming. Here, you use a special program counter to compare each new program version with its immediate predecessor and insert appropriate flags.

Because this comparator could not easily recognize whether a new line was a modification or an addition, all modifications would be counted as deletions and additions. This is exactly equivalent to the LOC accounting rules. You could even run the comparator counter after every modification and defect fix.

Another approach is to build such a comparator counter into the source-code control system. That way, every program update would be analyzed and every line automatically flagged with the date and version when it was added or deleted. You could also assign a number to every program fix, release, or version update and affix that number and date to every deleted, added, or modified line in each update. You could also include the developer's name, the fix number, the project name, or any other potentially useful information. With such a support system, you could determine when every change was made, when a defect was injected, or how much code was added and deleted with each update. These data are essential for effective quality management of large programs. Modern source-code control systems generally provide many of these capabilities.

Overall, the problem of counting deletions and modifications can be partially addressed with tool support, but it is still a difficult process that is both error-prone and apt to produce misleading results. The best approach is to make an accurate count for each small program and then use whatever automated tools you can obtain to identify and track all subsequent changes.

3.8   Other Size Measures

Although this chapter concentrates almost entirely on the line-of-code (LOC) measure, that is only one size-measurement option. As noted earlier, depending on the type of work you do, database elements, defect fixes, or pages might be more appropriate. Another useful and much more general size measure is called **function points**. The function-point measure was developed in the late 1970s and has become widely used. There is now a standards body, the International Function Point Users Group (IFPUG), that supports function points, and a considerable amount of literature is available (Garmus and Herron 2001; Jones 2000).

The principal point to remember is that no size measure is best for all situations. Whether you prefer LOC, database elements, or function points, the best strategy is to gather data on your estimated and actual size and time measures. Then analyze these data to see which measures and methods are best for you in each situation. Regardless of what I or anyone else says, if your data indicate that some measure and method is best for you, it probably is.

3.9   Summary

There are many reasons to measure software size. One of the most important is to help in project planning. The size measure should correlate to development effort, be precise, and be automatically countable. Typical size measures are database elements, source program lines of code, pages of design or text, and function points. Because there are many ways to define software size data, you must use precise definitions and carefully note the types of elements to be included in each count.

Size counters can be designed to count physical or logical product elements or lines. A third method combines these two: counting logical lines by using a coding standard and a physical counter. This is the approach the PSP uses to count LOC. For database work, count a selected set of database elements.

Properly designed tools can produce many useful size statistics. For each program version, for example, you need to know the number of added and deleted elements or lines. A practical way to get such data is with a program that compares each new program version with its immediate predecessor. This comparator then identifies and counts the added and deleted items.

Well-defined and consistently used size measures can provide the data needed to make accurate size and development time estimates. Size data are also useful for comparing the defect rates among programs. Here, you use the defect rate per hundred new and modified database elements or per thousand lines of new and modified code. When estimating maintenance workload for a program, however, consider total product size.

An effective software size measure must fit your and your team's needs. First, define the reason you want to use the measure and then gather historical data on both your work and the proposed measure. Then make sure that your measurement practices satisfy your intended purpose for the measure.

3.10   Exercises

The standard assignment for this chapter includes exercises R1 and R2 and uses the PSP0.1 process to write one or more programs. For the R1, R2, and program assignment kits, see your instructor or get them at **www.sei.cmu.edu/tsp/**. These kits contain the assignment specifications and the PSP0.1 process scripts. In completing this assignment, faithfully follow the PSP0.1 process, record all required data, and produce the R1 and R2 reports and the program report according to the specifications in the assignment kit.

References

Flaherty, M. J. "Programming Process Productivity Measurement System for System/370." *IBM Systems Journal* 24, no. 2 (1985): 168–175.

Garmus, D., and D. Herron. *Function Point Analysis.* Boston: Addison-Wesley, 2001.

Humphrey, W. S. *Managing the Software Process.* Reading, MA: Addison-Wesley, 1989.

Jones, C. *Software Assessments, Benchmarks, and Best Practices.* Boston: Addison-Wesley, 2000.

4

Planning

Software development plans are often incomplete and inaccurate. During the 27 years when I worked at IBM, we once needed a critical new function for the OS/360 programming system. The engineering estimate was $175,000. Naively, that is all the funding I requested. Some months later, the developers found that the work would cost $525,000. They had omitted many necessary tasks from their original plan. They had forgotten documentation; testing; the integration, build, and release processes; and quality assurance. Sure enough, however, the coding and unit test costs were about $175,000. They had made a pretty good estimate, but their plan was painfully (for me) incomplete. I had to make up the difference out of department funds.

The problem is that few software organizations have a planning process that ensures that plans are complete, thoroughly reviewed, and properly approved. Even worse, few software developers have the knowledge and experience to make sound plans. When you start a project, management typically states very clearly when they want the job done, but they are not usually very clear about much else. It is not that they are bad, lazy, or incompetent; it is just that, except for the schedule, most requirements are complex and cannot be easily described. By emphasizing the schedule, management gives the impression that it is their highest-priority concern. But, although the schedule is important, you must also address all of management's stated and implied goals. In addition, while doing this, you must do your best to meet management's desired schedule.

PSP training will help you to build the needed planning skills. Planning is the first step in the PSP for three reasons. First, without good plans you cannot effectively manage even modestly sized software projects. Second, planning is a skill that you can learn and improve with practice. Third, good planning skills will help you to do better software work. This chapter introduces software planning and provides a general overview of the planning process. It discusses what a plan is and what it should contain. It reviews the reasons why planning is important and it describes the elements of an effective planning process. It then discusses plan quality and how your work with the PSP will help you to do better work and be a more effective team member.

4.1   The Planning Process

What management really wants is a completed project *now*, at no cost. Anything else is a compromise. However, because they know that development takes time, they will push for the most aggressive schedule that you and your team will accept as a goal. Not unreasonably, they believe that projects with the shortest schedules finish before ones with longer schedules. Therefore, they will keep pushing until they believe that the schedule is the shortest one you will agree to meet. As developers, however, we are responsible for doing the work. With an impossibly short schedule, it is difficult if not impossible to make a usable plan. Then, without a plan, we are generally in such a rush to code and test that we cut corners and don't do as good a job as we could. Such projects generally take much more time than they would with a realistic plan.

Typically, when management asks for an aggressive date, the developers tell them that this date doesn't allow enough time to do the work. Management then insists that the date is firm, and the team generally caves in and agrees to do its best. Such teams start out in trouble and almost always end up in trouble. As Greg's team found in Chapter 1, the best answer to this problem is to make a detailed plan and to review it with management. Because most managers want a schedule you *can* meet, they will negotiate a thoughtfully made plan with you. If you present a convincing case, they will then end up agreeing to your schedule. To have such a debate, however, you must know how to make a plan and how to defend it to management. PSP training provides these skills. Later, on a team, the TSP shows you how to prepare for and handle the plan negotiations with management.

4.2   Why Make Plans?

In software engineering, as in other fields, our role as developers is to devise economical and timely solutions to our employer's needs. To do this, we must consider costs and schedules. The connection between cost estimating, scheduling, and the planning process can best be illustrated by an example. Suppose you want to put an addition on your home. After deciding what you want and getting several bids, most of which are around $24,000, you pick a builder who offers to do the job in three months for $20,000. Although this is a lot of money, you need the extra space and can arrange for a home-equity loan. You then sign an agreement and the builder starts the work. After about a month into the job, the builder tells you that, because of unforeseen problems, the job will take an extra month and cost an additional $4,000.

This presents you with several problems. First, you badly need the space, and another month of delay is a great inconvenience. Second, you have already arranged for the loan and don't know where you can get the extra $4,000. Third, if you get a lawyer and decide to fight the builder in court, all the work will stop for many months while the case is settled. Fourth, it would take a great deal of time and probably cost even more to switch to a new builder in the middle of the job.

After considerable thought, you decide that the real problem is that the builder did a sloppy job of planning. Although you do not know precisely what went wrong, the builder probably got low bids on some of the major subcontracts, such as the plumbing, plastering, or painting. You can endlessly debate what the job should cost, but essentially the problem was caused by poor planning. If you had originally been given the $24,000 price, you could have decided then whether to proceed with that builder and how to finance the work. The odds are good that at this point you will try to negotiate a lower price but continue with the current builder. Because the other bids were close to $24,000, you know this is a pretty fair price. You would not use this builder again, however, and would probably not recommend him to anyone else.

The problem with incompetent planning is that everybody loses: customers receive late and more costly products, management must tie up more resources, and the developer gets a bad reputation. To be successful, businesses must meet their commitments. To do our part, we must produce plans that accurately represent what we will do.

Planning is serious business. It defines commitments and supports business decisions. Well-thought-out plans will help you to make commitments that you can meet, and enable you to accurately track and report your progress. Personal planning skill will be even more important when you work on a development team. The overall team plan is most likely to be realistic when it is built from competently made team-member plans. As you practice the methods described in this and the next four chapters, you will learn how to make competent plans.

4.3   What Is a Plan?

"The project plan defines the work and how it will be done. It provides a definition of each major task, an estimate of the time and resources required, and a framework for management review and control. The project plan is also a powerful learning vehicle. When properly documented, it is a benchmark to compare with actual performance. This comparison permits the planners to see their estimating errors and to improve their estimating accuracy" (Humphrey 1989). Plans typically are used as the following:

☐ A basis for agreeing on the cost and schedule for a job

☐ An organizing structure for doing the work

☐ A framework for obtaining the required resources

☐ The standard against which to measure job status

☐ A record of what was initially committed

The connection between plans and commitments is extremely important. Every project starts as a new endeavor. At the outset, the project must be created out of thin air. New projects typically start with no staff. A manager, user, or customer must commit funds, and some workers and suppliers must be convinced to participate in the work.

For substantial projects, management's first step is to assemble a planning and proposal team and produce an overall plan. Without a clear and convincing plan, they will not be able to get funding, hire the staff, and arrange for all the facilities, supplies, and other support needed to do the work. Nobody wants to pay for an undefined job, and few people will work on a project that has unclear objectives. Because an accurate plan is the essential first step in creating a successful project, planning is an important part of every project.

4.4   The Contents of a Software Plan

The focus of this and the next three chapters is on the personal planning process and the products it produces. Although personal planning, team planning, and project management are all related, the objective here is to practice personal planning for small software projects. Because detailed planning is the key to accurate planning, learning to make accurate plans for small projects is the essential first step in learning how to make accurate plans for large projects.

In deciding what a plan should contain, consider the needs of the people who will use the plan and what they will do with it. PSP plans have two users: you and your customers. You need four things from a plan:

1. Job sizing: How big is this job and how long do you expect it to take?

2. Job structure: How will you do the work? What will you do first, second, and so on?

3. Job status: How will you know where you are? Will you finish on time and are the costs under control?

4. Assessment: How good was the plan? Did you make any obvious errors? What mistakes can you avoid in the future and how can you do a better planning job?

For your personal plans, the possible users are the PSP instructor, your coworkers, your manager, or an end user. These people also want four things from your plan:

1. What is the commitment? What will you deliver, when, and at what cost?

2. Will the product be what they want? Will there be any interim checkpoints on product performance and quality?

3. Is there a way to monitor progress? What kind of warning can they expect for cost, schedule, or quality problems? Will scope changes be clear and identifiable?

4. Will they be able to evaluate the job? Can they separate planning problems from poor management? Is there a way to assess product quality during the job?

Although these issues will not be very complex for the small programs developed with the PSP, they will clarify several points:

☐ The plan must be based on doing a defined piece of work. Otherwise, there is no way to make an accurate plan, and you could even build the wrong product.

☐ The job steps should be clearly defined and measurable. This will provide a framework for the plan and a way to track progress.

☐ You should check your plan with the customer, manager, or instructor before starting the work. This is always a good idea and is essential for any but the smallest jobs.

☐ Periodically report progress to your customers and managers. For any but the shortest projects, this will alleviate concern and build trust.

When you plan personal work, your objective is to estimate the cost and schedule of the job you will actually do. Then, once you complete the job, if the estimate differs from the actual result, you have a planning problem. Although there may have been development problems, the planning objective was to forecast what would actually happen. With the PSP, the saving grace is that the projects are simpler and more consistent than is typical for development projects. Although overall gross data on large projects are rarely helpful in planning the next job, the PSP data are. In addition, when estimating your own work, you decide how to do the job, you produce the plan, and you do the work. Then, when you are done, you can compare the plan with what you actually did.

4.5   Planning a Software Project

To make a personal plan, take the following steps:

1. Start with an explicit statement of the work to be done and check it carefully to ensure that you understand what is wanted. Even though the initial requirements will often change, start with the best requirements statement you can get.

2. Break any projects that take more than a few days into multiple smaller tasks and estimate each one separately. More detail means greater planning accuracy.

3. In making the estimates, compare this job with historical data on prior similar jobs.

4. Document the estimate and later compare it with the actual results.

5. When the requirements change, change the plan and get your customers and managers to agree with the new plan before you accept the change.

Before making an estimate, first ensure that the historical data you use are for similar work. On one project, for example, a software professional used historical data from a prior project to make the estimate. Partway through the job, he found that the work was taking three times longer than estimated. Although the number of requirements had increased a little, each one was taking much longer than expected. On examination, he found that the current requirements involved complex system functions, whereas the previous project concerned requirements for small, stand-alone applications. In this new work, he had to deal with many more people to resolve the system issues and to get the requirements approved. By tracking and analyzing his work, he could see the problem in time to alert management and get help.

The Planning Framework

The PSP planning framework is shown in Figure 4.1. The tasks you perform are shown in the rectangles; and the data, reports, and products are shown in the ovals. Starting with a customer need, the first step is to define the requirements. Next, to

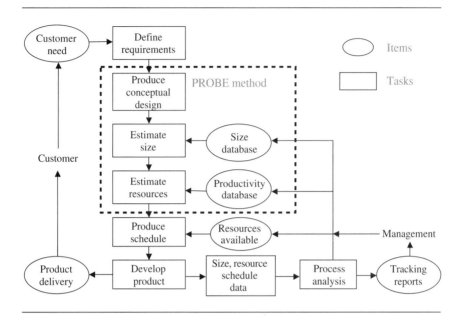

FIGURE 4.1 PROJECT PLANNING FRAMEWORK

relate your plan to the actual product you will build, produce a conceptual design. From the conceptual design, you can now estimate the size of the new product. Then, with a size estimate, use historical productivity data to estimate how long the work will take. Finally, starting with the planned project start date, spread your available working hours over the project calendar to produce the schedule. The final step is to calculate the date when you expect to finish the work.

　　With the plan in hand, and assuming that you have all of the needed information and facilities, you can start development. Then, during the job, you track the time you spend and the sizes of the products you produce. This provides the data you need to make future plans.

4.6　The Conceptual Design

To make an accurate plan, start with a conceptual design. It defines a preliminary design approach and names the product elements and their functions. Do not produce the complete design, but merely postulate the principal product parts and the functions they will perform. This is an abstraction process in which you say, "If I had parts that performed functions A, B, and C, I would know how to build this product."

There are many ways to build a product to meet almost any requirement, and these different approaches will generally involve different amounts of work. For example, out of 810 times that the PSP exercises were developed from the identical requirements statements, the size distribution was as shown in Table 4.1. Although some of this enormous size range is due to skill and experience variations and some from use of embedded language functions, the principal difference is from different design strategies. By producing the conceptual design, you can base your estimate on the particular design strategy you plan to follow. This helps you to make a realistic estimate.

Although the conceptual design is important, it is not the actual design—and you should not feel obliged to implement it. You produced it solely to make the plan. When you actually do produce the design, examine several approaches, brainstorm design ideas with associates, or examine the designs of previously developed products. For larger projects, it is even a good idea to do this while producing the conceptual design. A few minutes spent in such exploration can often reveal approaches that could reduce the development work by large factors. Don't feel constrained to implement a design just because it is the first one you thought of. Although it is possible that your first idea will turn out to be the best, be suspicious of it until you have examined one or two alternatives and found that it is still best.

When estimating a large product, producing a conceptual design can be a significant task. Though you may question the need to go into a lot of detail just to make an estimate, the issue is accuracy. If you need an accurate estimate, you must refine the conceptual design into sufficient detail to define parts that you know how to build. Even for fairly large programs, however, this need not take more than a few hours.

In producing the conceptual design, remember that the objective is to make a plan, not to produce the design. You want to spend just enough time thinking about the product's design so that your estimate is more than a guess. The trick is

TABLE 4.1 PSP PROGRAM SIZE RANGES IN LINES OF CODE (LOC)

Program Number	1	2	3	4	5	6	7	8
Maximum	613	872	560	578	338	542	1043	913
Upper Quartile	113	97	104	117	113	197	199	279
Average	88.3	91.5	93.2	98.4	89.5	164.1	162.9	232.4
Median	76	62	71	84	81	153	138	208
Lower Quartile	54	43	50	63	54	114	100	156
Minimum	7	8	9	29	4	22	17	33

to produce a conceptual design that provides enough guidance for estimating but does not delve too deeply into the design work itself. With the small programs like those in the PSP course, the conceptual design work should not take more than a few minutes, 20 at most.

The challenge with the PSP is to limit the time you spend on the conceptual design. Although a more complete design will always produce a more accurate plan, the objective with the PSP is to quickly produce the minimum design needed to make a reasonably accurate plan. Because there is no magical approach that works best for everyone, experiment with various methods until you find one that works well for you.

4.7 Plan Quality

The objective of the planning process is to produce an accurate plan. The next three chapters address how to measure, predict, and improve planning accuracy. As you make plans for your PSP programs, don't worry about the errors in your individual plans, as long as they appear to be random. Although you should strive to reduce estimating error, some error is unavoidable. The key, however, is to make unbiased or balanced plans. When you can make balanced plans, five out of about every ten plans will be overestimates and five will be underestimates. This is important because when you work on a TSP project, you and your teammates will make individual plans to combine into the team plan. If your plans are all balanced, the errors in the individual plans will tend to cancel each other out, resulting in a much more accurate team plan. The following chapters describe size measures, software estimating, and the PROBE method for producing balanced plans.

4.8 Planning Issues

Although most planning issues are covered in the following chapters, three general issues must be covered first: requirements creep, planning tools, and the statement of work. Although these issues will probably not be significant in writing the PSP exercise programs, they will be important when you work on a project team.

Requirements Creep

The requirements for engineering work always grow. On my team at SEI, team workload increases by an average of 1% per week: Over a 20-week plan cycle, the total work increases by about 20%. The first strategy for handling requirements creep is to plan for every proposed change and get all parties involved to agree to the cost and schedule consequences. Second, factor in a workload growth allowance during planning. I suggest you follow both strategies.

Estimating and Planning Tools

Many estimating and planning tools are available but they all require that you first make a development estimate. These tools can be helpful in checking estimates and in managing planning mechanics. Example cost estimating tools are COCOMO II, REVIC, and SEER, and example planning tools are Artemis Views, Microsoft Project, and Primavera.

The Statement of Work

Depending on the situation, a statement of work (SOW) can provide a useful record of your plan. It should contain a summary of customer and management agreements, key project assumptions, the names of the workers, and key dependencies. By attaching a copy of the Project Plan Summary form and sending the SOW to your management and the customer, you both document the plan and quickly identify any disagreements or misunderstandings. Though an SOW is usually helpful for a team, it is not generally required for individual work. When in doubt, however, produce an SOW and give it to your manager and the customer.

4.9   Summary

Planning is the first step in the PSP for three reasons. First, without good plans you cannot effectively manage even modestly sized software projects. Unplanned projects are often troubled from the start and are almost always in trouble at the end. Second, planning is a skill that you can learn and improve with practice. If you don't learn how to make good plans now, planning skills are almost impossible to pick up on the job. Third, good planning skills will help you to do better software work. Although the connection between planning and product quality is not obvious, unplanned projects are invariably under schedule pressure and the developers can rarely take the time to do an adequate job of requirements, design, or quality management.

In software engineering, as in other fields, the role of the developers is to devise economical and timely solutions to the employer's needs. This is the essential issue of the planning process: making plans that accurately represent what you will do. This in turn will help you to better manage your personal work and to be a more effective team member. Although personal planning is an important part of project planning, it is only a part. Many more issues are involved in producing a complete plan for a large project. These larger plans, however, are most likely to be realistic when they are composed of the multiple personal plans of the individuals who will do the work. As the accuracy and completeness of these elemental plans improves, their composite will be of higher quality. Conversely, when individual plans are poorly developed, they provide a poor foundation for the overall plan. The PSP will help you build the skills needed to make balanced and accurate personal plans.

Reference

Humphrey, W. S. *Managing the Software Process.* Reading, MA: Addison-Wesley, 1989.

5

Software Estimating

This chapter addresses size estimating. It starts with a brief description of conceptual design and then covers proxy-based estimating. Chapter 6 describes the PROBE method for using proxies to make size and time estimates. As shown in Figure 4.1 in Chapter 4 (see p. 63), the PSP planning process starts with the conceptual design. This provides the basis for the size and resource estimates. At the outset, you will know relatively little about the planned product, so your estimates will be least accurate. Because you must presumably commit to a delivery date, however, you must make the best estimate that you can. This chapter describes how to identify the parts of a planned product and estimate their sizes.

5.1 Size Estimating Principles

In principle, estimates are made by comparing the planned job with previous jobs. By breaking planned products into multiple smaller parts and comparing each part with data on similar parts of prior products, you can judge the size of the new product. This strategy works well for estimating almost any kind of development work. However, it requires data on the products you have developed and the work required to develop them. You also need a method for using historical data to make the estimates.

This divide-and-conquer estimating strategy has the advantage of scaling up. That is, once you have learned to make accurate estimates for the PSP exercises, you can use the identical methods to estimate larger jobs. The only difference is that you will have to divide bigger jobs into more parts or get data on larger parts.

In planning a PSP project, I use the term *product* to refer to the end item produced by the project and I use the term *parts* to refer to the elements of a product, whatever you plan to call them. Depending on the type of development, the parts could be systems, subsystems, components, classes, procedures, databases, or whatever term best applies to that particular product. For example, when I estimate a C++ program, the parts are classes. With Object Pascal, they would be objects, and with database work, they would be fields, tables, or queries. If the product's parts have even smaller elements, such as methods, functions, or procedures, I call them *items*.

5.2   The Conceptual Design

When first making a plan to develop a product, you may generally understand the requirements but little else. The estimating challenge is then to predict the size of this vaguely defined product and the time required to develop it. Because no one can know in advance how big a planned product will be or how long it will take to develop, estimating will always be an uncertain process. Therefore, you need to use the best product requirements and historical data you can get.

With the PSP, you make a size estimate first and then make the development time estimate. For the size estimate to be reasonably accurate, it must be based on an initial design concept, and that conceptual design must reflect the way you plan to build the product. As noted in Chapter 4 (see p. 63), the conceptual design defines a preliminary design approach and names the expected product parts and their functions. Do not produce the complete design during planning; just postulate the parts you will need and the functions they will perform.

For an accurate estimate, you must refine the conceptual design to the level of the parts you know how to build. Next, check for historical data on similar parts. If a part does not resemble anything in your historical records, see if you have refined the conceptual design to the proper level. Assuming you have a reasonably complete and well-structured parts database, you will likely find that the part is a composite of several more basic parts. If so, refine it into those more basic parts. If a conceptual part is at the right level and still does not look like any of your existing part data, estimate it as the first of a new kind of part. In doing so, compare this part to other product parts in the database to get a feel for their relationships and then make your best intuitive estimate of its size. Then, after you have completed the development work, measure the size of the new parts and enter these data into your database for use in estimating future work.

5.3   Proxy-Based Estimating

Consider the example of construction. In home building, the number of square feet of living space provides a basis for estimating construction costs. Few people, however, can visualize the house they want in terms of square feet. They think of number of bedrooms and bathrooms. Software estimating has similar problems. If we could judge the number of database relations or LOC for a product requirement, we could probably make a pretty good estimate of that product's size. Unfortunately, few people can directly judge how many LOC or database elements it would take to meet a product requirement.

What is needed is some proxy that relates product size to the functions we can visualize. A proxy is a substitute or a stand-in. Assuming it is easier to visualize the proxy than the size measure, the proxy can help you to judge a product's likely size. Examples of proxies are classes, tables, fields, or screens. The generalized proxy-based estimating process is illustrated in Figure 5.1.

Selecting a Proxy

The criteria for a good proxy are as follows:

- ☐ The proxy size measure should closely relate to the effort required to develop the product.
- ☐ The proxy content of a product should be automatically countable.
- ☐ The proxy should be easy to visualize at the beginning of a project.
- ☐ The proxy should be customizable to the needs of each project and developer.
- ☐ The proxy should be sensitive to implementation variations that affect development cost or effort.

These points are discussed in the following sections.

Related to Development Effort

To be useful, a proxy must have a demonstrably close relationship to the resources required to develop the product. By estimating the relative size of the proxy, you can accurately judge the size of the planned product. To determine the effectiveness of a potential proxy, obtain data on the products that you have developed and

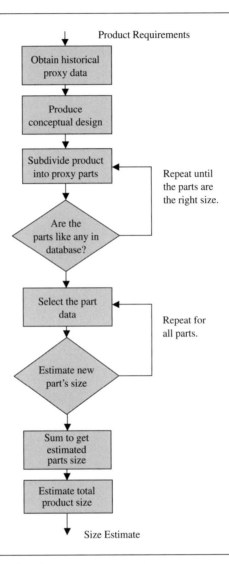

Product Requirements

Obtain historical
proxy data

Produce
conceptual design

Subdivide product
into proxy parts

Repeat until
the parts are
the right size.

Are the
parts like any in
database?

Select the part
data

Repeat for
all parts.

Estimate new
part's size

Sum to get
estimated
parts size

Estimate total
product size

Size Estimate

FIGURE 5.1 PROXY-BASED SIZE ESTIMATING

compare the proxy values with their development times. Using the correlation
method, determine if this or some other proxy is a better predictor of product size
or development effort. If the proxy does not pass this test ($|r| >= 0.7$), find another
one that does. You can quickly determine this by examining the data in a scatter
plot, like that shown in Figure 3.1 (see p. 39) and in Figure 5.2. The correlation

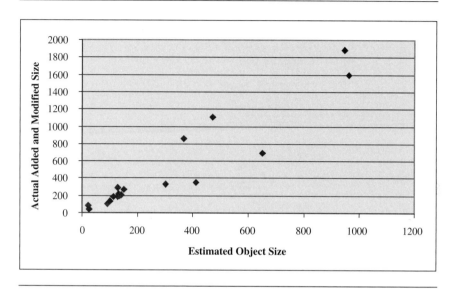

FIGURE 5.2 PART SIZE VERSUS ACTUAL SIZE (18 PASCAL PROGRAMS)

coefficient *r* is calculated by most PSP and TSP tools, but if you want to calculate it yourself, the formula for the correlation calculation is shown in Box 3.1 in Chapter 3 (see p. 36).

Because it is possible to get very high correlations with small amounts of data, statisticians use a significance measure to indicate the likelihood that a relationship either has predictive value or occurred by chance. The significance calculation is shown in Chapter 3 in Box 3.2 (see p. 37).

The Proxy Content Is Automatically Countable
Because estimating accuracy improves with more and better data, you will want a lot of proxy data. This suggests that the proxy should be a physical entity that can be precisely defined and automatically counted. If you cannot automatically count the proxy content of a product, there is no convenient way to get the data you will need to improve your estimating accuracy.

Easily Visualized at the Beginning of the Project
If the proxy is harder to visualize than the number of hours required to develop a product, you may as well estimate the hours directly. The usefulness of a proxy thus depends on the degree to which it helps you to visualize the size of the planned product. This in turn depends on your background and preferences. There will likely be no best proxy for all people or purposes. With suitable historical data, you could even use several different proxies in one estimate. The multiple-regression

method, usually introduced with the final PSP exercise program, can be helpful for this purpose.

Customizable to Your Project's Needs

Much of the difficulty people have with estimating methods results from using data from one group to plan work by another person or group. It is important, therefore, to use data that are relevant to your particular project. This suggests that you build a size and resource database for each type of product you develop. If the proxies you select are not suitable for some kinds of work, examine your data to identify more suitable proxies. After writing several programs, you should have enough data to identify useful proxies.

Sensitive to Implementation Variations

The proxies that are most easily visualized at the beginning of a project are application parts such as classes, inputs, outputs, database fields, forms, and reports. However, a good development estimate requires parts that closely relate to the product to be built and the labor to build it. This requires that proxy data be available for each implementation language, design style, and application category.

Possible Proxies

Many potential proxies could meet the criteria outlined above. The function-point method is an obvious candidate because it is widely used. Many people have found function points to be helpful in estimating resources. However, because function points are not directly countable in the finished product, there is no simple way for developers to get the data needed to improve their function-point estimating accuracy.

Other possible proxies are classes, database elements, forms, scripts, and document chapters. The data gathered during the PSP research show that database elements, classes, and document chapters generally meet the proxy criteria. For database work, developers have found that a count of all database elements is a reasonably accurate predictor of development effort. Example elements would be fields, tables, queries, and records.

Classes as Proxies

The principles of object-oriented design suggest that, for many kinds of programming, classes would be good estimating proxies. An application's conceptual parts would then be items that exist in the application environment. For example, in an automobile registration system, these might include automobiles, owners, registrations, titles, or insurance policies. In the conceptual design, you would select program classes that model these real-world conceptual parts. These highest-level product classes could then be visualized during requirements analysis. Classes thus potentially meet one of the requirements for a proxy.

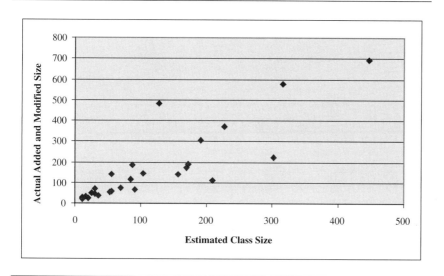

FIGURE 5.3 ESTIMATED VERSUS ACTUAL SIZE (27 C++ PROGRAMS: $r = 0.83$)

To determine whether class is a good size proxy, examine your historical data. Figure 5.2 shows the relationship between estimated object size and actual added and modified size for a family of 18 Object Pascal programs that I wrote during the PSP research work. Figure 5.3 shows similar data for a family of 27 C++ programs. Figures 5.4 and 5.5 compare these estimated part sizes (in LOC) with the hours spent developing these same Pascal and C++ programs. In both cases, the correlation and significance are very high. Because total program LOC correlates to development hours, classes thus meet the requirement that they closely relate to development effort.

Finally, as discussed in Chapter 3, classes are physical entities that can be automatically counted. Assuming that you use an object-oriented design methodology and programming language and that you gather size data on the classes you develop, classes will meet all of the criteria for an estimating proxy.

5.4   Using Proxies in Estimating

To use proxies in estimating, divide your historical size data into categories and size ranges. The construction example illustrates why this is important. When estimating the square feet in a house, a builder considers big rooms and small rooms and how many of each the buyer wants. The builder does this by room categories;

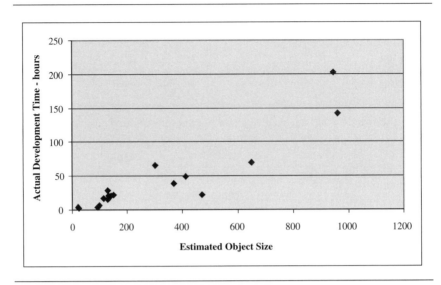

FIGURE 5.4 PASCAL ESTIMATED SIZE VERSUS ACTUAL HOURS ($r = 0.915$)

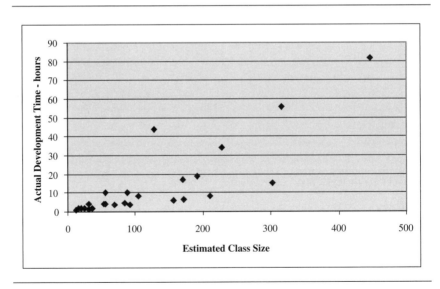

FIGURE 5.5 C++ ESTIMATED LOC VERSUS ACTUAL HOURS ($r = 0.829$)

for example, a big bathroom would likely be smaller than even a small family room.

Similarly, in estimating how many LOC a part contains, group the data into functional categories. Then estimate how many parts of each category are needed for the product, and the relative size of each part. Finally, decide how each part relates to its category, e.g., very small, small, medium, large, or very large. The Pascal and C++ categories I used with the PSP are shown in Table 5.1. At the top of Table 5.1, the C++ classes are listed in six categories. These data show that a medium-size C++ class item for mathematical calculations would have 11.25 LOC, while a very large calculation part would have 54.04 LOC.

The size of the parts you develop is also largely determined by your personal programming style. Some people prefer to group many items (or functions) into a few parts, while others prefer to create many parts with relatively few items. The estimating data should accurately reflect the languages and practices you use in developing software. Therefore, it is a good idea to use part size data derived from your own work.

TABLE 5.1 PARTS LOC PER ITEM

C++ Class Size in LOC per Item					
Category	Very Small	Small	Medium	Large	Very Large
Calculation	2.34	5.13	11.25	24.66	54.04
Data	2.60	4.79	8.84	16.31	30.09
I/O	9.01	12.06	16.15	21.62	28.93
Logic	7.55	10.98	15.98	23.25	33.83
Set-up	3.88	5.04	6.56	8.53	11.09
Text	3.75	8.00	17.07	36.41	77.66

Object Pascal Object Size in LOC per Item					
Category	Very Small	Small	Medium	Large	Very Large
Control	4.24	8.68	17.79	36.46	74.71
Display	4.72	6.35	8.55	11.50	15.46
File	3.30	6.23	11.74	22.14	41.74
Logic	6.41	12.42	24.06	46.60	90.27
Print	3.38	5.86	10.15	17.59	30.49
Text	4.40	8.51	16.47	31.88	61.71

In making a size estimate, first produce a conceptual design and identify its parts, and then decide on the functional category for each part and how many items it is likely to contain. Finally, determine whether each part falls into the very small, small, medium, large, or very large size range. From the relative-size table, you can then estimate the size of each part and calculate total estimated program size. There are various ways to produce the relative-size table, but the next section describes a relatively simple and reasonably accurate approach.

5.5   Producing the Relative-Size Table

The PROBE estimating method divides historical size data into categories that represent your kind of work. If, for example, you know the sizes of all the text-handling parts you previously developed, you can judge the likely size of a new text part. In my original PSP research work, I developed a total of 13 Pascal text objects, as listed in Table 5.2. Because of wide variation in the numbers of items per part, I normalized the data by the number of items and then sorted the data by LOC per item. This normalization results in the data shown in Table 5.2.

TABLE 5.2 PASCAL TEXT LOC PER ITEM

Object Name	Items	Object LOC	LOC per Item	Range
each-char	3	18	6.000	VS
string_read	3	18	6.000	
single_character	3	25	8.333	
each_line	3	31	10.333	S
single_char	3	37	12.333	
string_builder	5	82	16.400	
string_manager	4	82	20.500	M
list_clump	4	87	21.750	
list_clip	4	89	22.250	
string_decrementer	10	230	23.000	L
Char	3	85	28.333	
Character	3	87	29.000	
Converter	10	558	55.800	VL

The smallest number of LOC per item in Table 5.2 is now 6 and the largest is 55.8. Although this is nearly a 10-to-1 spread, it is somewhat more useful than the 30-to-1 spread without normalization. The value of knowing this range is clear when you consider the extreme case. Say, for example, you knew that the size range for text parts fell between 3 LOC and 3,000 LOC. This information would not be much help in picking the size of a new text part. Size ranges are thus most helpful if they are reasonably narrow.

The next step is to divide the size data into very small, small, medium, large, and very large size ranges. This provides an intuitive structure for judging part size. Some PSP and TSP support tools can generate the relative-size table for you, but you can easily make your own simple divisions by picking the largest and smallest values as the VL and VS sizes. Then pick the middle value for medium and the lower and upper quartile values as the S and L values, as shown in Table 5.2. If you wish to use a more mathematical method for selecting these values, the method I used to produce the values in Table 5.1 is given in Box 5.1.

BOX 5.1 PRODUCING A RELATIVE-SIZE TABLE

1. Divide the part sizes by the number of items in each part to give size per item.

2. Divide these item size data into functional categories that each have at least 6 to 8 members (calculation, text, and data, for example).

3. For each size value, take the natural logarithm of the size to give $\ln(x_i)$.

4. Calculate the average of these n logarithmic values: $\ln(x_i)_{avg}$.

5. Calculate the variance of the logarithmic values from their average:

$$\text{Var} = \frac{1}{n-1} \sum_{i=1}^{n} \left(\ln(x_i) - \ln(x_i)_{avg} \right)^2$$

6. Calculate the standard deviation: $\sigma = \sqrt{\text{Var}}$.

7. Calculate the logarithmic ranges: $\ln(\text{VS}) = \ln(x_i)_{avg} - 2\sigma$, $\ln(\text{S}) = \ln(x_i)_{avg} - \sigma$, $\ln(\text{M}) = \ln(x_i)_{avg}$, $\ln(\text{L}) = \ln(x_i)_{avg} + \sigma$, $\ln(\text{VL}) = \ln(x_i)_{avg} + 2\sigma$.

8. Calculate size ranges: $\text{VS} = e^{\ln(VS)}$, $\text{S} = e^{\ln(S)}$, $\text{M} = e^{\ln(M)}$, $\text{L} = e^{\ln(L)}$, $\text{VL} = e^{\ln(VL)}$.

5.6   Estimating Considerations

Estimating is a skill that you can develop and improve. The following paragraphs describe techniques you can use to improve your personal estimating accuracy. These methods involve reducing estimating error, controlling estimating bias, and handling the common problem of having to estimate with limited knowledge of the product to be built.

Improving Estimating Accuracy

Estimating is tricky business; it is part analysis, part design, part projection, and part calculated risk. Even when you use effective estimating methods and produce sound conceptual designs, you will still make mistakes. This is normal. If it happens more than about one-third of the time, however, reexamine your practices. Calculate the errors between the actual and planned times and sizes to see whether you can identify some of the causes of the variations.

Even if you continue making fairly large estimating errors, you can improve estimating accuracy by tracking and analyzing your estimates and, where you can, subdividing the estimates into parts. For example, suppose you have historical data showing that the standard deviation (or error) of your size estimates is 25%. If you estimate a large job as a single 10,000-LOC unit, the likely error would be 25%, or 2,500 LOC. This would mean that, about 65% of the time, the actual size for this program would fall between 7,500 and 12,500 LOC, or 10,000 LOC plus or minus one standard deviation. Next, suppose that before you estimated this 10,000-LOC program, you subdivided it into 100 parts and had each part independently estimated by 100 different estimators. Because the average of these estimates would be about 100 LOC, the size of the combined estimate would be 100 times the average, or 10,000 LOC.

Now, assuming that all of these 100 estimators had the same 25% estimating error, each estimate would have a standard deviation of 25 LOC. To find the likely error of the combined estimates, you would combine their variances to get the variance of the total estimate. Because the variance is the square of the standard deviation, you would then take the square root of the variance to get the standard deviation of the total estimate. The standard deviation of each estimate is 25 LOC, so the variance is 625, giving 62,500 as the variance of the total estimate. The standard deviation of the total is then the square root of this, or 250 LOC. This means that about 65% of the time, the combined estimate would have an expected error of 250 LOC, or one-tenth the standard deviation of your original 10,000-LOC estimate. Making the estimate in 100 parts reduced the expected error by ten times.

Dividing an estimate into parts can help you to better understand the planned product and make more accurate judgments about its size. However, you won't get

the statistical advantages of multiple estimates unless you use independent estimators. If you make all of the estimates yourself, you should still expect a 25%
error for the total estimate.

Estimating Bias

Estimating errors are of two general kinds. First, estimating accuracy will fluctuate by some average amount (the standard deviation). Second, the estimates may
have a bias. For example, you might tend to estimate 40% too low. Using the preceding example, for this 10,000-LOC program, your estimates would fluctuate
around 6,000 LOC, not 10,000 LOC. Next, with the 100 estimators, if each estimated 40% too low, the nominal 100-LOC programs would be estimated with a
bias of 40 LOC and a standard deviation of 25 LOC. Statistically speaking, the average of the sum of these estimates is the sum of their averages, so the combined
estimate would then be 100 times the average, or 6,000 LOC. That is, the bias of
40 LOC would affect every estimate, and the resulting estimate for the total program would be around 6,000 LOC.

Again, the combined error of the independent estimates would be 250 LOC,
meaning that about 65% of the time, the actual size would be expected to fall between 5,750 and 6,250 LOC. That is, it would be within about plus or minus 250
LOC of the biased average estimate of 6,000 LOC. Although this estimate looks
even worse than the original 10,000 estimate, it actually is a much better estimate.
In other words, the bias is likely to be a more consistent error that can be measured
and at least partially compensated for, whereas the variance is not. If you were to
gather data on many such estimates and calculate their biases, and if the estimating process were reasonably stable, you could make an accurate bias adjustment.

Estimate bias depends on the data you use, your estimating methods, and
your knowledge of the application. It also depends on how much design work you
have done, your degree of optimism about the job, and your estimating ability. The
amount of an estimator's bias will fluctuate over time, and it can be radically influenced by such factors as management pressure, personal commitment, or the
degree of error in the prior estimate.

To manage estimating bias, use an estimating method that relies on historical
data. Then, consistently use average values in your estimating. If, for example, you
believe that a new programming project has several very difficult functions, estimate the job in several parts and treat these difficult functions as relatively large.
For the overall job, however, try to have as many small parts as very large ones so
that the total estimate will come out to be about equal to your historical average.
If you do this, individual estimates may be high or low, but your estimates will be
correct on average. You will then have eliminated estimating bias.

An important objective of the PSP is to improve your ability to make estimates. Some developers' estimating errors swing quite widely between frequent

large underestimates and large overestimates. As they learn to use historical size data and to track their estimating experience, however, their estimating ability gradually improves. Even the most experienced estimators, however, occasionally make significant errors. By measuring and analyzing your estimates, you will learn how to make better estimates, and how to compensate for your estimating biases. For example, if you always estimate too low, you will soon recognize this trend and begin to reduce your bias. Over time, then, your estimates will tend to fluctuate around zero.

The PROBE method, described in Chapter 6, uses the linear-regression method to achieve better estimates. The basic philosophy behind PROBE is to provide a procedure and the data for making progressively more accurate estimates. The defined procedure helps to produce more consistent results, and the data from each estimate will help you to gradually reduce the standard deviation and bias of the estimates. Furthermore, by gathering and using your own estimating data, your estimating accuracy will improve.

Incomplete Knowledge Bias

In considering estimating accuracy, there is another important source of error. When you estimate the size of a new program before you have designed it, you will be uncertain about precisely how big it will be. The only way to completely compensate for this uncertainty would be to complete the design and implementation before making the estimate. Of course, this is impractical when you need an estimate and a plan before making a commitment. In this situation, your best alternative is to gather all of the available historical data, use an estimating method such as PROBE that compensates for incomplete knowledge bias, and utilize the judgment of any available experts to help you make the best possible estimate.

Although the lack of product knowledge will increase estimating variance, its most important impact is on estimating bias. Because bias is a natural consequence of early estimates, it is important that you learn as much about it as possible. One approach for large projects is to reestimate the program's size at several points during development. Assuming that you make all of the estimates yourself, they should become increasingly accurate as development progresses. Over time, as you gather data on more projects, you will learn how much error to expect at each phase. To properly use these data, you would then use different regression parameters for each development phase.

On a TSP project, you make new size and resource estimates after completing the requirements work, again after completing much of the design work, and again after coding. If you kept a record of the phase for each estimate, you could compare the estimates with the actual results during the project postmortem. This would enable you to understand and at least partially compensate for the incomplete knowledge bias.

Overcompensation

If you consistently make underestimates or overestimates, examine your data and estimating practices. If the problems are principally with size estimating, you may not be using appropriate historical data, or you could be making too gross a conceptual design. Often, you can substantially improve your estimates by making a more complete conceptual design. Don't overdo it, however, as you should not complete the design before making the estimate. The objective is to learn how to make accurate estimates before doing the work. Conversely, if the problem is principally with the time calculations, examine the variation among seemingly similar tasks. Try to understand the factors that cause some tasks to take longer than others, and figure out how to plan for these factors. Remember that if you estimate everything as an "average" project, on average you will be right. Good methods and personal data produce balanced plans; experience and skill gradually reduce planning errors.

If you alternately underestimate and overestimate, try to stabilize your estimating process. However, don't try to adjust each estimate to compensate for the error in the previous one. Such intuitive adjustments are almost impossible to control. The danger in adjusting your intuition is that you could lose your intuitive sense by trying to treat it analytically. Make your adjustments in the data and estimating methods.

If your estimating accuracy continues to oscillate, seek help from a PSP instructor, a TSP coach, or a teammate. Ask them to review your estimate and to raise issues and questions. By explaining your estimates, you will better see how to improve them. Always make your own estimates, but do not hesitate to have others review and comment on them.

Selecting an Abstraction Level

If you pick a reasonably detailed abstraction level for your estimates, you will have more data points. The smaller the abstraction, the more actual versus estimated data you will get from each project. Conversely, if you pick too small an abstraction level, you could have trouble visualizing the small proxies. For example, if the typical parts for your programs have items that average about 10 LOC and there are 5 items per part, then the parts will average about 50 LOC each. When you later use the PROBE method to estimate a 50,000-LOC system, you will then have to identify, categorize, and estimate the sizes of about 1,000 parts. This could be a substantial job.

Large Systems

For systems much larger than about 5,000 LOC, it could be a major job to reduce the conceptual design to low-level parts. TSP teams typically handle this problem by dividing systems into 10 to 20 or so major parts and estimating their sizes as a team. Generally, the combined experience of all team members provides enough historical data to enable TSP teams to make pretty good estimates, even before they have firm requirements.

Although such high-level abstractions are generally hard to categorize, once you have used PROBE on several projects, you will have learned how to use historical data to make size estimates, and you will have an intuitive feel for the sizes of even fairly large components and subsystems. Then, after completing some high-level design work, you will know enough to make much more detailed estimates.

Unprecedented Products

The PROBE method assumes that you can produce a conceptual design fairly quickly and that you can subdivide this design into familiar parts or components. Although this is not generally a problem for products of types that you have previously built, it is more difficult for new and unprecedented products. An *unprecedented product* is one whose size, complexity, performance, function, or some other important characteristic is so different from anything you have previously developed that you have no benchmarks to guide your planning or development work. The best solution in these cases is to resist making firm estimates for unprecedented products until you have completed a feasibility study and built some prototypes. This experience should provide the knowledge to refine the conceptual design to a level where you have historical data. If you can't do this, then you are no longer making an estimate, you are making a guess.

5.7 Summary

In project planning, estimates are generally required before you can begin development. At this early stage, you may generally understand the requirements but know little else about the product. Therefore, you will need a proxy to relate product size to the required product functions. The criteria for a good proxy are that its size should be closely related to the effort needed to develop the product and that it can be automatically counted. It should also be easy to visualize at the beginning of the job and be sensitive to language, style, and design differences that might affect the development effort.

In using a proxy, divide your data into ranges that correspond to the sizes of the proxy items in your database. With the PSP, the practice is to divide the proxy items into five size ranges: very large (VL), large (L), medium (M), small (S), and very small (VS).

6

The PROBE
Estimating Method

The principal objective of the estimating process is to produce accurate estimates. To do this, you must start with the best requirements you can get, obtain good historical data, and use a sound estimating method. Because your early estimates will likely have large errors, you also need a way to judge and improve your estimating accuracy. The PROBE method shows you how to obtain estimating data, how to use these data to make estimates, and how to measure and improve the accuracy of your estimates.

6.1 Estimating from Data

The PROBE method guides you in using historical data to make estimates. For example, in estimating the work to develop a database query system, you would first produce the conceptual design and then divide it into parts. Then you would estimate the number of elements in each part. For example, if you estimate a total of 80 elements and you know that each element has taken you, on average, 1.5 hours to develop, the total development-time estimate would be 120 hours, or 80 (the number of elements) times 1.5 (the time per element).

To make accurate estimates, however, you need a statistically sound way to determine the average time required to develop a part. The PROBE method shows you how to do this. Figure 6.1 shows data on 21 database projects. These are the same data shown in Figure 3.1 (see p. 39). The trend line for these data is calculated with a method called **linear regression**. It produces a line that accurately fits the data. The **trend line**, or **regression line**, is represented by the following equation:

$$\text{Development Time} = \beta_0 + \beta_1 * \text{EstimatedSize}$$
$$= 0.17 + 1.53 * 80 = 122.57$$

Here, $\beta_0 = 0.17$ and $\beta_1 = 1.53$. These β values are calculated by the PROBE method described in this chapter and they are determined mathematically to best represent the trend of the data. The β_1 value is the average development time required per database element, or about 1.5 hours per element, and β_0 is the overhead time. In other words, this equation indicates that, for a project with no elements, the development time would be 0.17 hour, or about 10 minutes. For larger projects, you would then add 1.5 hours per element.

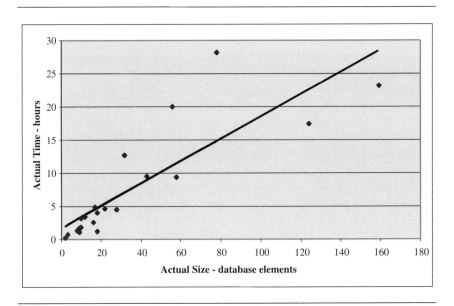

FIGURE 6.1 EXAMPLE DATABASE ESTIMATING DATA

6.2   Proxy-Based Estimating

The *PRO*xy-*B*ased *E*stimating (PROBE) method enables you to use any item you choose as the proxy, as long as it meets the criteria for a good proxy that are described in Chapter 5 (see pp. 71–74). Using one developer's data, the basic steps of the size estimating procedure are shown in Figure 6.2 and described in the following paragraphs. Because, at least initially, you will not have enough data to use the full PROBE method, several exception cases are described later in the chapter.

PROBE Step 1: The Conceptual Design

After you complete the conceptual design, you identify the parts of the product you plan to develop. You are now ready to make the size estimate.

PROBE Step 2: Estimate Parts Size

Following the methods described in Chapter 5, estimate the sizes of the conceptual design's parts. Do this by determining the part types and then judging the number of items (methods) for each part and the relative sizes of the items. Once you know whether an item is very small (VS), small (S), medium (M), large (L), or very large (VL), look up the item size in a table like Table 5.1 (see p. 77).

   For example, the size estimate made by Student 12 for Program 8 is shown in Table 6.1. She first named each added part in the conceptual design and determined its type. The first part, Matrix, was of the type *Data*. She next estimated that this part would likely contain 13 items and judged their relative size to be medium. Finally, she determined from Table 5.1 that a medium Data part would have 8.84 LOC per item. Multiplying this by the number of items resulted in 114.9 LOC. She then repeated this procedure for each added part to arrive at a total of 361 added-part LOC. After completing the project, she entered the actual sizes for these same parts.

   If a part has items of different types, estimate each part-item combination as a separate part. For example, if class A has items (methods) of type Char, Calc, and Print, treat these as three parts: AChar, ACalc, and APrint.

PROBE Step 3: Estimate the Sizes of the Reused Parts and Base Additions

In PROBE step 3, estimate the size of any other program parts (base, deleted, reused, and so on). For example, if you can find available parts that provide the functions required by your conceptual design, you may be able to reuse them. Provided that

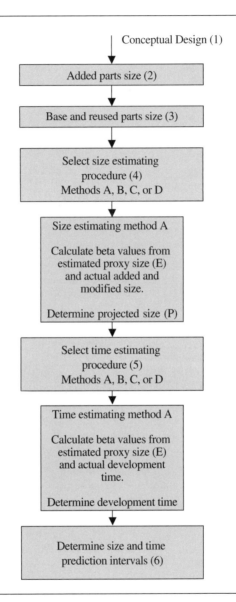

FIGURE 6.2 THE PROBE ESTIMATING METHOD

TABLE 6.1 THE PARTS ADDITION ESTIMATE

Parts Additions	Type	Estimated Items	Rel. Size	Size*	Actual Size*	Items
Matrix	Data	13	M	115	136	14
LinearSystem	Calc.	8	L	197	226	11
LinkedList	Data	3	L	49*	54*	3
Control	Logic				48	2
Total			**PA**	361	464	

these parts work as intended and are of suitable quality, reusing available parts can save considerable time. For any parts from the reuse library, note their names and sizes under *Reused Parts*. In the example shown in Table 6.2, Student 12 identified two reused parts with a total of 169 LOC.

PROBE considers two kinds of reused parts. First are the parts taken from a reuse library. The second, the *new-reusable* parts, are some of the added parts you have already estimated. Identify these as new-reusable parts if you plan to use them in developing other programs. It is good practice to build a library of useful parts when working in a new application environment. Then, when developing new programs, code you plan to add to the reuse library is new-reusable code. In Table 6.1, Student 12 planned to add three items to the LinkedList part, or 49 LOC of estimated new-reusable code. She noted these items with an asterisk beside their LOC estimates. Because she took the other LinkedList items from the reuse library, she included them as *Reused Parts*.

If you plan to modify an existing program, determine the size of the base program to be enhanced and the sizes of any changes you expect to make. Table 6.3

TABLE 6.2 REUSED PARTS ESTIMATE

Reused Parts		Estimated Size	Actual Size
LinkedList		73	73
DataEntry		96	96
	Total R	169	169

TABLE 6.3 SIZE ESTIMATING TEMPLATE

Student	Student 12	Date __5/1__
Program	Multiple Regression	Program # __8__
Instructor	Humphrey	Language __C++__
Size Measure	LOC	

Base Parts	Base	Estimated Deleted	Modified	Added
PSP Program 3	695	0	5	0
Total **B**	695 **D**	0 **M**	5 **BA**	0

Base Parts	Base	Actual Deleted	Modified	Added
PSP Program 3	695	0	18	0
Total	695	0	18	0

Parts Additions	Type	Estimated Items	Rel. Size	Size*	Actual Size*	Items
Matrix	Data	13	M	115	136	14
LinearSystem	Calc.	8	L	197	226	11
LinkedList	Data	3	L	49*	54*	3
Control	Logic				48	2
Total			**PA**	361	464	

90

TABLE 6.3 (continued)

Student   Student 12   Program   8

Reused Parts	Estimated Size	Actual Size
LinkedList	73	73
DataEntry	96	96
Total R	169	169

PROBE Calculation Worksheet (Added and Modified)

		Size	Time
Added size (A):	$A = BA + PA$	361	
Estimated proxy size (E):	$E = BA + PA + M$	366	
PROBE estimating basis used:	(A, B, C, or D)	A	A
Correlation:	(R^2)	0.62	0.58
Regression Parameters:	β_0 Size and Time	62	108
Regression Parameters:	β_1 Size and Time	1.3	2.95
Projected Added and Modified Size (P):	$P = \beta_{0\,size} + \beta_{1\,size}{}^*E$	538	
Estimated Total Size (T):	$T = P + B - D - M + R$	1397	
Estimated Total New Reusable (NR):	sum of * items	49	
Estimated Total Development Time:	Time $= \beta_{0\,time} + \beta_{1\,time}{}^* E$		1186
Prediction Range:	Range	235	431
Upper Prediction Interval:	UPI $= P + $ Range	773	1617
Lower Prediction Interval:	LPI $= P - $ Range	303	755
Prediction Interval Percent:		90	90

shows the completed PSP Size Estimating Template with the added and reused parts, the base parts, and the planned modifications. Student 12 identified 695 LOC of base code, 5 of which she planned to modify. She actually did modify 18 LOC.

Although developers occasionally get to develop entirely new programs, most of our work is enhancing existing programs. Here, base program size is the total size of the unmodified program before development. Base additions are for enhancements you make to the base program. If you know enough about the base product to do so, estimate base additions the same way you estimate added parts.

The reused category is only for unmodified parts. When modifying existing programs, the unmodified program is the base, and you estimate its additions, changes, and deletions. Even if the base program is unmodified, it is not considered reused unless it was specifically intended for reuse. The reused category is only for parts that come directly from the reuse library without *any* modification.

The final part of step 3 is to add all of the parts estimates to obtain the estimated proxy size (E), to be entered in the Size Estimating Template in Table 6.3. E is the number used by PROBE to make the size and time projections. In the example, Student 12 had a total of 361 LOC of parts additions, 5 LOC of modifications, and 0 LOC of base additions, resulting in a value of 361 + 5 + 0 = 366 LOC for E. This number is entered in the Estimated proxy size (E) space on line 2 of the PROBE Calculation Worksheet.

PROBE Step 4: The Size Estimating Procedure

In PROBE step 4, check your data to determine whether you can use PROBE method A. After you have used the PSP for a while, you will normally use method A to make size and time estimates. Later in the chapter, after examining the basic PROBE method A, you will learn how to use PROBE methods B, C, and D to make estimates with limited data.

With estimated proxy size E, you can calculate the projected program size P and total estimated development time. If, for example, historical data showed that your finished programs were generally about 25% larger than estimated, you might add a 25% fudge factor to each estimate. The PROBE method essentially does this but in a statistically sound way. As noted before, the method is called linear regression. Although these calculations are a little more complex than taking simple averages, they use historical data to produce a statistically sound estimate. The parameters β_0 and β_1 are used in the following equation to calculate projected added and modified size:

$$\text{Projected Added and Modified Size (P)} = \beta_0 + \beta_1 * E$$

When two sets of data are strongly related, you can use the linear regression method to represent that relationship. As Figure 5.2 (see p. 73) and Figure 5.3 (see p. 75) show, estimated part size and actual added and modified size are often closely correlated. This means that linear regression is often appropriate. The parameters β_0 and β_1 are calculated from your historical data. These calculations are described later with an example.

Finished programs usually contain more than just the parts specified in the conceptual design. For example, they will likely contain declaration and header code that is not included in the parts estimates. To account for this and for any other such code, you must use a factor that is based on your historical experience. Fortunately, the PROBE method accounts for this factor when it calculates the β_0 and β_1 parameters.

In the example shown in Table 6.3, the fact that $\beta_1 = 1.3$ indicates that Student 12's finished programs have historically been 30% bigger than the total of the estimated parts and modifications. In addition, the value $\beta_0 = 62$ indicates that, on average, she underestimated by 62 LOC. As shown in Table 6.3, the regression calculations result in a total of 538 projected added and modified LOC. In this case, because added and modified code were used in making the size estimate, total program size is calculated by adding the 695 LOC of base code and the 169 LOC of reused code, and subtracting the 5 LOC of modified code. The total estimate is then 1,397 LOC for the finished program. The modified LOC are subtracted because they would otherwise be counted twice: once in the 695 LOC of base code and again in the estimated proxy size (E). As noted in size accounting in Chapter 3 (see p. 42), a line of modified code is treated as both an added line and a deleted line.

PROBE Step 5: The Time Estimating Procedure

In PROBE step 5, again check your data to determine whether you can use PROBE method A for the time estimates. Although method A is also the preferred method for time estimates, you can also use alternative methods B, C, and D, which are described later in the chapter. Once you have obtained the β values for time, use them and the estimated proxy size (E) to calculate the estimated development time. Then enter the size and time estimates in the plan spaces in the Project Plan Summary shown in Table 6.4.

PROBE Step 6: The Prediction Interval

The final calculations on the PROBE Size Estimating Template are for the **prediction interval**. The prediction interval is a statistically determined range around your size or time estimate within which the actual value is likely to fall. For a 70% prediction interval, you would expect the actual time and size values to fall outside of this range about 30% of the time. The prediction interval is described in Chapter 7.

TABLE 6.4 PSP1 PROJECT PLAN SUMMARY

Student	Student 12	Date	5/1
Program	Multiple Regression	Program #	8
Instructor	Humphrey	Language	C++

Summary Size/Hour	Plan	Actual	To Date
	27.4	30.9	23.4

Program Size	Plan	Actual	To Date
Base (B)	695	695	
	(Measured)	(Measured)	
Deleted (D)	0	0	
	(Estimated)	(Counted)	
Modified (M)	5	18	
	(Estimated)	(Counted)	
Added (A)	533	464	
	(A&M – M)	(T – B + D – R)	
Reused (R)	169	169	
	(Estimated)	(Counted)	
Added and Modified (A&M)	538	482	2081
	(Projected)	(A + M)	
Total Size (T)	1397	1328	5161
	(A&M + B – M – D + R)	(Measured)	
Total New Reusable	49	54	294

Estimated Proxy Size (E)	366

Time in Phase (min.)	Plan	Actual	To Date	To Date %
Planning	146	166	710	13.3
Design	425	332	1220	22.8
Code	390	333	1639	30.6
Compile	30	16	288	5.4
Test	105	31	749	14.1
Postmortem	90	58	737	13.8
Total	1186	936	5343	100

Defects Injected	Actual	To Date	To Date %
Planning	2	6	3.5
Design	11	38	22.0
Code	26	129	74.5
Compile	0	0	0
Test	0	0	0
Total Development	39	173	100

Defects Removed	Actual	To Date	To Date %
Planning	0	0	0
Design	10	10	5.8
Code	19	72	41.6
Compile	10	61	35.3
Test	0	30	17.3
Total Development	39	173	100
After Development			

6.3   Estimating with Limited Data

Table 6.5 shows the four PROBE methods, the conditions for using them, and how they are used. These methods are also described in the PROBE Estimating Script in Table 6.6, the Size Estimating Template Instructions in Table 6.7, and the PROBE Calculation Worksheet Instructions in Table 6.8.

By choosing one of the four PROBE size estimating procedures, you decide how to calculate the β parameters. Base this choice on the quality of your data. Method A should be your first choice but it requires at least three, and preferably four, data points of *estimated proxy size* (E) and *actual added and modified size* that correlate with an $r >= 0.7$. If you can't use method A, try to use method B. This method uses *plan added and modified size* and *actual added and modified size*. Again, you must have at least three, and preferably four, data points that correlate with an $r >= 0.7$. If the data are not adequate for methods A and B, then use method C if you have at least some data on plan and actual added and modified size. If you don't have any data, you must use method D. With method D, you are not actually making a projection but merely guessing at a value to enter as

TABLE 6.5 THE FOUR ALTERNATE PROBE CALCULATION METHODS

Method	Data Used for Beta Values		Data Requirements
	Size	Time	
A	Estimated proxy size and actual program size	Estimated proxy size and actual development time	The data must correlate with $r >= 0.7$
B	Planned program size and actual program size	Planned program size and actual development time	The data must correlate with $r >= 0.7$
C	Planned program size if available and actual program size. Set $\beta_0 = 0$ and $\beta_1 =$ to-date actual size/to-date planned size. If planned data not available, set $\beta_1 = 1.0$	Planned program size if available and actual development time. If planned size data not available, use actual size. Set $\beta_0 = 0$ and $\beta_1 =$ to-date actual time/to-date planned size. If planned data not available, set $\beta_1 =$ to-date actual time/to-date actual size.	Some actual size and time data
D			No data

TABLE 6.6 PROBE ESTIMATING SCRIPT

Purpose	To guide the size and time estimating process using the PROBE method
Entry Criteria	• Requirements statement • Size Estimating template and instructions • Size per item data for part types • Time Recording log • Historical size and time data
General	• This script assumes that you are using added and modified size data as the size-accounting types for making size and time estimates. • If you choose some other size-accounting types, replace every "added and modified" in this script with the size-accounting types of your choice.

Step	Activities	Description
1	Conceptual Design	Review the requirements and produce a conceptual design.
2	Parts Additions	Follow the Size Estimating template instructions to estimate the parts additions and the new reusable parts sizes.
3	Base Parts and Reused Parts	• For the base program, estimate the size of the base, deleted, modified, and added code. • Measure and/or estimate the side of the parts to be reused.
4	Size Estimating Procedure	• If you have sufficient estimated proxy size and actual added and modified size data (three or more points that correlate), use procedure 4A. • If you do not have sufficient estimated data but have sufficient plan added and modified and actual added and modified size data (three or more points that correlate), use procedure 4B. • If you have insufficient data or they do not correlate, use procedure 4C. • If you have no historical data, use procedure 4D.
4A	Size Estimating Procedure 4A	• Using the linear-regression method, calculate the β_0 and β_1 parameters from the estimated proxy size and actual added and modified size data. • If the absolute value of β_0 is not near 0 (less than about 25% of the expected size of the new program), or β_1 is not near 1.0 (between about 0.5 and 2.0), use procedure 4B.
4B	Size Estimating Procedure 4B	• Using the linear-regression method, calculate the β_0 and β_1 parameters from the plan added and modified size and actual added and modified size data. • If the absolute value of β_0 is not near 0 (less than about 25% of the expected size of the new program), or β_1 is not near 1.0 (between about 0.5 and 2.0), use procedure 4C.
4C	Size Estimating Procedure 4C	If you have any data on plan added and modified size and actual added and modified size, set $\beta_0 = 0$ and $\beta_1 = $ (actual total added and modified size to date/plan total added and modified size to date).
4D	Size Estimating Procedure 4D	If you have no historical data, use your judgment to estimate added and modified size.

TABLE 6.6 (continued)

Step	Activities	Description
5	Time Estimating Procedure	• If you have sufficient estimated proxy size and actual development time data (three or more points that correlate), use procedure 5A. • If you do not have sufficient estimated size data but have sufficient plan added and modified size and actual development time data (three or more points that correlate), use procedure 5B. • If you have insufficient data or they do not correlate, use procedure 5C. • If you have no historical data, use procedure 5D.
5A	Time Estimating Procedure 5A	• Using the linear-regression method, calculate the β_0 and β_1 parameters from the estimated proxy size and actual total development time data. • If β_0 is not near 0 (substantially smaller than the expected development time for the new program), or β_1 is not within 50% of 1/(historical productivity), use procedure 5B.
5B	Time Estimating Procedure 5B	• Using the linear-regression method, calculate the β_0 and β_1 regression parameters from the plan added and modified size and actual total development time data. • If β_0 is not near 0 (substantially smaller than the expected development time for the new program), or β_1 is not within 50% of 1/(historical productivity), use procedure 5C.
5C	Time Estimating Procedure 5C	• If you have data on estimated—added and modified size and actual development time, set $\beta_0 = 0$ and $\beta_1 =$ (actual total development time to date/estimated – total added and modified size to date). • If you have data on plan – added and modified size and actual development time, set $\beta_0 = 0$ and $\beta_1 =$ (actual total development time to date/plan total added and modified size to date). • If you only have actual time and size data, set $\beta_0 = 0$ and $\beta_1 =$ (actual total development time to date/actual total added and modified size to date).
5D	Time Estimating Procedure 5D	If you have no historical data, use your judgment to estimate the development time from the estimated added and modified size.
6	Time and Size Prediction Intervals	• If you used regression method A or B, calculate the 70% prediction intervals for the time and size estimates. • If you did not use the regression method or do not know how to calculate the prediction interval, calculate the minimum and maximum development time estimate limits from your historical maximum and minimum productivity for the programs written to date.
Exit Criteria		• Completed estimated and actual entries for all pertinent size categories • Completed PROBE Calculation Worksheet with size and time entries • Plan and actual values entered on the Project Plan Summary

the plan added and modified size or the development time on the Project Plan Summary.

After selecting an estimating method, calculate the β_0 and β_1 values and verify that they are reasonable. If β_0 for size is larger than about 25% of the planned program's expected size, or β_1 is not between about 0.5 and 2.0, use method B; if

TABLE 6.7 SIZE ESTIMATING TEMPLATE INSTRUCTIONS

Purpose	Use this form with the PROBE method to make size estimates.
General	• A part could be a module, component, product, or system. • Where parts have a substructure of methods, procedures, functions, or similar elements, these lowest-level elements are called items. • Size values are assumed to be in the unit specified in size measure. • Avoid confusing base size with reuse size. • Reuse parts must be used without modification. • Use base size if additions, modifications, or deletions are planned. • If a part is estimated but not produced, enter its actual values as zero. • If a part is produced that was not estimated, enter it using zero for its planned values.
Header	• Enter your name and the date. • Enter the program name and number. • Enter the instructor's name and the programming language you are using. • Enter the size measure you are using.
Base Parts	If this is a modification or enhancement of an existing product • measure and enter the base size (more than one product may be entered as base) • estimate and enter the size of the deleted, modified, and added size to the base program After development, measure and enter the actual size of the base program and any deletions, modifications, or additions.
Parts Additions	If you plan to add newly developed parts • enter the part name, type, number of items (or methods), and relative size • for each part, get the size per item from the appropriate relative size table, multiply this value by the number of items, and enter in estimated size • put an asterisk next to the estimated size of any new-reusable additions After development, measure and enter • the actual size of each new part or new part items • the number of items for each new part
Reused Parts	If you plan to include reused parts, enter the • name of each unmodified reused part • size of each unmodified reused part After development, enter the actual size of each unmodified reused part.

the β values are still not within the desired ranges, use method C. For method C, with some size data, total the plan added and modified sizes for the programs for which you have data and total the actual added and modified sizes for the same programs. Then set β_1 equal to to-date total actual size divided by the to-date plan size and set β_0 to 0. If you don't have planned size data, set $\beta_1 = 1.0$. For method D, make your best guess.

For the time estimate, the guidelines are much the same. For example, if the time β_0 is larger than about 25% of the planned program's expected development

TABLE 6.8 PROBE CALCULATION WORKSHEET INSTRUCTIONS

Purpose	Use this form with the PROBE method to make size and resource estimate calculations.
General	The PROBE method can be used for many kinds of estimates. Where development time correlates with added and modified size • use the Added and Modified Calculation Worksheet • enter the resulting estimates in the Project Plan Summary • enter the projected added and modified value (P) in the added and modified plan space in the Project Plan Summary If development time correlates with some other combination of size-accounting types • define and use a new PROBE Calculation Worksheet • enter the resulting estimates in the Project Plan Summary • use the selected combination of size accounting types to calculate the projected size value (P) • enter this P value in the Project Plan Summary for the appropriate plan size for the size-accounting types being used
PROBE Calculations: Size (Added and Modified)	• Added Size (A): Total the added base code (BA) and Parts Additions (PA) to get Added Size (A). • Estimated Proxy Size (E): Total the added (A) and modified (M) sizes and enter as (E). • PROBE Estimating Basis Used: Analyze the available historical data and select the appropriate PROBE estimating basis (A, B, C, or D). • Correlation: If PROBE estimating basis A or B is selected, enter the correlation value (R^2) for both size and time. • Regression Parameters: Follow the procedure in the PROBE script to calculate the size and time regression parameters (β_0 and β_1), and enter them in the indicated fields. • Projected Added and Modified Size (P): Using the size regression parameters and estimated proxy size (E), calculate the projected added and modified size (P) as $P = \beta_{0Size} + \beta_{1Size} \text{*}E$. • Estimated Total Size (T): Calculate the estimated total size as T = P+B-D-M+R. • Estimated Total New Reusable (NR): Total and enter the new reusable items marked with *.
PROBE Calculations: Time (Added and Modified)	• PROBE Estimating Basis Used: Analyze the available historical data and select the appropriate PROBE estimating basis (A, B, C, or D). • Estimated Total Development Time: Using the time regression parameters and estimated proxy size (E), calculate the estimated development time as $Time = \beta_{0Time} + \beta_{1Time} \text{*}E$.
PROBE Calculations: Prediction Range	• Calculate and enter the prediction range for both the size and time estimates. • Calculate the upper (UPI) and lower (LPI) prediction intervals for both the size and time estimates. • Prediction Interval Percent: List the probability percent used to calculate the prediction intervals (70% or 90%).
After Development (Added and Modified)	Enter the actual sizes for base (B), deleted (D), modified (M), and added base code (BA), parts additions (PA), and reused parts (R)

time, or β_1 is not between about 0.5 and 2.0 times your historical hours/LOC, use method B; and if the β values are still not within the desired ranges, use method C. For method C, assuming that you have at least some size data, total the plan added and modified sizes for the programs for which you have data and total the actual development times for the same programs. Then set β_1 equal to the total actual development times divided by the total planned sizes and set β_0 to 0. For method D, make your best guess.

The final step in the PROBE method is to calculate the value of P, the projected program size, and the estimated development time and enter them on the Project Plan Summary. Enter the projected size for Added and Modified Size (A+M) in the *Plan* column; and the development time under Time in Phase, Total, in the *Plan* column.

For many types of software work, good correlations are likely for development time and added and modified size. If this is the case for your data, use the Calculation Worksheet in the PROBE Size Estimating Template (see Table 6.3, p. 91) to produce the projected value, P, as the Projected Added and Modified Size for the program. Then enter this value in the *Plan* column of the Project Plan Summary. However, if the best correlation was for some other combination of the size accounting types, you could use that. Then you would have to produce an appropriately modified PROBE Calculation Worksheet to calculate projected program size for the size accounting types you plan to use.

6.4   An Estimating Example

The following example shows the time-estimation calculations for the data in Table 6.9.

TABLE 6.9 EXAMPLE HISTORICAL DATA

Program Number	Estimated Proxy Size	Plan Added and Modified Size	Actual Total Hours
1		83	11.2
2		116	9.3
3		186	21.6
4	97	81	6.9
5	81	114	10.2
Totals	178	580	59.2

1. You have the estimated proxy size of E = 126 LOC.

2. As shown in Table 6.9, you have estimated proxy size data for only two programs, so you cannot use method A. Next, check the correlation between *Plan Added and Modified Size* and *Actual Total Hours* to determine whether you can use method B. Using the data values in Table 6.10 and the formulas shown in Box 3.1 (see p. 36), calculate the value of the correlation *r* as follows:

$$r = \frac{n * Sum(x * y) - Sum(x) * Sum(y)}{\sqrt{\left(n * Sum(x^2) - Sum(x)^2\right) * \left(n * Sum(y^2) - Sum(y)^2\right)}} =$$

$$r = \frac{5 * 7747.7 - 580 * 59.2}{\sqrt{(5 * 74498 - 580 * 580) * (5 * 830.14 - 59.2 * 59.2)}} = \frac{4402.5}{4828.7} = 0.9117$$

Because *r* >= 0.7, you can use method B.

Even though most PSP and TSP support tools make these calculations, you should understand how they are made. Box 6.1 gives the calculation method, and one of the PSP exercises is a program to calculate the regression parameters. The assignment kit for that program describes the calculations with an example.

3. Using the values in Table 6.10 with the formulas in Box 6.1, the regression parameters are as follows:

$$\beta_1 = \frac{Sum(x * y) - n * x_{avg} * y_{avg}}{Sum(x^2) - n * (x_{avg})^2} = \frac{7747.7 - 5 * 116 * 11.84}{74498 - 5 * 116^2} = 0.121987$$

$$\beta_0 = y_{avg} - \beta_1 * x_{avg} = 11.84 - 0.121987 * 116 = -2.31046$$

TABLE 6.10 EXAMPLE REGRESSION CALCULATIONS

Program Number	Estimated Proxy Size – x	Actual Hours – y	Size*Size x*x	Size*Hours x*y	Hours*Hours y*y
1	83	11.2	6,889	929.6	125.44
2	116	9.3	13,456	1,078.8	86.49
3	186	21.6	34,596	4,017.6	466.56
4	81	6.9	6,561	558.9	47.61
5	114	10.2	12,498	1,162.8	104.04
Total	580	59.2	74,498	7,747.7	830.14
Average	116	11.84			

Using these β values, calculate the estimated development time as follows:

Time $= \beta_0 + \beta_1 * E = -2.31046 + 126 * 0.121987 = 13.060$ hours

---

BOX 6.1 CALCULATING THE SIZE OR TIME PARAMETERS β_0 AND β_1

Start with n values of x and y, where x is the estimated proxy size (E) and y is the actual added and modified size or actual development time for the n programs:

$$\beta_1 = \frac{\sum\limits_{i=1}^{n} x_i y_i - n x_{avg} y_{avg}}{\sum\limits_{i=1}^{n} x_i^2 - n x_{avg}^2}$$

$$\beta_0 = y_{avg} - \beta_1 x_{avg}$$

6.5   Estimating Nonprogramming Tasks

Although most of the assignments in this book involve planning and developing small programs, two are for planning and producing reports. When working on almost any kind of project, the PSP methods can help you to plan, manage, and track your work. To estimate the time needed for the project's tasks, follow the decision tree shown in Figure 6.3. It illustrates the logic for selecting an estimating method. The following steps describe how to estimate the time needed to write a report that is estimated to have seven single-spaced pages. The developer's historical data are shown in Table 6.11 and the steps are numbered as shown in Figure 6.3.

1. Start with as clear an understanding of the task requirements as you can get.
2. Do you have a defined process for the task? It is difficult to make an intelligent plan with an ill-defined process for doing the work. It is also difficult to measure the work, track progress, or judge the quality of the result.
3. If the answer to step 2 is no, produce a simple process definition. This definition should divide the work into parts that represent between about 10% and 25% of the total job, and they must include the planning and postmortem steps. It is usually best to start with only four to eight steps. With experience and historical data, you can further refine this process.

TABLE 6.11 EXAMPLE REPORT-WRITING DATA

Job	Estimated Size x	Estimated Time	Actual Size	Actual Time y	x*x	x*y	y*y
494	6	900.00	4.00	556.00	36.00	3,336.00	309,136.00
498	6	600.00	5.00	575.00	36.00	3,450.00	330,625.00
501	6	830.00	5.00	1,003.00	36.00	6,018.00	1,006,009.00
502	3	415.00	5.00	431.00	9.00	1,293.00	185,761.00
507	5	600.00	3.50	431.00	25.00	2,155.00	185,761.00
Total	26	3,345.00	22.50	2,996.00	142.00	16,252.00	2,017,292.00

4. Do you have defined process measures? You need measures to plan your work, track your progress, and learn to make better plans in the future.

5. If your answer to step 4 is no, define at least size and time measures. For program development, include defect measures. For PSP planning purposes, you will need data for the time taken by each process step and the sizes of the products produced.

6. Do you have historical data? Historical data will help you to judge the size of the job and the effort required. The following example uses the data in Table 6.11 for writing documents.

7. Even if your answer to step 6 is no, you can usually identify some similar jobs and judge how long they took. If you have never measured any of your previous work, your estimates for new work could be off by three or more times. When estimates are this badly in error, they are generally too low. Under these conditions, using almost any relevant data will reduce your planning errors.

8. Estimate the size of the planned new product. In the example, the developer estimated that the report would require seven single-spaced pages.

9. To use PROBE, the estimated size data must correlate with the actual development time data with an $r >= 0.7$. In this case,

$$r = \frac{n * Sum(x * y) - Sum(x) * Sum(y)}{\sqrt{\left(n * Sum(x^2) - Sum(x)^2\right) * \left(n * Sum(y^2) - Sum(y)^2\right)}} =$$

$$r = \frac{5 * 16252 - 26 * 2996}{\sqrt{(5 * 142 - 26 * 26) * (5 * 2017292 - 2996 * 2996)}} = \frac{3364}{6144.5} = 0.5475$$

10. Because the answer to the question in step 9 is no, you must use PROBE method C and make an average estimate. With the data in Table 6.11, divide

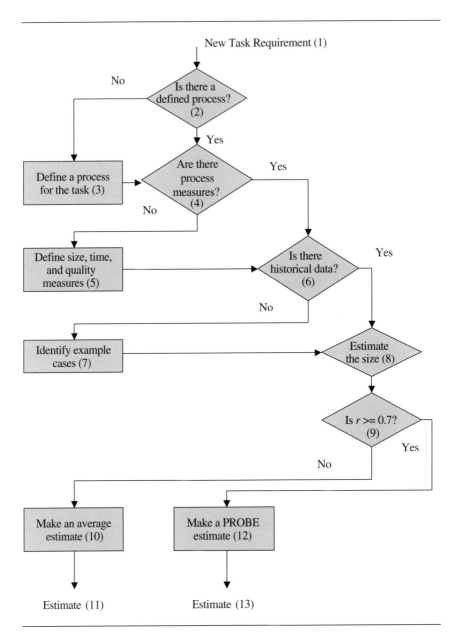

FIGURE 6.3 ESTIMATING NONPROGRAMMING TASKS

the total actual development time, 2,996 minutes, by the total estimated size of 26 pages to get a rate of 115.2 actual minutes per estimated page. For a job estimated to have seven pages, the development time would be 7 * 115.2 = 806.4 minutes or 13.4 hours.

11. Record the estimate.

12. If the answer to step 9 had been yes, you could have used PROBE method A or B. For method A, however, you would need a size proxy such as topic paragraphs with historical size data for various topic types and their sizes.

6.6   Considerations in Using PROBE

With experience and a growing volume of personal data, the PROBE method will help you to make progressively more accurate estimates and plans. The following discussion covers some of the more common questions about using PROBE.

Estimating Practice

While you are learning to make consistent estimates, your estimating accuracy will likely fluctuate widely, and your β_0 and β_1 parameters will change significantly from one program to the next. Over time, however, your estimates will tend to stabilize. Once the values of the regression parameters are reasonably stable, you can stop recalculating them for every program. Keep track of your estimating data, however, and periodically update the β parameters.

As you gain experience, your process will evolve and the data on some prior programs will no longer represent your current practice. When that occurs, drop the older data points and include only the newer and more representative ones. Always retain the data, of course, but only use data that represent how you currently work.

Estimating Judgment

In using any statistical method, you could get nonsensical results. For example, the β_0 and β_1 parameters represent a straight-line fit to the data. Because total program size is generally somewhat larger than estimated proxy size, you would expect β_1 to be somewhat larger than 1.0. A β_1 of 1.25, for example, would mean that on average, your total programs have an added and modified content that is about 25% larger than estimated part size.

If the data contain some wildly inaccurate estimates, however, it is possible to get almost anything for the β_0 and β_1 values. In fact, I have seen β_1 values as low as 0.05 and as high as 4.0 or more. A negative β_1 is even possible. When the value of β_1 is this far from 1.0, the linear regression method is likely to give misleading results. This would also be the case if the value of β_0 were a large positive or negative number. A large β_0 value would be one with an absolute value that was larger than the sizes of some small programs or a significant fraction of the size of the program you are currently estimating. When the linear regression parameters are obviously incorrect, use method C for the estimates. That is, add up all of the proxy size estimates and all of the actual added and modified sizes for these same programs. Then use the ratios of these totals to make the estimate.

Suppose the estimated proxy size for a new program is 137 LOC. Suppose also that you found the values of β_0 and β_1 to be 168 and 0.26, respectively. Even if your data correlated, when β_0 is large and β_1 is much less than 1.0, use an averaging method instead of linear regression. For example, if the sum of the proxy LOC estimates for the previous four programs was 427 LOC and the sum of the actual added and modified LOC for these same programs was 583 LOC, the ratio of these would be 1.365. In this case, set β_0 to 0 and β_1 to 1.365. With 137 proxy LOC for the new program, the added and modified size estimate for the new program would be 137 * 1.365 = 187 LOC.

Whenever either the size or time linear-regression parameters appear unreasonable, follow method C and use average values for the estimates. In addition, occasionally check your linear-regression estimates against an estimate made with average data. If the results are significantly different, check your calculations and reconsider the suitability of using linear regression. Differences of 20% to 30% should not concern you, but much larger errors, if they persist, could indicate that your estimating data is out of date or no longer appropriate. Furthermore, if your estimating accuracy starts to deteriorate, check your data and recalculate the β parameters.

Outliers

The reason for nonsensical values of β_0 and β_1 is often that you have included one or more **outlier** points in the data. An outlier is a data point where something unusual occurred, such as the requirements changed or you made an unusual mistake when producing the conceptual design. If you just made a larger-than-normal estimating error, you cannot discard that point. For every point you discard, describe in your assignment report the nature of the nonrecurring event that justified treating this point as an outlier. The reason to discard outlier points is that they can cause the regression method to produce nonsensical results. After removing any outliers, make sure you still have at least three points that show a reasonable correlation between program size and development hours—that is, $r >= 0.7$.

Another common cause of trouble is that all of the data are bunched in a narrow range. For example, if you had data for a large number of programs that all contained 75 to 100 database elements, you wouldn't have a wide enough range of data to give a reasonable trend. Another potential problem is having a lot of clustered data with one extreme point. For example, if you have 12 data points that all fall between 75 and 100 database elements and one point for 350 elements, you will likely get a high correlation. Unless you are confident that the extreme point was truly representative of your performance, the high correlation could be misleading. In that case, you should use method C.

Using Limited Data

Another problem, particularly when you are just starting to use the PSP, is having few historical data points. To use linear regression, you must have at least three sets of historical values. Therefore, you cannot use PROBE method A until you have estimated part data for at least three programs, and you can't use method B until you have estimated added and modified data for at least three programs. Until then, use method C, the averaging method, to make the size and resource estimates.

Overcompensation and Undercompensation

In addition to the overcompensation considerations discussed in Chapter 5 (see p. 83), normal statistical variation can also affect your estimating judgment. Analyze your estimating accuracy and make appropriate adjustments, but only after thoughtfully studying the data. If you attempt to correct your process for normal statistical fluctuations, you will almost certainly get worse results. The best approach is to consciously make corrections only when you change your process or identify erroneous or ineffective practices. Then maintain these changes consistently for several estimates, even if they appear to overcorrect for the previously observed problems.

Although you should follow a consistent estimating pattern and not worry about each error, this is almost impossible. The estimation process involves so many judgments that it is easily biased. The only reliable approach is to use a defined method and historical data. When you consistently use the same methods and are guided by the data, the statistical aberrations will be reduced. Though you must still make judgments, you can check them to ensure that they are reasonably balanced and consistent with the data. The regression method is essentially a way to use personal data to make estimates. If your estimates are consistently near the average values indicated by your data, your estimates will, on average, always be accurate.

6.7   Summary

The principal reason to estimate the size of a software product is to help you make plans. The quality of these plans will then depend on the quality of the estimates. This accuracy, in turn, will depend on the quality of the data and the soundness of the estimating methods you use. The PROBE method provides a statistically sound way to make estimates, and the PSP process will guide you in gathering and using the data you need to make accurate plans.

When using PROBE, you gather estimated and actual size and time data for each project. Then you divide the size data into categories and size ranges. The estimating process starts with a conceptual design followed by an estimate of the sizes of the proxy parts in that design. With the total estimated proxy size, the PROBE method shows you how to estimate program size and development time.

When estimating a large job as a single unit, there are two sources of error. First, estimating accuracy will fluctuate around some mean or average. Second, the estimate will typically have some bias. If you gathered data on many estimates and calculated the biases, and if the estimating process were reasonably stable, you could make an accurate bias adjustment. This, in fact, is what the PROBE method does.

Without data and without a defined estimating method, your estimates often will be inconsistent and unpredictable. By using the PROBE method and historical data on your personal work, you can minimize this error. Then, as you gather data and gain experience, you will make progressively better estimates. Of course, because estimating is an uncertain process, you should expect some estimating error. With the PROBE method, however, you can consistently make balanced estimates and judge the accuracy of your estimates.

6.8   Exercises

The assignment for this chapter is to use PSP1 to write one or more programs. The PSP1 process and the program specifications are given in the assignment kits, which you can get from your instructor or at **www.sei.cmu.edu/tsp/**. Each kit contains the assignment specifications, an example of the calculations involved, and the PSP1 process scripts. In completing this assignment, faithfully follow the PSP1 process, record all required data, and produce the program report according to the specifications given in each assignment kit.

7

Software Planning

Up to this point, we have examined estimating, but the objective of the planning process is to produce a plan. This chapter describes how to use the results of the estimating process to produce a project plan. Starting with a discussion of plan requirements, this chapter covers project and period plans, making schedules, and tracking and reporting progress. The chapter also discusses planning accuracy, plan changes, and management reporting. Although the change-management and reporting issues are not very significant for the PSP exercises, they will be more important when you work on a TSP team. Because the PSP methods can be extremely helpful in handling these plan-management issues, they are covered in this chapter.

7.1 Plan Requirements

In producing a plan, the result must meet certain requirements. The five basic requirements for a plan are that it be accessible, clear, specific, precise, and accurate. These topics are discussed in the following paragraphs.

Is It Accessible?

Accessibility is best illustrated by the case of a company that was fighting a major U.S. government lawsuit. At one point, they were required to provide all of the historical documents that related to a particular topic. Because the company was large, this material was scattered among thousands of files. The cost of searching all those files would have been prohibitive, so the company gave the plaintiff all the files that could possibly contain any of the desired data. Even though these files undoubtedly contained material the company didn't want released, they judged this problem to be minor compared to the costs of a detailed document review. Although the plaintiff knew that what he wanted was somewhere in the many thousands of pages of files, he might as well not have had it. In practical terms, it was inaccessible.

To be accessible, a plan must provide the needed information so that you can find it; it must be in the proper format; and it must not be cluttered with extraneous material. Although having complete plans is important, voluminous plans are unwieldy. You need to know what is in the plan and where it is. You should be able to quickly find the original schedule and all subsequent revisions. The defect data should be clear, and the program size data must be available for every program version. To be most convenient, these data should be in a prescribed order and in a known, consistent, and nonredundant format.

Is It Clear?

I find it surprising that even experienced developers occasionally turn in PSP homework that is sloppy and incomplete. Some items are left blank, others are inconsistent, and a few are obviously incorrect. Sometimes, even incomprehensible notes are jotted in the margins. Such work is not data and should be rejected. The fundamental point this book teaches is the importance of quality data. If the data are not complete and unmistakably clear, they cannot be used with confidence. If they cannot be used with confidence, there is no point in gathering them at all.

Is It Specific?

A specific plan identifies what will be done, when, by whom, and at what costs. If these items are not clear, the plan is not specific. For the PSP plans you produce, the data in the Project Plan Summaries specifically answer these questions. You will finish the numbered program on the prescribed schedule and for the cost of your total estimated time.

Is It Precise?

Precision is a matter of relating the unit of measure to the total magnitude of the measurement. If, for example, you analyzed a project that took 14 programmer years, management would not be interested in units of minutes, hours, or probably even days. In fact, programmer weeks would probably be the finest level of detail they could usefully consider.

For a PSP job that takes five hours, however, units of days or weeks would be useless. Conversely, units of seconds would be far too detailed. Here you are probably interested in time measured in minutes.

To determine an appropriate level of precision, consider the error introduced by a difference of one in the smallest unit of measure. A project that is planned to take 14 programmer years would require 168 programmer months. An uncertainty of one month would contribute an error of at most 0.6%. In light of normal planning errors, this is small enough to be quite acceptable. For a five-hour project, an uncertainty of one minute would contribute a maximum error of about 0.33%. A unit of measure of one minute would thus introduce tolerable errors, whereas units of an hour or even a tenth of an hour would probably be too gross.

Is It Accurate?

Although the other four points are all important, accuracy is crucial. A principal concern of the planning process is producing plans with predictable accuracy. As you plan the PSP work, do not be too concerned about the errors in each small task plan as long as they appear to be random. That is, you want to have about as many overestimates as underestimates. These are called **unbiased estimates**. As you work on larger projects or participate on development teams, the small-scale errors will balance each other out and the combined total will be more accurate. The PROBE method guides you in producing unbiased, or balanced, plans.

7.2 Project and Period Plans

As developers, we all use both project plans and period plans. A **period plan** is for a calendar period—a day, week, month, or year. Period plans concern activities that are scheduled on a calendar basis. Businesses run on period plans. They pay salaries at regular intervals, periodically bill customers, and pay dividends every quarter. We also live in a periodic world. We eat and sleep at regular intervals and work on specified days of the week.

The project estimates and plans cover the effort and cost to develop products. The products may be tangibles like programs and books, or intangibles like designs and test plans. **Project plans** are driven by the needs of the job. Some tasks must precede others, and various deliverables can be produced only when the proper preparatory work has been done.

Although period plans and project plans are different, they must be related. Much of the difficulty that organizations have with software development stems from mismanagement of this period-project relationship. When making a plan, you should start with an estimate of work to be done. If the estimate is incomplete or inaccurate, the resulting plan will almost certainly be incomplete and inaccurate. However, even with an accurate and complete estimate, if you don't do a competent job of relating the project estimates to the calendar, the resulting plan could still be troublesome.

To make a project schedule, spread the estimated work for the job over the available time. This mapping of project tasks to the calendar becomes the project schedule. It is a key element of the project plan. Because your work is about products and your life is in periods, however, both period plans and project plans are important to you. You cannot produce a competent plan without properly producing and relating the two.

The relationship of the estimate and schedule is shown in Figure 7.1. This is the planning framework originally covered in Chapter 4 (see p. 63). It shows that

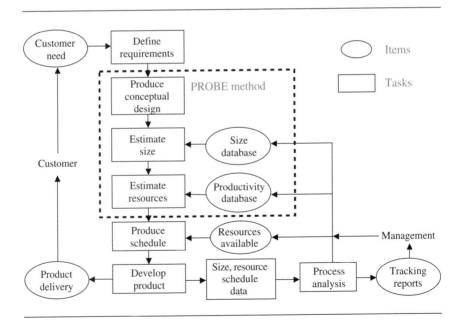

FIGURE 7.1 PROJECT PLANNING FRAMEWORK

the size and resource estimates are produced first and that these estimates are used to produce the schedule. However, the "Produce schedule" box has two inputs: the estimates and the available resources. The key question addressed now is, What resource information do you need and how do you combine it with the estimate to produce the schedule? That is the next subject in this chapter.

7.3   Producing the Schedule

To make a schedule, start by estimating the effort required to do the job. Then allocate these hours to the various project tasks. For the PSP exercises, spread the total hours over the phases using the To Date % from the projects completed to date. This assumes that the work for the new job will be distributed in much the same way it was for the prior jobs. It also assumes that each project phase requires only one task. For small projects like the PSP exercises, the projects are small enough that the phases can be considered as single tasks, and the work is similar enough from job to job that the To Date % provides reasonably accurate task estimates.

For larger team projects, there are normally many tasks per phase, and each project generally has a different To Date % time distribution. You must then estimate the time for each task. The PSP will help you do this if you have recorded the size and time for similar tasks. Then you can use the PROBE method for these tasks and use those estimates in your project planning. You will then be able to make accurate estimates, even for large projects. The key is to track time and size data for each kind of task and to use these data to make PROBE estimates whenever you have the data to do so. Even if you only have data on one task and even if these data are only for one team member, you can use the data until you have enough personal data to make a PROBE estimate.

Even if you have to use someone else's data, your estimate will be better than a guess. In one case, a large team was estimating the design work for the next project phase. They had completed the requirements work and concluded that there were about 600 classes to design in the next phase. The team was reluctant to guess at the time required to design a class because they would then multiply that guess by 600. One of the developers was ahead of schedule and had data on two classes she had already designed. The team used her data for the estimate. The result was within about 10% of the actual time the team spent.

Estimating Task Hours

To relate project estimates and period plans, you must decide how many hours you will spend each week working on project tasks. Then you can make the schedule.

On a TSP team, the hours spent on planned tasks are called **task hours**. Although you may work on many other project-related activities, if these activities are not specific tasks in your plan, that time is not task time. Task hours are part of the project plan, and normal working hours are part of the period plan. The rest of your working time is for those things you don't want to make the effort to plan, such as answering e-mail, attending meetings, helping coworkers, and so forth. To accurately plan this other work, you would have to measure and track all of these miscellaneous tasks. This is not usually worthwhile unless your work is billed by the hour and you need an accurate record.

Before estimating weekly task hours, consider the number of work hours in a year. A 52-week year of 40-hour weeks has 2,080 working hours. After accounting for vacations, holidays, sickness, and personal time, working hours are generally cut by 10% to 15%. In addition, in most engineering organizations, the developers spend 20 to 25 hours a week in meetings, handling e-mail, consulting on other projects, assisting marketing, or performing any of the other myriad tasks they generally must do. In a typical 40-hour workweek, it is not unusual for developers to put in only about 12 to 15 task hours. Many factors affect these hours, and they will vary substantially among individuals and even from week to week. Although most developers believe that they should aim for 20 or more task hours per week, few teams are able to achieve that many. Then, when their plans assume too many weekly task hours, their projects start out in trouble and they spend weeks struggling to recover. Until you have data on your own work, be conservative with your task-hour estimates.

Managing Task Time

The amount of time you spend on project tasks will fluctuate. First-time TSP team members generally start with a rate between 12 and 15 task hours per week. After a few weeks of work, they can often increase this task-hour rate to 15 to 17 hours, and some occasionally reach almost 20 task hours. Some experienced TSP teams can even reach 20 or more task hours in an average week, but they usually work more than 40 hours per week to do so. As with size and time estimating, the key is to gather data on your personal performance and to use these data in making estimates and plans.

With a realistic task-time plan, you can usually meet most of your schedule commitments. If your estimates are seriously off, when the inevitable schedule crisis comes, you can defer all routine work and devote 40 or more hours per week to the highest-priority tasks. For a brief period, you won't answer your mail, go to meetings, do paperwork, or even take coffee breaks. You will do nothing but work. If you plan for 15 to 20 weekly task hours, in a crunch you could easily double your task time. If you try to do this for any length of time, however, you will quickly burn out and the quality of your work will likely suffer.

In the long run, periodic crash efforts may help you to meet commitments, but they do not improve overall productivity. Although you will be very productive for short periods, when you get tired, your productivity will drop sharply. Just as in the fable of the tortoise and the hare, over the long term, if you make steady and orderly progress, you will generally outperform those who work in feverish spurts. Try to make realistic plans that leave a reasonable allowance for the normal events of your daily working life. This will provide a prudent cushion for the occasional last-minute crisis.

7.4　Making the Schedule

The PSP scheduling procedure is shown in Figure 7.2. This complex a procedure is not needed for the PSP assignments in this text, but you will use these methods with the TSP. Because most TSP tools will handle the scheduling and tracking calculations automatically, there is generally no need to do them by hand. To use these planning methods properly, however, you should understand how they work. The data in the following example are simplified versions of the data I gathered while writing the manuscript for the original PSP book (Humphrey 1995). The descriptions are keyed to the numbered items in Figure 7.2 and use the data shown in Tables 7.1 and 7.2.

1. **Estimate Resources:** Start with a resource estimate. For the PSP, this is the total estimated hours for the project.

2. **Estimate the Tasks:** For the PSP exercises, use the To Date % to allocate your time among the project phases. For larger projects, use data on prior similar tasks to estimate the time for the new tasks. Then enter the time for each task in the *Plan Hours* column on a Task Planning Template like that shown in Table 7.2.

3. **Estimate Weekly Task Hours:** Except for your first TSP project, use historical data to guide the task-hour estimate. To avoid getting overcommitted, base your estimates on personal data if you have it or on data from experienced TSP teams if you can get it.

4. **Calculate Available Hours:** If, like most developers, you spend at least some time on other projects, estimate the part of your task hours that you can commit to this project. Then enter these hours for each week, as shown in Table 7.1. As you do, consider both personal and other project commitments.

5. **Plan Task Dependencies:** Arrange the tasks in the rough order in which you expect to do them. This initial order should consider your current understanding of task dependencies. Don't worry too much about the precise task order because you will probably make many changes as the work progresses.

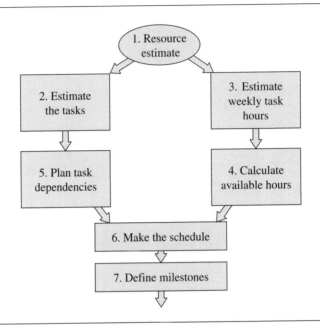

FIGURE 7.2 PSP SCHEDULE PLANNING

TABLE 7.1 SCHEDULE PLANNING TEMPLATE

Date	Week	Plan Hours	Cum. Hours	Actual Hours	Cum. Act. Hours	PV	Cum. PV	EV	Cum. EV
3/8	1	20	20			0.99	0.99		
3/15	2	20	40			0.53	1.52		
3/22	3	20	60			1.43	2.95		
3/29	4	10	70			0	2.95		
4/5	5	15	85			0	2.95		
4/12	6	15	100			2.94	5.89		
4/19	7	20	120			0	5.89		
4/26	8	15	135			0	5.89		
5/3	9	20	155			3.66	9.55		
5/10	10	15	170			0	9.55		
5/17	11	20	190			0	9.55		
5/24	12	20	210			2.94	12.49		
5/31	13	20	230			0	12.49		

TABLE 7.1 (continued)

Date	Week	Plan Hours	Cum. Hours	Actual Hours	Cum. Act. Hours	PV	Cum. PV	EV	Cum. EV
6/7	14	20	250			0	12.49		
6/14	15	20	270			4.37	16.86		
6/21	16	20	290			0	16.86		
6/28	17	20	310			0	16.86		
7/5	18	20	330			4.37	21.23		
7/12	19	20	350			0	21.23		
7/19	20	20	370			0	21.23		
7/26	21	20	390			3.66	24.89		
8/2	22	20	410			0	24.89		
8/9	23	20	430			0	24.89		
8/16	24	20	450			4.37	29.26		
8/23	25	20	470			0	29.26		
8/30	26	20	490			2.14	31.40		
9/6	27	20	510			0	31.40		
9/13	28	20	530			2.94	34.34		
9/20	29	20	550			0	34.34		
9/27	30	20	570			0	34.34		
10/4	31	20	590			4.37	38.71		
10/11	32	0	590			0	38.71		
10/18	33	0	590			0	38.71		
10/25	34	10	600			0	38.71		
11/1	35	20	620			0	38.71		
11/8	36	20	640			0	38.71		
11/15	37	20	660			4.37	43.08		
11/22	38	20	680			0	43.08		
11/29	39	20	700			0	43.08		
12/6	40	20	720			3.66	46.74		
12/13	41	20	740			0	46.74		
12/20	42	20	760			2.94	49.68		
12/27	43	0	760			0	49.68		
1/3	44	20	780			0	49.68		
1/10	45	20	800			0	49.68		
1/17	46	20	820			2.94	52.62		

TABLE 7.2 THE TASK PLANNING TEMPLATE

Phase	Task	Plan Hours	Cum. Plan Hours	PV	Cum. PV	Plan Week	Actual Hours	Actual Week	EV	Cum. EV
Plan	Book Plan	15.10	15.10	0.99	0.99	1				
Draft	Preface	8.14	23.24	0.53	1.52	2				
Draft	Chapter 1 Draft	21.70	44.94	1.43	2.95	3				
Draft	Chapter 2 Draft	44.75	89.69	2.94	5.89	6				
Draft	Chapter 3 Draft	55.60	145.29	3.66	9.55	9				
Draft	Chapter 4 Draft	44.75	190.04	2.94	12.49	12				
Draft	Chapter 5 Draft	66.45	256.49	4.37	16.86	15				
Draft	Chapter 6 Draft	66.45	322.94	4.37	21.23	18				
Draft	**Planning Drafts**	**0**	**322.94**	**0**	**21.23**	**18**				
Draft	Chapter 7 Draft	55.60	378.54	3.66	24.89	21				
Draft	Chapter 8 Draft	66.45	444.99	4.37	29.26	24				
Draft	Chapter 9 Draft	32.55	477.54	2.14	31.40	26				
Draft	**Quality Drafts**	**0**	**477.54**	**0**	**31.40**	**26**				
Draft	Chapter 10 Draft	44.75	522.29	2.94	34.34	28				
Draft	Chapter 11 Draft	66.45	588.74	4.37	38.71	31				
Draft	Chapter 12 Draft	66.45	655.19	4.37	43.08	37				
Draft	**Design Drafts**	**0**	**655.19**	**0**	**43.08**	**37**				
Draft	Chapter 13 Draft	55.60	710.79	3.66	46.74	40				
Draft	Chapter 14 Draft	44.75	755.54	2.94	49.68	42				
Draft	Chapter 15 Draft	44.75	800.29	2.94	52.62	46				
Draft	**All Drafts**	**0**	**800.29**	**0**	**52.62**	**46**				

For small jobs, ranking the tasks in order is relatively simple. However, for larger projects, it is often necessary to work together with your teammates to identify the task dependencies. If you find it helpful, you can also use a critical path scheduling system such as PERT (Zells 1990).

6. **Make the Schedule:** Starting with the first task, check the planned cumulative hours. In Table 7.2, the first task takes 15.10 hours. From Table 7.1, the plan shows 20 cumulative hours for week 1, so the first task will be finished in week 1. Enter "1" in the *Plan Week* column for that task. For the second task, the Preface, the cumulative hours are 23.24. The planned cumulative hours in

Table 7.1 first exceed this value in week 2, so the planned week for completing the second task is 2. Continue this process until you have entered the planned completion weeks for all the tasks.

7. **Define Milestones:** Finally, to facilitate project tracking and reporting, identify the key project milestones and list their planned completion dates. In Table 7.2, these are shown in bold as zero-hour tasks. Check the TSP support tool you will use to see what convention it uses to identify milestone tasks.

You now have a personal plan. For a team plan, you will also need to know the key task dependencies, task responsibilities, and principal checkpoints.

7.5 Earned Value

When planning a project with many tasks, you will need a way to track and report progress, particularly when you complete tasks in a different order than originally planned. If all the tasks take an equal amount of time or if there are only a few tasks, this might not be difficult, but projects typically have many tasks of differing types and sizes. The *Earned Value* (*EV*) measure provides a convenient way to address this tracking and reporting problem (Boehm 1981; Humphrey 1989). The EV method establishes a value for every task, regardless of its type. Whenever you complete a task, you earn this EV amount. To judge progress against the plan, merely compare the EV each week with the planned earned value, or PV, for that week. If the cumulative EV equals or exceeds cumulative PV, you are on or ahead of schedule.

To calculate PV, determine every task's estimated percentage of the total task hours for the entire project. That is that task's planned value. You earn the earned value when you complete the task. For example, for a project of 1,000 total task hours, a 15-hour task would have a planned value of 1.5. When you completed this task, you would earn 1.5 EV, which would then be added to the total project EV. Note that there is no partial credit for partially completed tasks. The earned value credit is given only when the task is completed. If the task is half done, it contributes nothing. For tasks that are so big that you want intermediate progress measures, break them into subtasks. Even when tasks take much more (or less) than the planned time, their EV is unchanged and is the planned value (PV) that was established when making the plan.

Earned value is particularly useful when there are frequent plan changes. It is also a surprisingly accurate way to measure project status and to estimate the project's completion date. In using EV, however, keep the following limitations in mind:

☐ The EV method assumes that the rate of task completion in the future will be roughly the same as what it was in the past. If this is not the case, EV-based projections will not be accurate.

□ The EV method measures progress relative to the plan. If the plan is inaccurate, the EV projections will also likely be inaccurate. The EV method corrects planning errors when these errors are roughly the same for every project phase. That is, if you estimated project size as 10 KLOC and it turned out to be 25 KLOC, the EV projections could still be accurate. If, however, the development plan was accurate but the test plan was badly underestimated, the EV projections would be accurate for the development work but inaccurate for testing.

□ The EV method assumes that the project's resources are uniform. If the staffing level increases, the EV projections will be pessimistic, and if the staff has recently been cut, the projections will be optimistic.

Generally, when plans are based on historical data, the EV method will provide accurate projections when the planned time distribution across the job phases is consistent with the historical To Date percentages. When the distribution by phase is unrealistic, the EV method will not provide accurate projections.

Depending on the project's size and expected duration, plan in sufficient detail to provide frequent status feedback. For example, for a 100-hour project stretching over five to six weeks, at least ten subtasks are required to provide one or two checkpoints a week. Although you will want to see regular EV progress, do not track yourself to death. My rule of thumb is that one checkpoint per week is not enough, and one per day is too many. I prefer two to four task completions a week. This requires that tasks be planned to take less than ten hours each.

7.6   An Earned Value Example

Tables 7.1 and 7.2 show simplified versions of the actual task and schedule plans I used for writing the draft of the first PSP book (Humphrey 1995). I had expected to spend 800.29 hours to write this draft and, based on my planned available time, estimated that I would finish in late January. As shown in Table 7.1, I planned a vacation in October (weeks 32 and 33), when I expected to accomplish nothing on the manuscript. I calculated that the draft would take 52.62% of the total book-writing time of 1,520.89 hours. Table 7.2 lists the planned completion dates for the draft chapters, together with the chapter PVs.

My early progress in writing the manuscript is shown in Tables 7.3 and 7.4. As is clear, I did not write the chapters in the planned order. I wrote the preface, then Chapter 11, and then Chapter 6. Next, I wrote Chapters 1, 2, and 3 in order. I then finished Appendix A before starting Chapter 4. Note several important messages here. First, even though this was my fourth book, my plan was not very accurate. I had originally planned to start the book with the material in Chapter 13. As writing progressed, however, I realized that this was not the right way to start this book so I made a new design. Because I didn't add any new work, however, I could still use earned value to track progress against the original plan.

Later, I decided that the statistical material covered in many of the chapters should be treated more completely in a new Appendix A. Until I included this work in my plan, however, working on Appendix A did not earn EV credit. By now, getting EV credit had become so important to me that I kept delaying work on Appendix A until I changed the plan. Because I didn't have a TSP tool to do it for me, I had to manually recalculate the EV for all the tasks, as shown in Tables 7.3 and 7.4. The Appendix A tasks had the same planned work distribution by phase as the rest of the book, so the manuscript draft was still planned to take 52.62% of the job. Adding these tasks, however, did reduce the EV for all the work done so far. Though I later made more changes in chapter order and content, the EV system enabled me to track progress and accurately estimate when I would finish the job.

TABLE 7.3 EXAMPLE SCHEDULE PLANNING TEMPLATE

Date	Week	Plan Hours	Cum. Hours	Actual Hours	Cum. Act. Hours	PV	Cum. PV	EV	Cum. EV
3/8	1	20	20	12.60	12.6	0.93	0.93	0	0
3/15	2	20	40	33.47	46.07	0.50	1.43	0.93	0.93
3/22	3	20	60	25.70	71.77	1.32	2.75	0.50	1.43
3/29	4	10	70	16.58	88.35	0	2.75	0	1.43
4/5	5	15	85	22.05	110.40	0	2.75	4.09	5.52
4/12	6	15	100	32.93	143.33	2.75	5.50	0	5.52
4/19	7	20	120	32.08	175.42	0	5.50	4.09	9.61
4/26	8	15	135	25.80	201.22	0	5.50	0	9.61
5/3	9	20	155	34.58	235.80	3.42	8.92	0	9.61
5/10	10	15	170	31.65	267.45	0	8.92	4.07	13.68
5/17	11	20	190	29.65	297.10	0	8.92	0	13.68
5/24	12	20	210	31.95	329.05	2.75	11.67	0	13.68
5/31	13	20	230	46.68	375.73	0	11.67	6.84	20.52
6/7	14	20	250	31.88	407.61	0	11.67	2.75	23.27
6/14	15	20	270			4.09	15.76		
6/21	16	20	290			0	15.76		
6/28	17	20	310			0	15.76		
7/5	18	20	330			4.09	19.85		
7/12	19	20	350			0	19.85		
7/19	20	20	370			0	19.85		*(continued)*

TABLE 7.3 (continued)

Date	Week	Plan Hours	Cum. Hours	Actual Hours	Cum. Act. Hours	PV	Cum. PV	EV	Cum. EV
7/26	21	20	390			3.42	23.27		
8/2	22	20	410			0	23.27		
8/9	23	20	430			0	23.27		
8/16	24	20	450			4.09	27.36		
8/23	25	20	470			0	27.36		
8/30	26	20	490			1.99	29.35		
9/6	27	20	510			0	29.35		
9/13	28	20	530			2.75	32.10		
9/20	29	20	550			0	32.10		
9/27	30	20	570			0	32.10		
10/4	31	20	590			4.09	36.19		
10/11	32	0	590			0	36.19		
10/18	33	0	590			0	36.19		
10/25	34	10	600			0	36.19		
11/1	35	20	620			0	36.19		
11/8	36	20	640			0	36.19		
11/15	37	20	660			4.09	40.28		
11/22	38	20	680			0	40.28		
11/29	39	20	700			0	40.28		
12/6	40	20	720			3.42	43.70		
12/13	41	20	740			0	43.70		
12/20	42	20	760			2.75	46.45		
12/27	43	0	760			0	46.45		
1/3	44	10	770			0	46.45		
1/10	45	10	780			0	46.45		
1/17	46	10	790			2.75	49.20		
1/24	47	10	800			0	49.20		
1/31	48	10	810			3.42	52.62		

TABLE 7.4 EXAMPLE TASK PLANNING TEMPLATE

Phase	Task	Plan Hours	Cum. Plan Hours	PV	Cum. PV	Plan Week	Actual Hours	Actual Week	EV	Cum. EV
Plan	Book Plan	15.10	15.10	0.93	0.93	1	13.8	2	0.93	0.93
Draft	Preface	8.14	23.24	0.50	1.43	2	35.3	3	0.50	1.43
Draft	Chapter 1 Draft	21.70	44.94	1.32	2.75	3	28.6	10	1.32	10.93
Draft	Chapter 2 Draft	44.75	89.69	2.75	5.50	6	62.5	10	2.75	13.68
Draft	Chapter 3 Draft	55.60	145.29	3.42	8.92	9	41.2	13	3.42	20.52
Draft	Chapter 4 Draft	44.75	190.04	2.75	11.67	12	27.3	14	2.75	23.27
Draft	Chapter 5 Draft	66.45	256.49	4.09	15.76	15				
Draft	Chapter 6 Draft	66.45	322.94	4.09	19.85	18	67.6	7	4.09	9.61
Draft	**Planning Drafts**	**0**	**322.94**	**0**	**21.23**	**18**				
Draft	Chapter 7 Draft	55.60	378.54	3.42	23.27	21				
Draft	Chapter 8 Draft	66.45	444.99	4.09	27.36	24				
Draft	Chapter 9 Draft	32.55	477.54	1.99	29.35	26				
Draft	**Quality Drafts**	**0**	**477.54**	**0**	**31.40**	**26**				
Draft	Chapter 10 Draft	44.75	522.29	2.75	32.10	28				
Draft	Chapter 11 Draft	66.45	588.74	4.09	36.19	31	57.5	5	4.09	5.52
Draft	Chapter 12 Draft	66.45	655.19	4.09	40.28	37				
Draft	**Design Drafts**	**0**	**655.19**	**0**	**43.08**	**37**				
Draft	Chapter 13 Draft	55.60	710.79	3.42	43.70	40				
Draft	Chapter 14 Draft	44.75	755.54	2.75	43.45	42				
Draft	Chapter 15 Draft	44.75	800.29	2.75	49.20	46				
Draft	Appendix A Draft	55.60	855.89	3.42	52.62	48	68.8	13	3.42	17.10
Draft	**All Drafts**	**0**	**855.89**	**0**	**52.62**	**48**				

7.7   Comments on the EV Example

This example illustrates the importance of task size. The tasks shown in Tables 7.2 and 7.4 averaged 44.5 hours each with a maximum of 66.45 hours and a minimum of 8.14 hours. Furthermore, out of the 48-week schedule, this plan earned EV in only 18 of the 48 plan weeks. This does not provide enough feedback to manage even a one-person job like this. This is a simplified example, however, because my actual book-writing process had 21 tasks for each chapter, with 10 of them used to produce the chapter drafts. By getting feedback on my progress every week, I had a highly motivating sense of steady progress. This helped me to maintain my productivity.

In addition, as shown in Tables 7.3 and 7.4 and Figure 7.3, my plan for writing the first PSP book was seriously off. At 14 weeks I had reached 23.3 EV, which is the level planned for week 23. This meant that I was nine weeks ahead of schedule and would finish the manuscript four months ahead of the plan. To make these calculations, I used the same method that TSP teams use to track their work. The kinds of data TSP teams use are shown in Figure 7.3. In 14 weeks, I had earned 23.3 points of EV: a rate of 1.66 EV points a week. To finish the manuscript, I had to earn 52.62 – 23.3 = 29.32 more EV. At my historical rate, this would take 17.66 more weeks, meaning that I would finish 16 weeks ahead of schedule, or in week 32 instead of the planned week 48. This assumed that I would continue working at the same rate and that nothing would change the size of the tasks.

Another important conclusion can be drawn from Figure 7.3. The row for *To-date hours for tasks completed* compares the planned time for the completed tasks with the actual times. The work done to date was planned to take 378.5 hours, but it actually took me 402.6 hours, an underestimate of 6.37%. However, I averaged 63% more task hours than planned, which more than compensated for my 6% project underestimate. I had based the task-hour estimate on my previous book, for which I had averaged 26 hours per week. Because I did not believe I could maintain that same rate on the new book, I used a more conservative 20 hours per week. This was not a planning system problem, but rather an error in planning judgment. Because I was able to work at home and didn't have any children around to distract me, I was able to achieve an unusually high task-hour rate. I suggest that you not use these data as an example, at least until you have data on your own personal task-hour experience.

TSP Week Summary - Form WEEK

Name	Watts Humphrey	Date 7-Jun
Team	PSP	
Status for Week	14	Cycle
Week Date	6/7	

Weekly Data	Plan	Actual
Project hours for this week	20.0	31.9
Project hours this cycle to date	250.0	407.6
Earned value for this week	0.0	2.8
Earned value this cycle to date	11.7	23.3
To-date hours for tasks completed	378.5	402.6
To-date average hours per week	17.9	29.1

FIGURE 7.3 THE TSP WEEKLY SUMMARY REPORT FORM

A planning system based on historical data will accurately project future performance if you continue working as before. I had not expected to spend so many hours per week, but I was wrong. By using the earned value system, I recognized this planning error after only a few weeks. After the first month of a two-year project, I could see that I would finish the manuscript draft much earlier than planned. After the first ten weeks, I could confidently commit to finishing the manuscript draft four months early. That is when I actually did complete it.

I had the reverse problem in writing the final manuscript. Because I obtained a great deal of feedback from manuscript reviews, the rewriting process took much longer than planned. However, by using earned value tracking, I could quickly recognize and adjust for this problem. With all of these changes, I sent the final manuscript to the publisher in June, exactly as planned a year and a half earlier.

7.8 Estimating Accuracy

It is helpful to think about estimating with an analogy to throwing darts at a target to get a number. Assume that your historical data have values for ten prior throws that clustered around 100, with a couple at 80 and one out at 60. Statistically, your new estimate is like another dart throw. The presumption is that its likely value is best represented by the variation of the previous throws. If, however, you use a bow and arrow, or switch to a different-sized dart, or stand twice as far away, your previous data will not be a good predictor of the error in the new throw.

With PROBE, the quality of an estimate is a direct function of the quality of the historical data. As shown in the dart-throwing example, however, it also depends on the degree to which these data correspond to what you plan to do. For example, if you changed your design method, built a much larger program, or developed an unfamiliar type of application, your historical data might not produce a very accurate plan. You could still use the PROBE method, but you should recognize the likely higher estimating error.

Process stability is also important. With the PSP exercises, you will use several different processes and learn a number of new methods. Because these changes will probably cause fluctuations in your performance, the quality of your estimates will likely have similar fluctuations. Although this instability is a necessary part of learning, a more stable process will probably improve your estimating accuracy.

7.9   The Prediction Interval

When using the regression method to make estimates, you can calculate the likely error in each estimate. The prediction interval gives the range within which the actual program size or development time will likely fall. Figure 7.4 shows actual data for nine programs, as well as the 70% prediction interval for the ninth estimate. This prediction interval shows the range within which the actual values have a 70% chance of falling. As the figure shows, seven of the nine points are between the upper and lower prediction ranges, and two are very near the lower prediction interval limit.

As you can also see from Figure 7.4, when the data points cluster closely around the regression line, the prediction interval range is narrower. This means that when you have historically made accurate estimates, the prediction interval for the next estimate will be narrow. Similarly, when your estimating errors have been large, the prediction interval will be large.

The prediction interval is very sensitive to outlier points. As discussed in Chapter 6 (see p. 106), outlier points are points that are unusual in one or more respects. Do not exclude points simply because they were bad estimates. Only do so if they do not represent what you plan to do. In this example, the developer had actually written ten programs, but he excluded one because he had misunderstood the requirements and started over partway through the job. The effect of including an outlier point can be seen in Figure 7.5. Including the tenth point raises the regression line above six of the ten data points, thus introducing an estimating bias. In addition, with this point, the 70% prediction interval includes 90% of the data points. An excessively large prediction interval indicates data problems. In this case, the prediction interval includes many more of the points than it should. A wide 70% prediction interval that included only about 70% of the points, however, would merely indicate a lot of variation in the data.

The prediction interval calculations are given in Box 7.1 and are described in the assignment kit for one of the PSP exercise programs. Many TSP tools automatically calculate the prediction interval, but to make these calculations yourself, write the appropriate program or produce a spreadsheet to do the calculations.

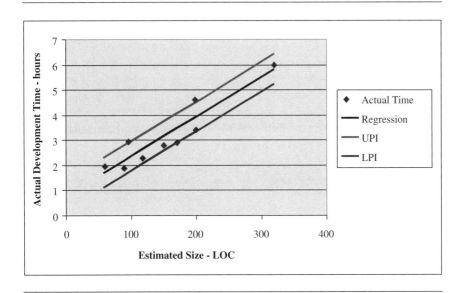

FIGURE 7.4 THE PREDICTION INTERVAL

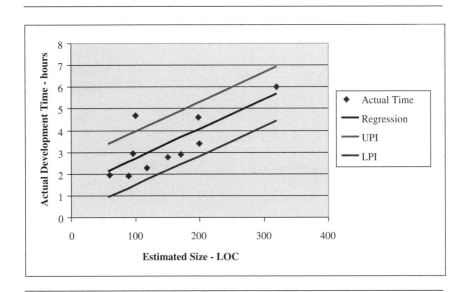

FIGURE 7.5 PREDICTION INTERVAL WITH OUTLIER POINT INCLUDED

BOX 7.1 CALCULATING THE PREDICTION INTERVAL

1. To determine the likely error of a regression projection for the term x_k from a set of n data values x_i and y_i, first calculate the variance of the y_i terms from the regression line:

$$\text{Variance} = \sigma^2 = \frac{1}{n-2} \sum_{i=1}^{n} (y_i - \beta_0 - \beta_1 x_i)^2$$

Standard Deviation $= \sigma = \sqrt{\text{Variance}}$

2. Find the value $t(p, d)$ of the t - distribution for $p = 70\%$ or 90% and $d = n - 2$ degrees of freedom (values for the t - distribution are shown in Table 3.1 on p. 38).

3. Calculate the value of the prediction interval range:

$$\text{Range} = t(p, d)\sigma \sqrt{1 + \frac{1}{n} + \frac{(x_k - x_{avg})^2}{\sum_{i=1}^{n}(x_i - x_{avg})^2}}$$

Here, x_{avg} is the average of the x terms, and x_k is the term for which the estimate is made and the prediction interval is to be calculated.

4. Calculate the upper and lower prediction intervals, UPI and LPI, where y_k is the estimate ($y_k = \beta_0 + \beta_1 x_k$).

UPI $= y_k +$ Range

LPI $= y_k -$ Range

7.10   Alerting Management to Changes

With sound plans and the EV tracking system, you can see precisely where you stand on a job. If you are ahead of schedule and believe that this rate of progress will continue, you could tell management about the improvement. Similarly, if you are falling behind, you could warn management and possibly even get their help. When you have schedule problems, don't just hide your head; talk to your manager and see what he or she can do to help. Although Brooks' law says that adding staff late in a project will delay it, with a plan and a defined process, adding trained people will usually accelerate the work (Brooks 1995). When you have a detailed plan and precise status measures, you can explain the issues to management and help them resolve any problems that block your progress. When you have problems, use your managers, but give them the data they need to help you.

An example shows how management can often help in ways you might not have considered. Some years ago, before everybody had workstations, I was walking through the machine room of IBM's Poughkeepsie programming development laboratory late one night and heard loud cursing. This poor programmer was late finishing testing and was frustrated because the file hardware kept failing. He told me that this machine failed so often that he could not get his program tested. He was developing the I/O software for a new file system and he was under intense pressure to finish it.

The next morning, I called the vice president in charge of the file hardware and discovered that they had a warehouse full of these machines. They couldn't ship them until the program was ready. The VP arranged to have four machines delivered to the machine room that morning, along with a maintenance engineer to keep them running. This accelerated the testing and the program was soon completed. If you have a problem that you can't handle, go to your managers for help. With good schedule planning and tracking information, you can explain the problems clearly enough so that they can help you solve them.

7.11   Planning Considerations

Planning is a learning process: You learn from each estimate and plan, from evaluating your data, and from reviewing your process. The best time for this learning is during the project postmortem. Based on experience with PSP estimating and planning, I have developed some planning guidelines. The following sections describe three aspects of planning: motivation, productivity, and part-time assignments.

Motivation

Earned value tracking can cause you to delay starting tasks that do not earn EV credit. With the first version of this book, for example, I was reluctant to work on the unplanned Appendix A. When I finally adjusted my plan to assign EV credit to it, however, I had no further problems. Promptly assign EV credit to essential new tasks. Conversely, if some partially completed task is no longer necessary, drop the remaining work on that task from the plan. Remove the earned value for the deleted work and increase the value of everything else you have done.

Even when you are working productively, if you cannot sense steady progress, it is easy to get discouraged. This is one reason why software developers spend so little time validating requirements and documenting designs: such work rarely feels very productive. When you are in a hurry and do not seem to be making progress, you are likely to switch to something that feels more productive. Because most developers view coding and testing as productive, that is where they prefer to spend their time. By showing progress during *all* phases of a programming job, however, the EV method can actually make the early requirements and design work feel productive, thereby improving the quality and productivity of your work.

The key is to adjust your plan with new task additions and deletions whenever necessary. I do so about every week or two. For small task changes, make minor plan adjustments, but for major task additions or deletions, redo the plan. Because every project is unique, however, the only general guideline is to regularly check whether the plan represents the way you are actually working. If it does not, either change the plan or, if the plan is still the right way to do the work, follow the plan.

Productivity

When you use the regression method and your productivity is improving, your historical data will tend to produce overestimates. This is a problem when you use data from an evolving process because the regression method uses average productivities and not productivity trends. If your productivity has been changing, adjust your planning process to use only your most recent data.

Part-Time Assignments

One of the more common problems developers face is multiple project assignments. When management is shorthanded, they often resort to assigning developers to several projects. Although it is normal to have some cleanup work to do on a project you are just completing or to be called back to help on a previous job, it is almost impossible to be productive on more than one major project at a time. Occasional interruptions to give temporary help are rarely a problem, but it is unreasonable to expect developers to give priority to more than one project at a time. Part-time assignments are troublesome for three reasons: task time, task switching, and team coordination.

1. **Task Time:** When simultaneously assigned to several projects, you must divide your weekly task hours among all the projects. If you were averaging 15 task hours per week and you were assigned to 3 projects, you could expect to average only 5 hours per week on each. It is hard enough to get much done in 15 hours a week, let alone 5. Even with 2 projects, an average of 7.5 task hours a week would still not provide enough time to accomplish very much.

2. **Task Switching:** We all have task-switching problems when we are interrupted in the middle of a challenging task. It is hard enough to produce a complex design, for example, without having to do it in short, disconnected bursts of time. Every time you return to the task, you must reconstruct the mental context for the work before you can make further progress. Even then, if you did not stop with a fully documented record of the work done to date, there is a good chance you will overlook something critical.

3. **Team Coordination:** In addition to the task-time and task-switching problems, multiple assignments make team coordination very difficult. When some team members are also assigned to different projects, it is hard for the others to arrange team meetings, inspection reviews, or design sessions. The full-time team members will not know where the part-time members are or be able to rely on them for help. This is inefficient and it destroys team spirit. Without a cohesive and dedicated group, teams rarely have the energy and enthusiasm that produces truly great work.

7.12   Summary

The PROBE method shows you how to use historical data to produce accurate estimates. Then, once you have estimated the size and development time for a project, you can produce the project schedule. With an estimate of the hours you will spend on project tasks each week, you can spread the estimated development time over the project schedule. Weekly task hours are typically about 50% or less of the normal working time. With an estimate of weekly task hours and a detailed task plan, you can calculate when each task will start and end. You can also set dates for the key project milestones. The milestone dates then provide intermediate project goals and a basis for reporting job status.

Earned value provides a way to measure and track job progress. It establishes a planned value for every task based on that task's percentage of total project development time. When you complete a task, you earn the planned value for that task and it is added to your project's cumulative earned value. Earned value provides a common measure for the value of every task, regardless of the type of work involved. A task gets earned value only when it is completed. Partially completed tasks get no credit.

When using the PROBE method, you use your data to make size and development time estimates and to calculate the likely error of these estimates. The prediction interval gives the 70% or 90% range around an estimate where the actual development time or product size will fall 70% or 90% of the time. Although the prediction interval is not a forecast, it does provide a useful guide to the expected error of the estimate.

7.13   Exercises

The standard assignment for this chapter includes exercises R3 and R4 and uses PSP1.1 to write one or more programs. For the R3, R4, and program assignment kits, see your instructor or get them at **www.sei.cmu.edu/tsp/**. These kits contain the assignment specifications and the PSP1.1 process scripts. In completing this assignment, faithfully follow the PSP1.1 process, record all required data, and produce the R3, R4, and program reports according to the specifications given in the assignment kits.

References

Boehm, B. W. *Software Engineering Economics.* Englewood Cliffs, NJ: Prentice-Hall, 1981.

Brooks, F. P. *The Mythical Man-Month.* Reading, MA: Addison-Wesley, 1995.

Humphrey, W. S. *Managing the Software Process.* Reading, MA: Addison-Wesley, 1989.

———. *A Discipline for Software Engineering.* Reading, MA: Addison-Wesley, 1995.

Zells, L. *Managing Software Projects.* Wellesley, MA: QED Information Sciences, Inc., 1990.

8

Software Quality

Software quality is a question of scale. With traditional methods, software developers produce their code as best they can and then they review this code, hold team inspections, and run tests. Their objective is to find and fix as many of the program's defects as they can. Although this approach has traditionally produced programs that run and even run pretty well, it has not produced code that is of high enough quality or sufficiently safe and secure to use for critical applications.

Perhaps the best way to explain the quality problem is by examining some data. Table 8.1 shows the defect densities of the programs delivered by organizations at various CMM maturity levels (Davis and Mullaney 2003). The CMM, or Capability Maturity Model, was introduced by the Software Engineering Institute to help organizations assess the capability of their software groups. At CMM level 1, typical defect content is about 7.5 defects per thousand lines of code. By the time organizations get to CMM level 5, they have applied all of the traditional software quality methods to find and fix the program's defects. These methods generally include requirements inspections, design inspections, compiling, code inspections, and a lot of tests. Although the improvement from CMM1 to CMM5 is significant, today's large-scale software systems have millions of lines of code.

TABLE 8.1 DELIVERED DEFECT DENSITIES BY CMM LEVEL

CMM Level	Defects/KLOC	Defects/MLOC
1	7.5	7,500
2	6.24	6,240
3	4.73	4,730
4	2.28	2,280
5	1.05	1,050

Therefore, a delivered 1,000,000-LOC program produced by a CMM level-5 organization would likely have about 1,000 undiscovered defects.

The key question is, How many defects can a program have and still be considered a quality product? When a million-line program has thousands of defects, it is almost certainly not of high enough quality to be safe or secure. With 100 defects per million LOC, it would have much higher quality, but most of us would still probably not feel safe riding in an airplane or driving a car controlled by such software. At 10 defects per million LOC, we might begin to consider the point debatable, and at 1 defect per MLOC, most of us would agree that, although not completely satisfied, we would begin to think that program quality was approaching an acceptable level.

So what would it take to get 1 or 10 defects per million LOC? I counted one of my C++ programs and found that a 996-LOC listing had 30 pages. Assuming that the data for your programs were similar, a 1,000-LOC program would, on average, have about a 30-page listing. At one defect per KLOC, level-5 organizations are then getting quality levels of about one delivered defect in every 30 pages of source-program listings. Although one defect in 30 pages is not bad when compared with other human-produced products, it is still 1,000 defects per MLOC. To get 100 defects per MLOC, we must have only one defect left in 300 listing pages, and for 10 defects per MLOC, we could miss at most one defect in 3,000 pages of listings. I cannot imagine reviewing and inspecting 3,000 pages of listings and missing at most one single defect. As this seems like a preposterous challenge, what can we do?

The answer, of course, is that people cannot inspect 3,000 pages and be confident of missing no more than one single defect. At one defect in 30 pages, today's level-5 organizations are near the limit of what people can achieve with the present commonly used methods. To get better quality levels, we must change our approach. Instead of searching for defects, we must focus on the process. We must measure the likelihood of a 1,000-LOC module having defects. If we could devise a process that would assure us, at development time, that a 1,000-LOC component had less than a 1% chance of having a defect, our systems would have about 10 defects per MLOC.

The PSP has process quality measures that help you to do this. However, because many of the required quality actions involve both personal and team work, you need the help of teammates to produce the highest-quality software. Then, to further improve product quality, you must improve the quality of your process. This requires measuring and tracking your personal work. This chapter relates process quality to product quality and shows how to use the PSP data to measure, track, and improve process quality. After defining software quality, the chapter covers the economics of quality, personal quality practices, quality measurement and management, PSP improvement practices, and defect prevention. A section at the end of the chapter discusses ways to use PSP quality-management methods when enhancing large existing products. Although the chapter's focus is principally on personal practices, the methods described are even more effective when used by all the members of a development team.

8.1   The PSP Quality Strategy

To produce a high-quality software system, each of that system's parts must also be of high quality. The PSP strategy is to manage the defect content of all parts of a system. By doing this, you will produce consistently reliable components that can then be combined into high-quality systems. Though the quality benefits of this strategy are important, the productivity benefits are even more significant. Software productivity generally declines with increasing product size (Boehm 1981). The primary reason is that it takes longer to find and fix defects in a big product than in a small one. Therefore, as products get larger, the greater volume of code both increases the number of defects and makes each defect harder to find. The common result is a great deal more time spent in testing.

With very high-quality parts, the software development process scales up without losing productivity. As you add high-quality elements to a high-quality base product, testing need only address the new parts. Although there could be systemic problems, the bulk of the defects will be localized. Hence, with high quality, you can largely retain small program productivity when developing larger products.

8.2   What Is Software Quality?

The principal focus of any software quality definition should be on the users' needs. Crosby defines quality as "conformance to requirements" (Crosby 1979). The key questions therefore are, Who are the users, What is important to them, and How do their priorities relate to the way that you build, package, and support products?

Product Quality

To answer these questions, we must consider the hierarchical nature of software quality. First, the product must work. If it has so many defects that it does not perform with reasonable consistency, the users will not use it regardless of its other attributes. This does not mean that defects are always the highest priority, but that they can be very important. If a minimum quality level is not achieved, nothing else matters. Beyond this quality threshold, the relative importance of performance, safety, security, usability, compatibility, functionality, and so forth depend on the user, the application, and the environment. However, if the software product does not provide the right functions when the user needs them, nothing else matters.

Although these user priorities are generally recognized as paramount, development organizations typically devote most of their time to finding and fixing defects. Because the magnitude of this fix process is often underestimated, most projects become preoccupied with defect repair and ignore the other more important user concerns. When a project team is struggling to fix defects in testing, it is usually late and the pressures to deliver are so intense that all other concerns are forgotten. Then, when the tests finally run, everyone is so relieved that they ship the product. However, by fixing these critical test defects, the product has reached only a minimum quality threshold. What has been done to make the product usable or installable? What about compatibility, performance, safety, or security? Has anyone checked the documentation or made the design suitable for future enhancement? Because of the excessive time required to fix defects, little or no time has been spent addressing the issues that are ultimately more important to the users.

With fewer test defects, projects can address the quality aspects that customers feel are most important. Product and process quality thus go hand in hand. A heavy reliance on testing is inefficient, time-consuming, and unpredictable. Then, when the development groups finally stop testing, they deliver a poor-quality product to the users. Though defects are only part of the quality story, they are the quality focus of the PSP. Defects are not the top priority, but effective defect management is essential to managing cost, the schedule, and all other aspects of product quality. Because defects result from errors by individuals, to effectively manage defects, you must manage personal behavior. You are the source of the defects in your products and you are the only person who can prevent them. You are also the best person to find and fix them.

8.3   The Economics of Software Quality

Software quality is an economic issue. You can always run another test or do another inspection. In most large systems, because every new test exposes new defects, it is hard to know when to stop testing. Although everyone agrees that quality is important, each test costs money and takes time. The key fact in optimizing life-cycle quality costs is that the cost of finding and fixing defects increases sharply in later life-cycle phases. However, it doesn't just cost a little more; the difference is enormous. To see why these costs are so high, consider the steps involved in finding and fixing defects:

1. The user experiences a problem and determines that it is a software problem.
2. The user reports the problem to a software specialist.
3. The software specialist verifies that there is a software problem.
4. The specialists reports the source of the problem to a developer.
5. The developer determines what is wrong with the product.
6. The developer fixes the product.
7. A development group inspects the fix to ensure that it is correct.
8. A test group tests the fix to ensure that it fixes the problem.
9. The test group tests the fix to ensure that it doesn't cause other problems.
10. The developers change the documentation to reflect the fix.
11. The release group rebuilds the product with the fix included.
12. The release group distributes the rebuilt product to the users.
13. The user installs the rebuilt product.
14. The user confirms that the fix actually corrected the problem.

Although every fix may not involve every cost element, the longer the defect is in the product, the greater its impact. Finding a requirements problem during customer use can be very expensive. Finding a coding defect during a code review, however, will cost much less. The objective, therefore, must be to remove defects from the requirements, the designs, and the code as soon as possible. By reviewing and inspecting every work product as soon as you produce it, you can minimize the number of defects at every stage. This also minimizes the volume of rework and the rework costs. It also improves development productivity and predictability as well as accelerating development schedules.

Testing is expensive for two reasons. First, a test produces a symptom, and then someone must find and fix the defect. Though these find-and-fix times can be short for many defects, occasionally they can take many hours or even days. Second, testing is expensive because each test checks only one set of operating conditions. Even relatively simple systems produce many possible data values, operating parameters, error conditions, and configuration combinations. Because some defects will affect program behavior under only limited conditions, finding most of the defects in testing would require running a very large number of tests. Even then, you could only be confident that the system would run when it was used in exactly the way it was tested.

Although testing can be very effective at identifying performance, usability, and operational problems, it is not an effective way to remove volumes of defects. Think about it this way: if you knew that you had to do some repetitive task thousands of times, wouldn't it be a good idea to find out the fastest and most effective way to do it? A great deal of data is available on the time required to find and fix software defects. These data all agree that the later a defect is found, the more it costs to find and fix it. Table 8.2 shows a summary of published data from several sources, and Figure 8.1 shows defect-repair data for a Xerox TSP team. Figures 8.2 and 8.3 show PSP data on the fix times for the 664 C++ defects and 1,377 Pascal defects I found while developing 72 module-size programs during my early PSP work. Fix times are clearly much longer during testing and use than in the earlier phases. Although this pattern varies somewhat by language and defect type, the principal factor determining defect fix time is the phase in which the defect was found and fixed.

Figure 8.4 shows a histogram of the per-defect times for 810 developers for the final four exercise programs in a PSP class. The times reflect the average time required to find and fix a defect in design reviews, code reviews, and testing. These data are for 3,240 programs that had a total of 87,159 LOC and included a total of 28,251 defects.

Even during development, unit testing is much less effective at finding and fixing defects than either design reviews or code reviews. The testing histogram at

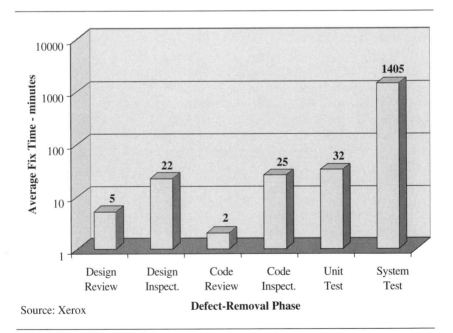

Source: Xerox

FIGURE 8.1 DEFECT-REPAIR TIME FOR A XEROX TSP TEAM

TABLE 8.2 COST OF FINDING AND FIXING DEFECTS

Reference	Inspection	Test	Use
IBM (Remus and Ziles 1979)	1	4.1 times inspection	
JPL (Bush 1990)	$90–$120	$10,000	
Ackerman et al. 1989	1 hour	2–20 hours	
O'Neill 1994	0.26 hour		
Ragland 1992		20 hours	
Russell 1991	1 hour	2–4 hours	33 hours
Shooman and Bolsky 1975	0.6 hour	3.05 hours	
vanGenuchten 1994	0.25 hour	8 hours	
Weller 1993	0.7 hour	6 hours	

the back of Figure 8.4 has many low rates, and the code review (CR) bar in the middle indicates many programs for which the developers found and fixed nearly 10 defects per hour or more. The zero-defect cases at the left were for programs that had no defects in that phase. The zero-defect design review bar (DLDR) is high because few developers find many defects in design reviews until they start measuring and managing the quality of their personal work.

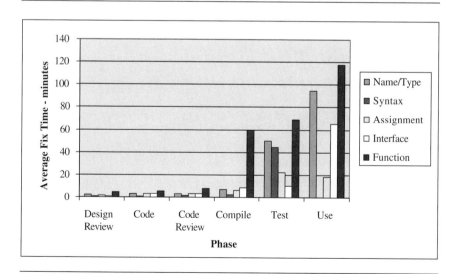

FIGURE 8.2 AVERAGE DEFECT FIX TIME (C++)

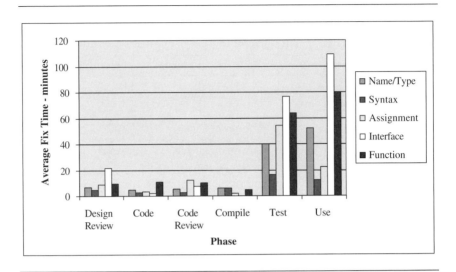

FIGURE 8.3 AVERAGE DEFECT FIX TIME (PASCAL)

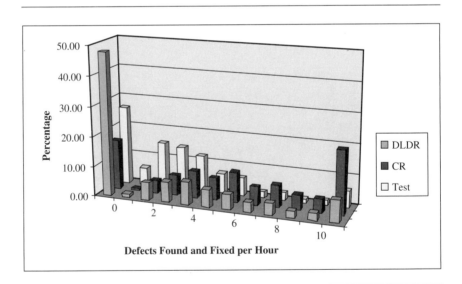

FIGURE 8.4 DEFECTS FOUND AND FIXED PER HOUR (3,240 PSP PROGRAMS)

Some people argue that the easy defects are found by inspections and the difficult ones are left for testing, but I have seen no data to support this. The PSP data show that, for every defect type and for every language measured, defect-repair costs are highest in testing and during customer use. Anyone who seeks to reduce development cost or time must focus on preventing or removing every possible defect before they start testing.

8.4   Defect Types

Defect tracking is important for all defect categories. Although developers will initially spend most of their time finding and fixing simple coding and design mistakes, their principal objective must be to deliver quality products. Therefore, they should be particularly concerned about the defects that they miss. Capers Jones, a well-known writer on software quality, reports that the distribution of delivered defects by type is as shown in Table 8.3. This table uses a conversion factor of 100 LOC per function point (Jones 2004).

The data in Table 8.3 show the importance of quality in every step of the development process. Although defective fixes account for only one in six of overall defect volume, they can be much higher for widely used products. With some IBM products, for example, fix errors accounted for over half of the customer-reported problems and an even higher percentage of service costs. The customer impact of defective fixes is high because many users install them shortly after receiving them. In other words, fix errors compound customer dissatisfaction because they affect users when they are already most unhappy with the product.

The data on error-prone modules also show why disciplined quality practices are so important. With IBM's OS/360 system, for example, only 4% of the modules accounted for over half of the customer-reported problems. For the IMS system,

TABLE 8.3 DELIVERED DEFECTS PER FUNCTION POINT AND KLOC

Defect Types/Origin	Defects/Function Point	Defects/KLOC
Requirements	0.23	2.3
Design	0.19	1.9
Coding	0.09	0.9
Document	0.12	1.2
Defective fixes	0.12	1.2
Total	0.75	7.5

only 31 of the 425 modules were responsible for 57% of the customer-reported defects (Jones 2004). When developers measure and manage the quality of their work, the inspection and test phases find many more of the requirements and design defects that are most important to users.

8.5   Personal Quality Practices

Most software professionals agree that it is a good idea to remove defects early, and they are even willing to try doing it. Beyond that, there is little agreement on how important this is. This is why, for example, developers will spend hours designing and coding a several-hundred-LOC program module and then spend only 10 or 15 minutes looking it over for any obvious problems. Although such superficial reviews may find something, the odds are against it. In fact, such cursory checks are usually a waste of time. To see how important it is to develop quality practices, and to begin to appreciate the enormous cost and schedule benefits of doing high-quality work, consider data on the numbers of defects in typical products and the costs of finding and fixing them.

Data for several thousand programs show that even experienced developers inject 100 or more defects per KLOC. Typically, about half of these defects are found during compiling and the rest must be found in testing. Based on these data, a 50,000-LOC product would start with about 5,000 defects, and it would enter testing with about 50 or more defects per KLOC, or about 2,500 defects. Again, about half of these defects would be found in unit testing at a rate of about two to three defects per hour, and the rest must be found in system-level testing at a cost of 10 to 20 or more hours each. Total testing times would then be about 13,000 to 25,000 hours. With roughly 2,000 working hours in a year, this would require 12 to 18 or more months of testing by a team of five developers.

With the PSP, you will use design reviews and code reviews to find defects before testing. Then, on a TSP team, you will also use inspections. When they do proper reviews and inspections, TSP teams typically find close to 99% of the defects before even starting system-level testing. Test times are then cut by ten times or more. Instead of spending months in testing, TSP teams need only a few weeks (Davis and Mullaney 2003).

If reviews and inspections are so effective, you might wonder why more organizations don't do them. There are two reasons. First, few organizations have the data to make sound quality plans. Their schedules are based largely on guesses, and their guesses are often wildly unrealistic. Then, when they treat these plans as accurate projections, there is no apparent reason to spend much time on reviews and inspections. However, during testing, the quality problems become clear, at which point all the developers can do is test and fix until they get the product to work. The second reason why organizations typically do not do reviews and inspections is that without PSP data, the developers do not know how many defects they inject or what it costs to find and fix them. Therefore, neither they nor their organizations can appreciate the enormous benefits of finding and fixing essentially all of the defects before they start testing.

8.6   Quality Measures

To improve quality, you must measure quality. The key questions then are these: what do you measure and how do you use the resulting data? Before we can use the data, we must decide on the quality measures. The defect content of a finished product indicates the effectiveness of the process for removing defects. This, however, is an after-the-fact measure. To manage the quality of our work, we must measure the work, not just the work products. The available work measures are **defect-removal yield**, **cost of quality**, **review rates**, **phase-time ratios**, and the **process quality index (PQI)**.

The Yield Quality Measure

Figure 8.5 shows a filter view of the defect-removal process. By viewing defect removal as a sequence of filters that progressively remove defects, one can define useful defect-removal measures.

Yield measures the efficiency of each filtering phase at removing defects. The yield of a phase is the percentage of product defects that are removed in that phase. For example, if a product contained 20 defects at the start of unit testing and seven were found during testing, the unit test yield would be $100*7/20 = 35\%$. Yield, however, also considers the defects injected, as well as those removed in each phase. Thus, if you made a mistake while fixing the first 6 defects and injected a seventh defect, which you then found, you would have found 6 of the 20 defects present at phase entry and injected and fixed one more. The phase yield would then be based on finding 7 of 21 possible defects, for a 33% phase yield.

The yield of a phase, or **phase yield**, can be calculated for any phase. Thus, there is unit test yield, code review yield, compile yield, and so forth. There is also something called **process yield**, which refers to the percentage of defects that were removed before the first compile. Thus, if 100 defects were injected during requirements, design, and coding, and if 68 of them were found in all of the reviews and inspections up to but not including compile, the process yield would be 68%.

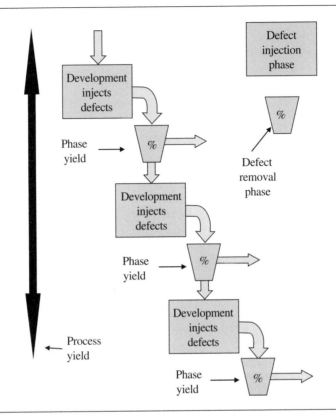

FIGURE 8.5 THE DEFECT-REMOVAL FILTERING PROCESS

Process yield can also be calculated for other phases, so if these same 100 defects had been injected in all of the phases up to system testing and 28 more defects were found in compiling, unit testing, and integration testing, then 68 + 28 = 96 defects would have been found before starting system testing. The process yield before system testing would then be 96%. When used without a phase name, process yield refers to the yield before compiling. If your development environment does not have a compile phase, then process yield will be measured up to but not including unit testing. Otherwise, when the phase name is included, phase yield can be calculated for any phase. The process yield, or yield-before-compile for a typical PSP class, is shown in Figure 8.6. Although most developers start with low process yields, their yields increase sharply when they start using design and code reviews.

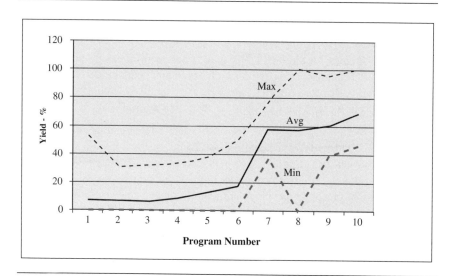

FIGURE 8.6 YIELD FOR 12 DEVELOPERS ON 10 PSP EXERCISES

The Cost of Quality (COQ)

The cost-of-quality measure should more properly be called the cost of poor quality. Juran describes **cost of quality** as a way to "quantify the size of the quality problem in language that will have impact on upper management" (Juran and Gryna 1988). COQ thus defines quality in cost terms that can easily be related to other aspects of a business. The cost of quality has three principal components: failure costs, appraisal costs, and prevention costs (Crosby 1983; Mandeville 1990; Modarress and Ansari 1987). Their definitions are as follows:

1. **Failure costs:** The costs of diagnosing a failure, making necessary repairs, and getting back into operation

2. **Appraisal costs:** The costs of evaluating the product to determine its quality level

3. **Prevention costs:** The costs of identifying defect causes and devising actions to prevent them in the future

To strictly follow these COQ definitions, appraisal costs should include the costs of running test cases or of compiling when there are no defects. Similarly, the defect-repair costs during inspections and reviews should be counted as failure costs. For the PSP, however, we use somewhat simpler definitions:

□ **Failure costs for the PSP:** The total cost of compiling and testing. Because defect-free compile and test times are typically small compared to total compile and test times, they are included in failure costs.

□ **Appraisal costs for the PSP:** The total times spent in design and code reviews and inspections. Inspections and design and code reviews are covered in Chapter 9. Because defect-repair costs are typically a small part of review and inspection costs, the PSP includes them in appraisal costs.

If the inspection and review fix times or the defect-free compile and test times were large enough to consider, however, you could measure them and use more precise cost-of-quality definitions. For personal process-management purposes, however, the simpler definitions are easier to track and equally useful.

The costs of prototype development, causal analysis meetings, and process improvement action meetings should be classified as prevention costs. The times spent in improving design methods, defining coding standards, and initiating personal defect tracking are all effective at reducing defect-injection rates, and are defect-prevention activities. The PSP does not provide measures for defect prevention, however, as this work typically involves cross-team and cross-project activities. To be most effective, defect-prevention work should span multiple projects and be incorporated into organization-wide processes and standards. The PSP cost-of-quality (COQ) measures are defined as follows:

□ **Failure COQ:** 100*(compile time + test time)/(total development time)

□ **Appraisal COQ:** 100*(design review time + code review time)/(total development time)

□ **Total COQ:** Appraisal COQ + Failure COQ

□ **Appraisal as a % of Total Quality Costs:** 100*(Appraisal COQ)/(Total COQ)

□ **Appraisal to Failure Ratio (A/FR):** (Appraisal COQ)/(Failure COQ)

The A/FR measure is useful for tracking personal process improvement. Figure 8.7 shows the A/FR results for 12 developers on 10 PSP exercises. Figure 8.8 shows the relationship of A/FR to test defects for these same developers. The number of test defects is typically much lower for higher values of A/FR. Although a high A/FR implies lower defects, too high a value could mean that you are spending excessive time in reviews. The PSP guideline is an A/FR of about 2.0.

Review Rate Measures

Although yield and COQ measures are useful, they measure what you did, not what you are doing. To do quality work, we need measures to guide what we do while we are doing it. In design or code reviews, the principal factors controlling yield are the time and the care a developer takes in doing the review. The review

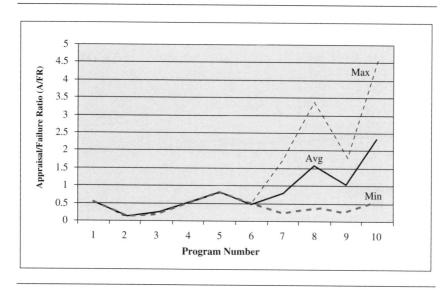

FIGURE 8.7 A/FR (12 DEVELOPERS)

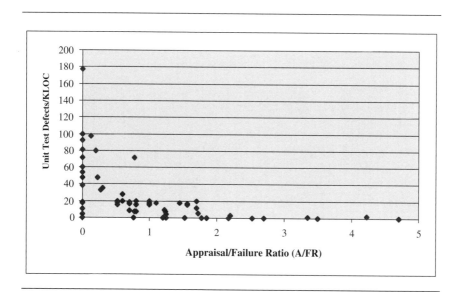

FIGURE 8.8 A/FR VERSUS UNIT TEST DEFECTS (12 DEVELOPERS)

rate and phase ratio measures provide a way to track and control review times. The review rate measure is principally used for code reviews and inspections, and measures the LOC or pages reviewed per hour. If, for example, you spent 20 minutes reviewing a 100-LOC program, your review rate would be 300 LOC per hour. There is no firm rate above which review yields are bad. However, the PSP data show that high yields are associated with low review rates, and that low yields are typical with high review rates. Figure 8.9 shows yield data for 810 developers.

The front set of bars is a histogram of yield for low review rates, and the back bars represent high review rates. The trends can be seen most clearly by looking at the bars for zero-yield reviews at the left and 100%-yield reviews at the right. The highest review rate had the highest percentage of zero-yield reviews. A zero-yield review is a high-tech way to waste your time. The PSP rule of thumb is that 200 LOC per hour is about the upper limit for effective review rates and that about 100 LOC per hour is recommended as the target review rate. The best guideline is to track your own review performance and find the highest rate at which you can review and still consistently get review yields of 70% or better.

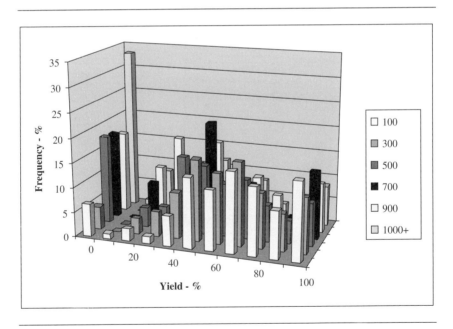

FIGURE 8.9 YIELD VERSUS REVIEW RATE (810 DEVELOPERS)

Phase Ratio Quality Measures

Another set of useful quality measures is the ratio of the time spent in two process phases. For example, the ratio of design review time to design time. To measure process quality, the PSP uses the ratios of design to coding time, design review to design time, and code review to coding time. One would expect that increases in design time would tend to improve product quality while correspondingly reducing coding time. The data in Figure 8.10 for 810 developers show that this is generally the case. The front bars represent developers who spent half as much time designing as coding; the back represents developers who spent twice as much time designing as coding.

Although there is no clear cutoff point below which quality is poor, a 1-to-1 ratio of design to coding time appears to be a reasonable lower limit, with a ratio of 1.5 being optimum. Again, this optimum point varies widely by individual and program type, but a useful rule of thumb is that design time should at least equal coding time. If it doesn't, you are probably doing a significant amount of design work while coding. As shown in Table 8.4 (p. 150), because developers typically inject more than twice as many defects per hour in coding, designing while coding is not a sound quality practice.

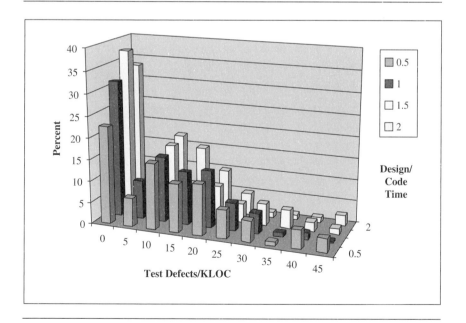

FIGURE 8.10 DEFECTS/KLOC VERSUS DESIGN/CODE TIME (810 DEVELOPERS)

TABLE 8.4 DEFECT-INJECTION AND -REMOVAL RATES
(3,240 PSP PROGRAMS)

Phase	Hours	Defects Injected	Defects Removed	Defects/Hour
Design	4,623.6	9,302		2.011
DLDR	1,452.7		4,824	3.321
Code	4,159.6	19,296		4.639
Code Review	1,780.4		10,758	6.043

Another useful ratio is for review time divided by development time. In the PSP, the general guideline is that you should spend at least half as much time reviewing a product as you spent producing it. This means that for every hour of coding, for example, you should spend at least half an hour doing a code review. The same ratio holds for design and design review time, requirements and requirements review time, and so forth.

One way to determine the reasonableness of these review ratios is by comparing defect-injection and -removal rates. Table 8.4 shows the defect-injection rates for detailed design and coding for the same 810 developers on the 3,240 programs they wrote with PSP2 and PSP2.1. The developers injected 9,302 defects in 4,624 hours of design and injected 19,296 defects in 4,160 hours of coding. These rates are 2.01 defects injected per hour in detailed design and 4.64 defects injected per hour during coding. The table also shows the defect-removal rates for these same developers in design reviews and code reviews. Here, the average removal rates are 3.32 defects per hour in design review and 6.04 defects per hour in code review. The ratios of these rates indicate that these developers must spend at least 76.8% of their coding time in code reviews to expect to find the defects they inject. Similarly, they must spend at least 60.5% of their design time in design reviews to find their design defects.

The PSP guideline of 50% is sufficiently close to these values to provide a simple and easy-to-remember target. However, you should view it as a minimum, with the optimum closer to 70%. As you gather data on your own performance, select the guideline that best fits your personal data.

The Process Quality Index (PQI)

Suppose that you followed all of these guidelines, that you spent as much time designing as coding, and that you met the 50% guidelines for design and code review times. Would this guarantee high quality? Unfortunately, no. Success depends on how you spend your time. Did you follow sound design practices and perform high-yield reviews?

These questions imply the need for at least two other measures. The first is to evaluate the quality of your code reviews. If you followed the code-review process (see Chapter 9) and used an up-to-date code-review checklist, you would probably have a high-yield review. The best indicator of this would be finding very few defects while compiling. In the PSP, 10 or fewer defects per KLOC during compiling is considered low. Without a pretty good code review, you are unlikely to get this low a number. Unfortunately, if your environment doesn't use a compile phase, this measure is not available. In these cases, you can use the data on the coding-type defects found in unit testing and, on a TSP team, the coding-type defects found during inspections and unit testing. For these purposes, defect types 10 through 50 can be considered coding-type defects.

The design review measure is somewhat more complex. Although the number of defects found in unit testing could be a useful measure of design quality, it also includes code quality. If, however, your compile defects/KLOC were below 10, then code quality is probably pretty good and the unit test defects would measure design quality. Thus, without data on compile defects, you cannot interpret the unit test defect measure. The suggested PSP measure specifies that if the compile defects/KLOC are less than 10, unit test defects/KLOC of 5 or less indicates a quality design. The process quality index (PQI) quality criteria are as follows:

- □ Design/Code Time = design time/coding time, with a range from 0.0 to 1.0
- □ Design Review Time = 2*design review time/design time, with a range from 0.0 to 1.0
- □ Code Review Time = 2*code review time/coding time, with a range from 0.0 to 1.0
- □ Compile Defects/KLOC = 20/(10 + compile defects/KLOC), with a range from 0.0 to 1.0
- □ Unit Test Defects/KLOC = 10/(5 + unit test defects/KLOC), with a range from 0.0 to 1.0

The process quality index is obtained by multiplying these five values together. Figure 8.11 shows the PQI profiles for six programs. The two programs with the poorest-quality profiles (numbers 5 and 6) were the only ones with defects after unit testing. The data in Figure 8.12 show that programs with PQI values above 0.4 historically have had no defects found after unit testing. The PQI goal, however, should be 1.0.

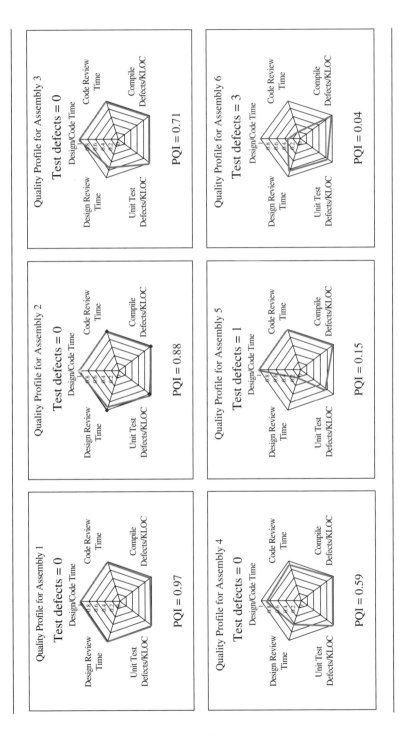

FIGURE 8.11 PROCESS QUALITY INDEX (6 PROGRAMS)

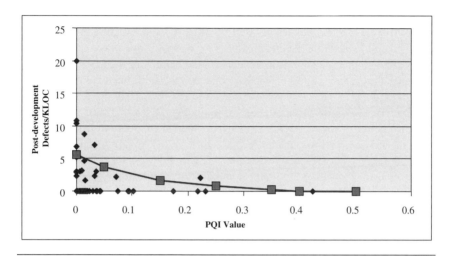

FIGURE 8.12 PQI VALUES VERSUS POST-DEVELOPMENT DEFECTS

8.7 Quality Management

It takes extraordinary skill and discipline just to get a reasonably sized program to run. Although the program may have remaining defects, the fact that it runs at all is an achievement; and though we may celebrate this feat, society now needs higher-quality software than individuals normally produce. We therefore need methods for producing high-quality products even though we personally inject defects. This requires measures to guide our improvement actions.

One can view the software process as the combination of two competing processes: defect injection and defect removal. The defect content of the finished product comes from the difference between these two processes. Thus, relatively small changes in process yield can cause large changes in the defect content of the finished product.

For example, in developing a million-LOC program, the developers would likely inject about 100 defects per KLOC, or 100,000 defects. If the process yield was 75%, 25,000 defects would be left for compiling and testing. If, again, as the PSP data show, about half of these defects were found during compiling, 12,500 defects would be left to find in testing. With four levels of testing, each with a 50% yield, 781 defects would still remain in the delivered product, for a defect level of 0.8 per KLOC. This is a rather good level of quality by current industrial standards. Suppose, however, that the process yield fell to 50%. Then 50,000 defects would remain for compiling and testing. If the yields of the other process steps remained the same, the final number of defects in the delivered product would double to 1,562, or 1.6 defects per KLOC. Thus, a 33% reduction in yield would double the number of delivered defects.

Although this is a significant increase in the number of defects shipped to the customer, the customer impact is modest compared to the impact on testing. If, as the data show, the average cost to remove defects in testing is 10 or more hours per defect, the 12,500 defects originally left for testing would take 125,000 or more programmer hours, or about 60 programmer years. With the reduced inspection yield of 50%, this number would double to 25,000 defects and 120 programmer years. Thus, a 33% reduction in review and inspection yields would cause 50 to 60 developers to spend another year testing and fixing the product. Even with this extra year, the final product would still have twice as many defects as with the original 75% yield.

From a yield-management point of view, the final number of defects is the residual of the yields of all of the process phases. If any single phase for any product component has low yield, some percentage of the defects it misses will impact every subsequent phase and degrade the final product. This degradation will also impact the costs of maintenance, of support, and of using the product, as well as the costs of all subsequent product enhancements. Poor-quality work has a lasting effect, so it is important that every developer manage the quality of his or her personal work. Not only will quality work save you time and effort, it will produce savings throughout the product life cycle.

8.8   Personal Quality Management

To effectively manage software quality, you must focus on both the defect-removal and the defect-injection processes. For example, some days you might inject a lot of defects because you are sick, have personal problems, or did not get enough sleep. Regardless of your training, skill, or motivation, there is a distinct probability that any action you take will produce an error. Even when I am extremely careful, close to 5% of all my changes contain mistakes that later require correction. This is true whether I am writing programs, doing financial calculations, or editing a manuscript. I have thus learned to expect such errors and to check my corrections and keep checking them until I find no more errors.

For software, the change process is the most error-prone activity (Levendel 1990). The percentage of fixes that generate defects is rarely less than 20% and it is generally much higher. When people recognize this problem and work to address it, they can bring the percentage of fix errors down to 5% or less (Bencher 1994).

Some of the most error-prone programming actions involve interpreting requirements and making design decisions. Errors are also likely during logic design and coding. Some percentage of fix decisions will be in error, as will a fraction of all keystrokes. Even expert typists make mistakes, though they make no design decisions. The quality strategy must therefore recognize that every action has a probability of injecting a defect. The challenge is to identify the defect sources and to prevent them, or to devise actions to consistently detect and remove all the defects that slip through.

The PSP's recommended personal quality-management strategy is to use your plans and historical data to guide your work. That is, start by striving to meet the PQI guidelines. Focus first on producing a thorough and complete design and then document that design with the four PSP design templates that are covered in Chapters 11 and 12. Then, as you review the design, spend enough time to find the likely defects. If the design work took four hours, plan to spend at least two, and preferably three, hours doing the review. To do this productively, plan the review steps based on the guidelines in the PSP Design Review Script described in Chapter 9. If you finish all of the steps in less than the planned time, check to see if you skipped anything or made any mistakes. Then, in the code review, follow the PSP Code Review Script described in Chapter 9. Make sure that you take the time that your data say you must take to do a quality job.

Although it is most desirable to find and fix all defects before testing, this is rarely possible. Reviews and inspections are performed by people, and people make mistakes. Because we cannot always expect to reach 100% yield in code reviews or inspections, testing must be part of every software quality strategy. But reviews, inspections, compiling, and testing are each most effective at finding different kinds of defects. For example, in design reviews, people will quickly see problems that would be extraordinarily hard to find in testing. Similarly, some system problems that are very hard to visualize in a review or inspection show up right away in testing.

In practice, this means that when you do careful personal reviews, you will find most of the defects and find them rapidly—but you will miss some. Then, when your team does thorough design and code inspections, the inspectors will find many of the defects that you missed. Some will be mistakes and others could be errors that you could not see because, every time you looked, you saw what you meant to do, rather than what you actually did.

The compiler will find other types of defects, as will every phase of testing. Surprisingly, however, when developers and their teams use reasonable care throughout the process, their finished products have essentially no defects. Of course, there is no way to know for certain that these products are defect-free, but many TSP teams have delivered products for which users have not reported defects. In short, quality work pays in reduced costs, shorter schedules, and higher-quality products.

What is right for you today will not likely be best forever. Not only will you develop new skills, but the technology will change, you will have a different working environment, and you will face different problems. You must thus continually track and assess the quality of your work. When improvement progress slows, set new goals and start again. Be alert for new techniques and methods, and use your data to determine what works best for you.

8.9   Managing Product Quality

The software quality problem is becoming more challenging every year. Initially, the issue was to get programs to run. That involved running a few tests until the program did what it was supposed to do. As systems have become more complex, the testing workload has grown until it now consumes about half of the development schedule. The PSP quality strategy addresses this issue by removing as many defects as possible before testing. This strategy has improved both product quality and development productivity. A study of TSP team results found that quality improvements of one to two orders of magnitude were common. Figure 8.13 shows the defect levels typical of shipped products at organizations at various levels of CMM maturity, together with the average defect level of the products shipped by a couple of dozen TSP teams (Davis and Mullaney 2003). Because

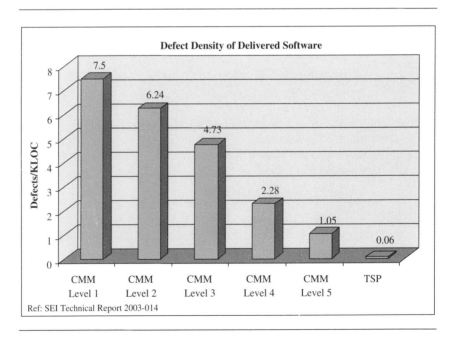

FIGURE 8.13 CMM AND TSP DEFECT LEVELS

most of the TSP teams were in organizations at CMM levels 1 and 2, the 0.06 average defect/KLOC was an improvement of about 100 times.

The challenge we face is that these quality levels are not adequate. The increasing importance of safety and security and the growing use of software to control safety and security in critical systems means that one defect per KLOC is not acceptable. In fact, even 100 defects per million lines of code (MLOC) is potentially dangerous. With today's multimillion-LOC systems, we must strive for 10 defects per MLOC or less. The question is, how can we possibly do this?

As noted earlier, this would require that developers miss only one single defect in 3,000 pages of listings, so we must devise the highest-quality processes we can create; and then we must measure and improve these processes so that the likelihood of having one defect in a one-KLOC module is less that 1%. That is what the PQI measure is designed to accomplish. The strategy is for you to follow a high-quality personal process with every product element. Then, your TSP team should follow a measured and managed team process to inspect and test that product element before including it in the system. When the data for any module look questionable, the team pulls it and reexamines it to determine whether it should be reinspected, reworked, or even completely replaced. What is exciting is how well this strategy works. Forty percent of the TSP teams have reported delivering defect-free products. And these teams had an average productivity improvement of 78% (Davis and Mullaney 2003). Quality isn't free—it actually pays.

8.10 PSP Improvement Practices

In software development, we rarely have the opportunity to develop brand-new products. Most of our work involves enhancing and fixing existing products, and many of these products have unknown and questionable quality histories. A question that I am often asked is, "How can I use the PSP on this kind of work?" In considering this question, the first point to remember is that the PSP is based on six principles:

1. To have predictable schedules, you must plan and track your work.
2. To make accurate and trackable plans, you must make detailed plans.
3. To make accurate detailed plans, you must base the plans on historical data.
4. To get the data needed to make accurate plans, you must use a defined and measured personal process.
5. To do high-quality work, you must measure and manage the quality of your development process.
6. Because poor-quality work is not predictable, quality is a prerequisite to predictability.

Although the PSP course focuses on how to apply these principles when developing new or modified module-size programs, the principles are equally applicable to modifying and enhancing large existing systems. In fact, these same principles also apply to developing requirements, designing hardware devices, and writing books.

The PSP principles can be used and are very effective for maintaining and enhancing existing products, but the quality benefits are more variable. The governing factors are the size of the existing product, the nature of the enhancement work, the historical data available, the quality of the existing product, the goals for the work, and the skills and resources available. There are many ways to design processes for maintenance and enhancement work but the example processes in Chapter 13 suggest ways to define such a process to best fit your needs.

8.11   Defect Prevention

Although detecting and fixing defects is critically important, it is an inherently defensive strategy. For the quality levels required today, we must identify the defect causes and devise steps to prevent them. By reviewing the data on the defects you and your team find during development and testing, you can establish a personalized defect-prevention effort. Possible strategies are to focus on defect types in any of the following categories:

- □ Those found in final program testing or use
- □ Those that occur most frequently
- □ Those that are most difficult or expensive to find and fix
- □ Those for which you can quickly identify preventive actions
- □ Those that most annoy you

The TSP process suggests a procedure for doing this through analyzing every defect found after unit testing. The key is to review every test and user-reported defect, gather the essential data, and establish an explicit prevention strategy. Then, start with a narrow defect category. Once you see what works best, you will have a better idea of how to proceed. The focus in reviews is on finding and fixing defects. Defect prevention, however, requires a more detailed study of the defects. You need to determine what caused them before you can devise ways to prevent them. Then you must work to consistently prevent these defects in the future. A suggested approach is as follows:

1. Select a defect type or class for analysis.
2. Summarize the causes of the defect. In team reviews, it is often helpful to use

Ishikawa or wishbone diagrams (Schulmeyer and McManus 1999). I have not found them necessary for the PSP but you may want to try them. An example is shown in Figure 8.14.

3. Look for trends or patterns in the data that suggest larger or more pervasive problems. An example might be a class of problem that gives you trouble right after an extended period of nonprogramming work.

4. Now that you understand the errors that caused the defects, determine why you made them. Some potential causes are poor or inadequate communication, education gaps, transcription errors, and incomplete or imprecise processes.

5. Devise ways to prevent these problems in the future.

6. Analyze actions that have worked in the past and ensure that you retain them and build on them.

7. Test your defect-prevention ideas on at least one PSP-size program and incorporate those that work in a process update.

8. Recycle through steps 1 through 7 until you run out of time or have no more useful ideas.

Although this approach is effective at a team or project level, it can be difficult to implement by yourself (Gale et al. 1990; Mays et al. 1990). One way to proceed when you run out of good ideas is to hold occasional defect-prevention brain-

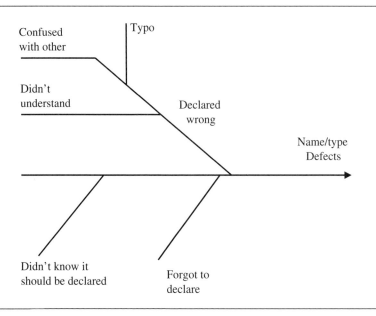

FIGURE 8.14 ISHIKAWA DIAGRAM

storming sessions with some team members. As you get more ideas, consider forming a defect-prevention group.

Try to hold these sessions on a set schedule, with the frequency controlled in part by how much software development you and your teammates do. It probably should not be more often than monthly and no less often than quarterly. If you do action planning too often, you will not have enough time to gauge the effectiveness of your previous actions. Conversely, if you wait too long, your progress will be slower and you are less likely to remember the defect causes. Therefore, do your first defect-prevention studies as soon as you have enough data to analyze. Data on 15 to 30 system-test or user-generated defects should provide enough data for useful analysis. Waiting much longer risks getting overburdened with data and unnecessarily fixing defects you could have prevented with a more timely review.

After implementing the resulting actions, be guided by your ideas. When you think another session would be productive, even if it is the next day, do it. When you run out of ideas, establish a schedule for the next review. Initially, set it a month away. Then, if the monthly reviews become less productive, space them further apart. Don't waste time holding a defect-prevention meeting if you don't have any new ideas. However, do not stop doing them entirely. Again, if you can get one or more teammates to help, you will be more productive. To start a defect-prevention effort, do the following.

1. Use your PSP data to establish a priority for the defect types to initially address. First pick a narrow class of problems and define explicit actions to prevent them.

2. Change your process to accomplish these actions. These changes may include changing forms, adding checklist items, or modifying standards. When practical, devise automated aids to help with transcription and oversight problems. Other automated defect-prevention actions will likely involve too much work to implement by yourself.

3. Conduct a prototype walk-through of the preventive measures to ensure that they are convenient, sustainable, and effective. Then make the indicated changes and insert the new methods into your standard process.

8.12 Summary

To improve the quality of your software, focus on the process required to consistently produce quality products. Seek the most effective methods for finding defects and the most effective ways to prevent them. The costs of finding and fixing defects escalate rapidly the longer the defects remain in the product, and the most cost-effective strategy is to ensure that all program elements are of the highest quality when they are first produced.

Although defects are only one facet of software quality, that is the quality focus of this book. Defects are rarely the users' top priority, but they are an essential focus of the PSP. This is because defects are most economically and effectively handled at the individual level. If the elemental programs in a system have many defects, the entire development process will be overwhelmed by the time-consuming and expensive process of finding and fixing defects during testing.

Software quality is an economic issue. You can always run another test or do another inspection. However, few organizations have the data to make sound quality plans. The PSP provides the data needed to calculate measures for yield, cost of quality, rates and ratios, and the process quality index (PQI). Process yield refers to the percentage of total defects removed before compiling and testing, and the cost-of-quality measure quantifies the quality problem in economic terms. The principal cost-of-quality elements are failure costs, appraisal costs, and prevention costs. These data are used to measure and evaluate the quality of your development process and to identify ways to improve it.

The software process can be viewed as the combination of two competing processes: defect injection and defect removal. The defect content of the finished product is then governed by the difference between the output of these two processes. Because the result is the difference of two large numbers, relatively small changes in either process can make a large difference in the final result. To effectively manage software quality, you must focus on both the removal and the injection processes. Although detecting and fixing defects is critically important, it is an inherently defensive strategy. To make significant quality improvements, identify the causes of the defects and then take steps to eliminate the causes, thus preventing the resulting defects.

References

Ackerman, A. F., L. S. Buchwald, and F. H. Lewski. "Software Inspections: An Effective Verification Process." *IEEE Software* (May 1989): 31–36.

Bencher, D. L. "Technical Forum." *IBM Systems Journal* 33, no. 1 (1994).

Boehm, B. W. *Software Engineering Economics.* Englewood Cliffs, NJ: Prentice-Hall, 1981.

Bush, M. "Improving Software Quality: The Use of Formal Inspections at the Jet Propulsion Laboratory." Twelfth International Conference on Software Engineering, Nice, France (March 26–30, 1990): 196–199.

Crosby, P. B. *Quality Is Free: The Art of Making Quality Certain.* New York: New American Library, 1979.

———. "Don't Be Defensive about the Cost of Quality." *Quality Progress* (April 1983).

Davis, N., and J. Mullaney. "Team Software Process (TSP) in Practice." SEI Technical Report CMU/SEI-2003-TR-014 (September 2003).

Gale, J. L., J. R. Tirso, and C. A. Burchfield. "Implementing the Defect Prevention Process in the MVS Interactive Programming Organization." *IBM Systems Journal* 29, no. 1 (1990).

Jones, C. Personal e-mail, 2004.

Juran, J. M., and F. M. Gryna. *Juran's Quality Control Handbook, Fourth Edition.* New York: McGraw-Hill Book Company, 1988.

Levendel, Y. "Reliability Analysis of Large Software Systems: Defect Data Modeling." *IEEE Transactions on Software Engineering* 16, no. 2 (February 1990): 141–152.

Mandeville, W. A. "Software Costs of Quality." *IEEE Journal on Selected Areas in Communications* 8, no. 2 (February 1990).

Mays, R. G., C. L. Jones, G. J. Holloway, and D. P. Studinski. "Experiences with Defect Prevention." *IBM Systems Journal* 29, no. 1 (1990).

Modarress, B., and A. Ansari. "Two New Dimensions in the Cost of Quality." *International Journal of Quality and Reliability Management* 4, no. 4 (1987): 9–20.

O'Neill, D. Personal letter, 1994.

Ragland, B. "Inspections are Needed Now More Than Ever." *Journal of Defense Software Engineering* 38. Software Technology Support Center, DoD (November 1992).

Remus, H., and S. Ziles. "Prediction and Management of Program Quality." *Proceedings of the Fourth International Conference on Software Engineering, Munich, Germany* (1979): 341–350.

Russell, G. W. "Experience with Inspections in Ultralarge-Scale Developments." *IEEE Software* (January 1991): 25–31.

Schulmeyer, G. G., and J. I. McManus. *Handbook of Software Quality Assurance.* New York: Van Nostrand, 1999.

Shooman, M. L., and M. I. Bolsky. "Types, Distribution, and Test and Correction Times for Programming Errors." *Proceedings of the 1975 Conference on Reliable Software, IEEE, New York,* catalog no. 75, CHO 940-7CSR: 347.

vanGenuchten, M. Personal conversation, 1994.

Weller, E. F. "Lessons Learned from Two Years of Inspection Data." *IEEE Software* (September 1993): 38–45.

9

Design and Code Reviews

Doing thorough design and code reviews will do more to improve the quality and productivity of your work than anything else you can do. In addition to reviewing your personal work, you should also review everything you use as a basis for this work. This includes the program's requirements, the high-level design, and the detailed design. Then, after you write the program, review it before compiling or testing it. If you find problems, fix the defects, correct faulty logic, simplify the program's structure, and bring the code up to your personal and team coding standards. If a program is unclear or confusing, add comments or rewrite it to make it simpler and cleaner. Make your programs easy to read and to understand.

Produce programs that you would be proud to publish and to show to your friends. If you do this on a project, you will produce better programs. You will also cut team testing time from months to weeks or even days, make your individual and your team's work more predictable, and have a more enjoyable and rewarding job. This chapter describes design and code reviews, why they are important, how to do them, and how to use your personal data to improve your reviewing skills.

9.1   What Are Reviews?

There are many ways to review software products. The principal methods are inspections, walk-throughs, and personal reviews. An **inspection** is a structured team review of a software product. Inspections were introduced by Mike Fagan in 1976 and are being used by a growing number of leading software organizations (Fagan 1976; Fagan 1986; Humphrey 2000). **Walk-throughs** are less formal and follow a presentation format, with an audience raising issues and asking questions. Although both walk-throughs and inspections can be effective and are used by TSP teams, they are not part of the PSP, which is a personal process. In addition, they should be done only after each developer has personally reviewed his or her work product.

In a **personal review**, you examine a product that you have developed before you give it to anyone else. Your objective is to find and fix as many of its defects as you can before anyone else implements, compiles, inspects, tests, or even reads the program. You should review the requirements before you start on the design and then review the design before implementing it. On a TSP team, you should also have team members inspect all your products after you have reviewed them and fixed all of the defects you found.

9.2   Why Review Programs?

When developers regularly produce programs that run correctly the first time, ask them how they do it. You will find that they are proud of their work. They carefully review each program before they compile or test it. They don't want anyone to see their product until they are sure it is something they are proud of. If you want quality products, you must personally review and rework them until you are satisfied with their quality.

In my early PSP research, I wrote 72 Pascal and C++ programs. The relative times it took me to fix defects are shown in Table 9.1. On average, it took eight times longer to find and fix a Pascal defect during testing than it did in the code review. The average code review time to find and fix a defect in both Pascal and C++ was between one and two minutes. The average time to find and fix a defect in unit testing was longer for both languages and was even longer after unit testing. This fix time, however, was made up of a lot of fixes that took only a few minutes and a few that took much longer.

My data for these programs also show that the fix time is essentially the same for most defect types. The principal exception was typographical defects, which took about five times as long to find and fix in unit testing as in the code

TABLE 9.1 RELATIVE DEFECT FIX TIMES

Products	Relative Code Review Fix Time	Relative Unit Test Fix Time	Relative Post-Unit Test Fix Time
47 Pascal programs	1	8	16
25 C++ programs	1	12	60

review. This was true for both the Pascal and C++ programs. Figure 8.1 (see p. 138) shows similar data for a Xerox TSP team. This figure has an exponential scale, so although finding and fixing defects took only a few minutes in code reviews, they averaged over 20 hours each in system testing.

Until they learn how to do effective code reviews, many developers write programs as fast as they can and immediately compile and test them. The compiler then leads them from one problem to the next. When the program finally compiles, they are so relieved that they try to run it. However, when programs have compile defects they almost certainly have test defects. If the first test doesn't find defects, the developers will likely declare victory and ship. Then all of the program's remaining defects must still be found, either in system testing or by the user. That is when finding defects becomes truly expensive. Reviewing a program is like reviewing a draft paper. Professional writers will tell you that the secret of good writing is rewriting. Writing good programs is much the same. Few programmers can

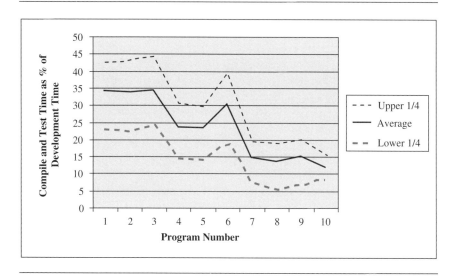

FIGURE 9.1 COMPILE AND TEST TIME RANGE (810 DEVELOPERS)

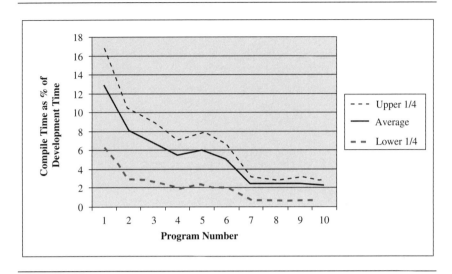

FIGURE 9.2 COMPILE TIME RANGE (810 DEVELOPERS)

write a perfect program on the first try. Many waste a lot of time compiling and testing a defect-prone first draft. Even after all this work, they still produce programs with numerous patches and many remaining defects.

Many developers, when they start PSP training, spend more than one-third of their time compiling and testing. Figure 9.1 shows the average and the upper and lower quartiles for the percentage of development time a group of 810 experienced software developers spent writing ten PSP exercise programs. On Program 1, one-quarter of the developers spent over 43% of their time compiling and testing, and three-quarters of them spent at least 23% of their time compiling and testing. The average compile and test time for these developers was 34%. By the end of PSP training, they were doing design and code reviews, and their average compile and test percentage dropped from 34% to 12%, or only about one-third of the time they had spent at the beginning of the course.

As shown in Figure 9.2, the improvement in compile time was even more dramatic. At the beginning of the course, average compile time was about 13% of development, and it dropped to about 2% by the end of the course. This improvement not only saved the developers time, but also made their development process more predictable and produced higher-quality products. Developers often argue that the compiler finds defects faster than they could and that they spend the saved compile and test time doing the reviews. As shown in Figure 9.3, however, these same 810 developers spent about 8% of their time in reviews on Program 10, while their compiling time was cut by 11%. The reduced test time and improved product quality are a free bonus.

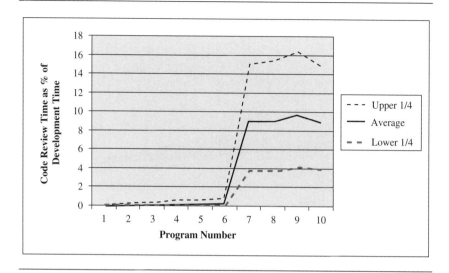

FIGURE 9.3 CODE REVIEW TIME RANGE (810 DEVELOPERS)

Although the correlation between compile and test defects is not very good for groups, Figure 9.4 shows that it is often quite good for individuals. Furthermore, Figure 9.5 shows that when developers find a lot of defects during compiling, they usually will have a lot of defects during testing. The dark bars in Figure 9.5 show

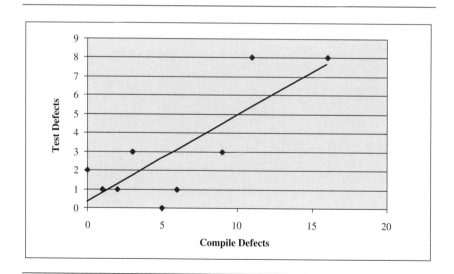

FIGURE 9.4 COMPILE VERSUS TEST DEFECTS, STUDENT 1 ($r = 0.808$)

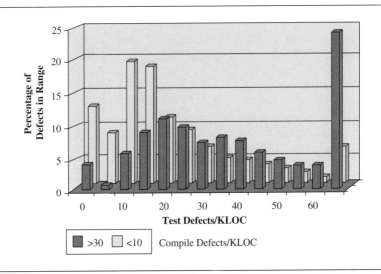

FIGURE 9.5 COMPILE VERSUS TEST DEFECT HISTOGRAM (810 DEVELOPERS)

the test defects for programs that had 30 or more compile defects per KLOC, and the light bars are for those with 10 defects or less per KLOC during compiling.

By examining your own PSP data, you will see that it is fastest and cheapest to find and fix problems before you design the wrong function or implement an erroneous design. A little time spent reviewing a program can save much more than the review time during compiling and testing. More importantly, when everyone on a development team does thorough design and code reviews, integration and system testing time is cut by a factor of five to ten or more. That is why TSP teams typically deliver on or ahead of schedule.

9.3   Review Principles

Each person is different. Until you have data on your own performance, you cannot know the most effective way for you to review programs. By using the PSP, however, you can gather your own data and see what works best for you. Try the methods that work for others and experiment with techniques you think may be better. Learn from the facts, let the data talk, and use your judgment. Give each method a fair trial but be guided by what the data tell you. Regardless of what I or anyone else may say, if your data support a particular method, then that is probably the right method for you.

The PSP process takes advantage of the fact that people are error-prone but that their errors are predictable. It is not that we are incompetent, just that we are human; and as humans, we tend to repeat our mistakes. By using our personal defect data, we can most efficiently look for the defects that we are most likely to make. The principles of the personal review process are as follows:

1. Personally review all of your own work before you move on to the next development phase.

2. Strive to fix all of the defects before you give a product to anyone else.

3. Use a personal checklist and follow a structured review process.

4. Follow sound review practices: review in small increments, do reviews on paper, and do them when you are rested and fresh.

5. Measure the review time, the sizes of the products reviewed, and the number and types of defects you found and missed.

6. Use these data to improve your personal review process.

7. Design and implement your products so that they are easy to review.

8. Review your data to identify ways to prevent defects.

By following these principles, you will improve your personal productivity and you will produce substantially better products. The reasons why these eight principles are so important are explained in the following paragraphs.

Review Your Products to Find and Fix All of Their Defects

Before doing a review, define your objective. Are you striving to improve the product or are you just glancing over the product so you can say you did a review? To avoid wasting your time, strive to find and fix the product's defects. Once you have made this your objective, the only rational goal is to find and fix all of the defects. Again, if that is not your goal, you are likely to waste your time by doing a superficial review. When you use the PSP on a TSP team, even though you will want your teammates to inspect your products as well, you should first thoroughly review them.

Although it is hard to be completely objective about your own work, it is even harder for other people to know what you intended to do. Therefore, once you finish drafting a requirement, producing a design, or writing some code, review it yourself to make sure it is what you intended to produce. By making this first check yourself, the reviews other people do will be more efficient. They won't be distracted by your obvious errors and can concentrate on the more subtle issues that you might have missed.

Your unique knowledge of your own work enables you to see things that others will miss, but the reverse is equally true. You will occasionally miss defects because you can't see them. We often see what we intended to do and not what we actually did. Although the review process is most effective for finding almost all kinds of defects, it is a human process and error-prone. Therefore, when working on a TSP team, complement your reviews with inspections and do thorough unit tests, integration tests, and system tests. By tracking and analyzing all of the defects that you find and miss, you will do better reviews, be more productive, and produce essentially defect-free products.

Use a Checklist and Follow a Structured Review Process

Checklists help you to completely and precisely follow a procedure. To do the job properly, you must follow the checklist exactly. How would you feel if you boarded a flight and heard the pilot tell the copilot they didn't have time to do the preflight checklist? Experienced pilots rigorously complete the checklist before every flight. Their lives and ours depend on the aircraft being fully prepared for flight. Even though they may have checked the identical items one hour earlier, they will completely re-review the entire checklist. Like the pilot, you need to be convinced that missing even one item could have serious consequences.

Reviewing a program is such an apparently obvious activity that it seems almost pointless to define a checklist and a process for doing it. However, a defined process is essential. When people just scan through their programs looking for errors, they rarely find very many. To do a truly effective review, you must follow an orderly process, use sound review practices, and measure your work. Without a defined process, you cannot define the measures, and without measures, you will not have the data to evaluate and improve your reviews. The key is to take the time, preferably during the postmortem for each program, to analyze the defects you found and missed, and to determine how to do a better review the next time.

Follow Sound Review Practices

Based on the experiences in developing over 30,000 programs in PSP courses, three review practices stand out as consistently effective. First, review relatively small amounts of material at any one time. Second, do the review on paper. Third, if possible, do the review when you are rested and refreshed. If that is not possible, at least take a short break first. These practices are discussed further in later sections of this chapter.

Measure Your Reviews

The biggest problem with reviews is convincing developers to take the time to do them properly. Somehow, manually searching through a program to find and fix its defects seems slow and laborious when a powerful computer, a compiler, and a debugging facility are waiting to be used. You can read all that I or anyone else says on the subject of reviews, but the only way to convince yourself is to measure your own reviews.

Use Data to Improve Your Reviews

Human performance is extraordinary. Each year, countless world records are broken, and performances that were once considered impossible become routine. Although this is a marvelous testament to the ability of people to surpass seemingly insurmountable barriers, it doesn't happen by accident. On close examination, you will find that these record-breaking performances are only for regularly measured events. When human performance is measured only occasionally, it doesn't seem to change much from year to year.

Although we know that measured human performance improves every year, why does it? Some have argued that better equipment, training, and diet contribute, but their effects are limited. A comparison between the performance of horses and people is instructive. Figure 9.6 shows 130 years of data for the time it takes men

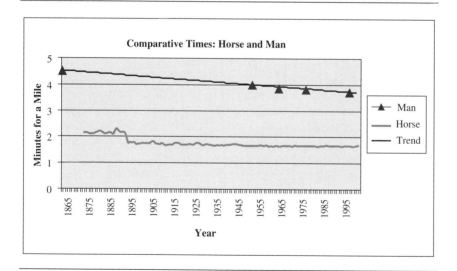

FIGURE 9.6 RECORD TIMES FOR THE MILE: MEN AND HORSES

and horses to run a mile. Whereas the world record for men has steadily improved, the winning times for horses in the Kentucky Derby have not changed significantly in over 100 years. Both men and horses benefited from better training, equipment, and diet, but only men improved consistently. The difference is motivation, and the key to motivation is feedback. The key to feedback, of course, is data.

Without measures, we have no objective way to know how well we are doing. Being essentially an optimistic species, we tend to remember what worked and forget what didn't. Although this keeps us happier, it also makes us complacent and less motivated to improve. Even worse, without measures, we cannot know how to improve, or even if we are improving. This is why a fundamental principle of PSP reviews is measurement.

Produce Reviewable Products

The seventh principle of PSP reviews is to produce products that are easy to review. This requires a lot of comments in the code and a precise and clearly documented design. To consistently produce such products, you must have both design and coding standards, and you must use them. Furthermore, as you find defects that could have been prevented with a better standard, update the standard.

Use Data to Prevent Defects

By just gathering defect data, you will be more conscious of your mistakes and make fewer of them. Figure 9.7 shows data on the defect-injection rates of 810 developers for 10 PSP programming exercises. It indicates that their defect-injection rates declined even before they used the quality methods introduced with Program 7. Defect measurement appears to be largely responsible for the 33% improvement from 120 defects per KLOC at the beginning to 80 defects per KLOC for Program 4.

You can use PSP defect data to reduce your personal defect-injection rate. Although there is not generally time to do this during the PSP course, when you work on a TSP team, consider forming a group of teammates to periodically review defect data and devise ways to prevent the highest-priority problems. There are many ways to prioritize defects—for example, by frequency, by total time to fix, by severity, or even by level of annoyance. Because these methods all have advantages and disadvantages, pick the approach that most appeals to you and then be guided by your data.

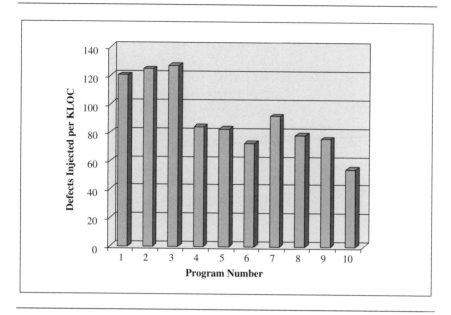

FIGURE 9.7 DEFECTS INJECTED PER KLOC (810 DEVELOPERS)

9.4 The PSP Code Review Process

The PSP Code Review Script is shown in Table 9.2. The code review entry criteria call for a complete design and a source-code listing of the program to be reviewed. You must also have copies of the Code Review Checklist, the coding standard, and the defect standard. The checklist that I used for my C++ programs is shown in Table 9.3.

In conducting the review, I first printed a listing and then went through the entire program line by line for each major checklist entry. That is, after checking that the program covered all of the design and that the includes were complete, I again reviewed every line for initialization errors. Then, I did the same for calls, names, and all subsequent entries in the checklist until I was done. At the end, I checked the exit criteria to make sure I had checked every box and fixed all of the defects. The reasons for printing a listing rather than reviewing on the screen are discussed on p. 194.

TABLE 9.2 PSP CODE REVIEW SCRIPT

Purpose	To guide you in reviewing programs
Entry Criteria	• A completed and reviewed program design • Source program listing • Code Review checklist • Coding standard • Defect Type standard • Time and Defect Recording logs
General	While following this process • do the review from a source-code listing; do not review on the screen! • record all time spent in the Time Recording log (LOGT) • record all defects found in the Defect Recording log (LOGD)

Step	Activities	Description
1	Review	• Follow the Code Review checklist. • Review the entire program for each checklist category; do not try to review for more than one category at a time! • Check off each item as it is completed. • For multiple procedures or programs, complete a separate checklist for each.
2	Correct	• Correct all defects. • If the correction cannot be completed, abort the review and return to the prior process phase. • To facilitate defect analysis, record all of the data specified in the Defect Recording log instructions for every defect.
3	Check	• Check each defect fix for correctness. • Re-review all design changes. • Record any fix defects as new defects and, where you know the number of the defect with the incorrect fix, enter it in the fix defect space.

Exit Criteria	• A fully reviewed source program • One or more Code Review checklists for every program reviewed • All identified defects fixed • Completed Time and Defect Recording logs

TABLE 9.3 CODE REVIEW CHECKLIST

Student _____ Date _____

Program _____ Program # _____

Instructor _____ Language _____C++_____

Purpose	To guide you in conducting an effective code review
General	• Review the entire program for each checklist category; do not attempt to review for more than one category at a time! • As you complete each review step, check off that item in the box at the right. • Complete the checklist for one program or program unit before reviewing the next.

Complete	Verify that the code covers all of the design.				
Includes	Verify that the includes are complete.				
Initialization	Check variable and parameter initialization. • at program initiation • at start of every loop • at class/function/procedure entry				
Calls	Check function call formats. • pointers • parameters • use of '&'				
Names	Check name spelling and use. • Is it consistent? • Is it within the declared scope? • Do all structures and classes use '.' reference?				
Strings	Check that all strings are • identified by pointers • terminated by NULL				
Pointers	Check that all • pointers are initialized NULL • pointers are deleted only after new • new pointers are always deleted after use				
Output Format	Check the output format. • Line stepping is proper. • Spacing is proper.				
() Pairs	Ensure that () are proper and matched.				
Logic Operators	• Verify the proper use of ==, =, ||, and so on. • Check every logic function for ().				
Line-by-line check	Check every line of code for • instruction syntax • proper punctuation				
Standards	Ensure that the code conforms to the coding standards.				
File Open and Close	Verify that all files are • properly declared • opened • closed				

9.5   The Code Review Checklist

A checklist is a specialized form for your personal use in doing reviews. When you use a checklist to do a review, the completed checklist copy is your record of the review. The checklist also disciplines your work and guides you through the review steps. Because you will likely change the checklist as you improve your reviews, it was designed as a separate script that you can change without changing the review process. It also simplifies the review script. When reviewing large programs, review them in parts and complete a checklist for each part. The several columns on the right of Table 9.3 enable you to use one checklist to review four separate parts of a program.

Building the Checklist

The PSP process requires that you develop your own review checklist and that you check off each item as you complete it. To build the checklist, start with the PSP Defect Type standard that was introduced with PSP0. It is shown again in Table 9.4. By gathering defect data, you will soon discover that some of these categories cause a lot of trouble, while others are not worth much attention. I found that four areas—syntax, function, interface, and assignment—accounted for 97% of all my compile and test defects.

Next, examine your defect logs to determine the defect types you encounter most frequently. Then devise checks to find them. Merely specifying "verify the logic" or "check the punctuation" is not adequate. Add concrete guidelines like "Check that all pointers are initialized to NULL" or "Verify the proper use of = and ==." When I examined my C++ defect data, I expanded the four most troublesome defect types into three or four subcategories, as shown in Table 9.5. These were not additional defect types, but more refined categories of the existing types. To produce this table, I used the descriptions recorded with each defect. This refinement enabled me to focus my reviews on the specific defect types that occurred most frequently. The percentages in the right-hand column show the total number of defects found in reviews, compiling, and testing.

A defect list sorted in frequency order is called a **Pareto distribution**. The defect type frequency shown in Table 9.5 is shown as a Pareto distribution in Figure 9.8. Using a Pareto distribution of your defects, construct a review checklist that focuses on the most prevalent types first. Although such a refined defect standard can be very helpful, its content will change as your process improves. I have found that the best practice is to use the ten basic PSP defect types and make sufficiently detailed comments to enable me to produce more precise defect categories whenever I update my checklists. In developing a checklist, also start with a well-designed coding standard.

TABLE 9.4 PSP DEFECT TYPE STANDARD

Type Number	Type Name	Description
10	Documentation	Comments, messages
20	Syntax	Spelling, punctuation, typos, instruction formats
30	Build, Package	Change management, library, version control
40	Assignment	Declaration, duplicate names, scope, limits
50	Interface	Procedure calls and references, I/O, user formats
60	Checking	Error messages, inadequate checks
70	Data	Structure, content
80	Function	Logic, pointers, loops, recursion, computation, function defects
90	System	Configuration, timing, memory
100	Environment	Design, compile, test, other support system problems

Because I based this PSP Code Review Checklist on my experiences writing C++ programs, it may not precisely fit your needs. To build a checklist that suits you, first review your defect data to see where you should focus the most attention. In addition, be careful about how you group the items on the checklist. For example, you could group all punctuation items together, as they can generally be searched for as a group. If you believe some action should be taken on every review, state it that way. However, if you believe that a checklist item is needed only under certain conditions, word it to indicate that. For example, if you want to recheck the design of any loop constructs that had defects in the design review, then your checklist should explicitly say something like "Recheck the design of every loop construct that was changed either during or since the design review."

Updating the Checklist

Examine the Pareto distribution for your defects every four or five programs to ensure that you are still focusing on the defect types that you most frequently miss in the reviews. If your data show a lot of change, do these analyses more often. By doing this, you will become more conscious of some defect types and stop injecting them. When you do, drop that defect type from the checklist. In the PSP course, do this analysis during the postmortem for every exercise program.

TABLE 9.5 EXPANDED DEFECT TYPE STANDARD

Purpose		To facilitate causal analysis and defect prevention	
Note		The types are grouped in ten general categories. • If the detailed category does not apply, use the general category. • The % column lists an example type distribution.	
No.	**Name**	**Description**	**%**
10	Documentation	Comments, messages, manuals	1.1
20	Syntax	General syntax problems	0.8
21	Typos	Spelling, punctuation	32.1
22	Instruction formats	General format problems	5.0
23	Begin-end	Did not properly delimit operation	0
30	Packaging	Change management, version control, system build	1.6
40	Assignment	General assignment problems	0
41	Naming	Declaration, duplicates	12.6
42	Scope		1.3
43	Initialize and close	Variables, objects, classes, and so on	4.0
44	Range	Variable limits, array range	0.3
50	Interface	General interface problems	1.3
51	Internal	Procedure calls and references	9.5
52	I/O	File, display, printer, communication	2.6
53	User	Formats, content	8.9
60	Checking	Error messages, inadequate checks	0
70	Data	Structure, content	0.5
80	Function	General logic	1.8
81	Pointers	Pointers, strings	8.7
82	Loops	Off-by-one, incrementing, recursion	5.5
83	Application	Computation, algorithmic	2.1
90	System	Timing, memory, and so on	0.3
100	Environment	Design, compile, test, other support system problems	0

Be careful not to drop defect types unless you no longer encounter them. If you still make a lot of off-by-one errors, for example, but find them all in the code review, you cannot stop reviewing for that defect type. If you did, you would then have to find more of them during testing. This is why you should look at the Pareto distribution sorted by both the defects you find and those that you miss.

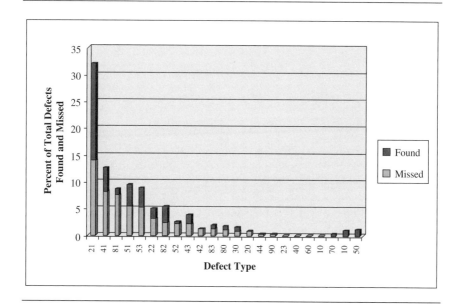

FIGURE 9.8 PARETO DISTRIBUTION OF C++ REVIEW DEFECTS

To add items to your checklist, sort the Pareto distribution in the order of the defects you miss, as in Figure 9.8. However, keep items on the list based on a Pareto distribution that is sorted by the number of defects you find by type. You should also do a sort based on the total fix times to make sure you are addressing all of the most important defects.

Reviewing against Coding Standards

Your principal interest in a code review is to ensure that all of the details are correct. Here is where a coding standard can be a big help. It should require that you initialize every parameter before use and that you first null all new pointers and then later delete them. It should also call for robustness checks to ensure that all calls have the proper parameter values, overflows are detected, and I/O errors do not disrupt program operation. Each procedure should check for erroneous input and provide clear error messages in the event of problems.

By reviewing against defined standards, you can ensure that your programs comply with the established system interfaces, the reuse criteria, the commenting guidelines, the header formats, the naming conventions, and so on. Although your programming practices will be influenced by the particular application and system environment, establish a consistent set of personal practices. Once you have decided on your practices, incorporate them in your standards and check them in your reviews. They will help you to prevent problems, to identify problems during testing, and to protect your users from the often unpleasant consequences of using defective software.

Using a Checklist

When doing a precise task like a code review, most people find it difficult to review more than one topic at a time. For example, if you attempted to simultaneously check for name/type defects and for Boolean logic problems, you would be likely to concentrate on the name/type defects and overlook Boolean logic problems, or the reverse. Partway through the review, you might realize this and then start to concentrate on the other defect type and slight the first. As a result, you would probably not do a proper review for either defect type. You can address this problem by dividing the checklist into sections with similar characteristics. By looking for all of the name/type problems at once, for example, you are likely to be both quicker and more effective.

After an item has been on your checklist for some time, you may tend to follow it superficially. If your review experience is like mine, periodically review your data to see how you are doing. For example, on the name/type check, see how many of these defects you catch in the reviews. If you are missing a lot of them, be more careful during your next review and see if you can devise a way to be more effective.

The Review Strategy

You may also have problems reviewing multiple small routines or procedures. For example, when reviewing a class with several methods, establish a review strategy. Suppose, for example, that the class has a control method and three application methods. If the methods each have about 50 to 75 lines of source code, you might consider reviewing the entire class in one pass through the checklist. To decide if this would be a sound strategy, look again at Table 9.3 (see p. 175) and picture how you would likely do the review.

1. To ensure that the code covered all of the design, review each method to ensure that all of the required functions are included.
2. To check the includes, examine each method to ensure that the proper includes are entered for each library function.
3. To check for initialization problems, walk through the logic of all methods.

When you review in this way, you will jump back and forth among the methods. As you examine one method, you will likely build a mental context that you may lose when you switch to another. These context switches take time, cause errors, and often result in low-yield reviews. When programs are even moderately complex, it pays to review each separable part as a unit. You would then complete the entire checklist for each part before going on to the next part. To see if this is the best approach for you, try one strategy with several programs or parts of programs, and try another strategy with some others. The data on defects per hour, LOC per hour, and yield (or percentage of defects found) should help you to decide which approach is most effective for you.

With a large hierarchical program, your design review strategy will likely follow a top-down pattern. For the code review, however, it is often best to start reviewing at the bottom. For example, consider a main routine that calls various procedures. One of these procedures, in turn, calls a file-handling routine. Start the code review with the lowest-level procedures that depend on no others—in this case, the file-handling routine. After reviewing the code in the lowest-level procedures, move up to the procedures that call them. As part of this higher-level review, check to ensure that every call is consistent with the procedure specifications. However, because you have just reviewed the lower-level procedures, you need not examine them further. By following this order, you can trust the procedural abstractions when you encounter them in the higher-level code reviews. If you don't follow such a strategy, you will keep tracing through the called procedures just to be sure that they do what they are supposed to do.

This strategy applies only when you are reviewing your own code. Here, you have a context for the reviews and probably remember the overall design, or have some design records or notes that explain the program's purpose and structure. When you start at the lowest level and work up, you are looking for local issues and ensuring that all of the coding details are correct. However, when reviewing unfamiliar code, you will likely want to follow more of a top-down strategy, at least until you understand the program's overall structure and behavior.

9.6 Design Reviews

Some design problems are extremely hard to find in source code. Examples are security problems, safety problems, state-machine design mistakes, and interface issues. Over 90% of Internet software vulnerabilities are due to software defects, and these are usually design problems. Similarly, system safety is also increasingly a software problem. All parts of safe and secure systems must be properly designed, and the design must be of high quality. This requires thorough design reviews. This chapter covers the more general design review considerations; Chapters 10, 11, and 12 cover design and design verification.

One problem with attempting to decipher a program's logic from the source code is the volume of material to be reviewed. Even simple source programs can involve several pages of documentation. A condensed design format such as pseudocode, precise mathematical notations, or standardized functional abstractions is much easier to understand. For example, name authentication is critical for security management and it is easy to lose track of name status when mired in coding details.

When reviewing source code for design defects, it is also easy to be distracted by coding problems. Obvious coding errors get in the way and make it much more difficult to visualize the larger design issues. A focus on design while reviewing code can also cause you to overlook many coding problems. To produce high-quality products, review your designs before writing the code. Then review the code too.

Another reason to review the design before writing the code is that you are much more likely to produce smaller, neater, and more understandable programs. You will also save the time that you would have spent coding incorrect logic. When you implement an incorrect design and then later review it, you will unconsciously try to minimize changes. Then you will try to correct the design to preserve as much of the existing code as possible. Because you no longer have the single priority of producing a quality design, however, design quality will almost certainly suffer.

An additional reason to review the design before implementation is that you are more likely to see and incorporate potential design improvements. This can be particularly important if you design the way I do. When faced with a logic problem, for example, I usually see some "obvious" way to solve it. Sometimes this way is sound, but occasionally it is not. With a little reflection, I will often see a neater solution that takes less code, has a cleaner structure, and is faster and easier to understand and to modify. If you design this way, and if you implement your designs before reviewing them, you will have made a large investment in this initial design.

When you review the design after writing the code, you are more likely to stick with a poor but workable design, even if it does not cleanly fit the functional need. With each new problem, you will patch this design, and soon it will be so complex that you will have trouble understanding it yourself. The practice of designing while coding is the cause of many code thickets in big systems. Such programs are often impossible to modify or even to fix. Clean designs are more likely to stay clean, even when modified. Patched-up designs generally get more complex with every change.

9.7   Design Review Principles

The PSP2 Design Review Script is shown in Table 9.6 and a basic Design Review Checklist is shown in Table 9.7. Some helpful design review guidelines are as follows:

- ☐ Produce designs that can be reviewed.
- ☐ Follow an explicit review strategy.
- ☐ Review the design in stages.
- ☐ If the design is incomplete, review the code.
- ☐ Verify that the logic correctly implements the requirements.
- ☐ Check for safety and security issues.

TABLE 9.6 PSP2 DESIGN REVIEW SCRIPT

Purpose		To guide you in reviewing detailed designs
Entry Criteria		• Completed program design • Design Review checklist • Design standard • Defect Type standard • Time and Defect Recording logs
General		Where the design was previously verified, check that the analyses • covered all of the design and were updated for all design changes • are correct, clear, and complete Where the design is not available or was not reviewed, do a complete design review on the code and fix all defects before doing the code review.
Step	**Activities**	**Description**
1	Preparation	Examine the program and checklist and decide on a review strategy.
2	Review	• Follow the Design Review checklist. • Review the entire program for each checklist category; do not try to review for more than one category at a time! • Check off each item as you complete it. • Complete a separate checklist for each product or product segment reviewed.
3	Fix Check	• Check each defect fix for correctness. • Re-review all changes. • Record any fix defects as new defects and, where you know the defective defect number, enter it in the fix defect space.
Exit Criteria		• A fully reviewed detailed design • One or more Design Review checklists for every design reviewed • All identified defects fixed and all fixes checked • Completed Time and Defect Recording logs

TABLE 9.7 PSP2 DESIGN REVIEW CHECKLIST

Student _____   Date _____

Program _____   Program # _____

Instructor _____   Language _____

Purpose	To guide you in conducting an effective design review
General	• Review the entire program for each checklist category; do not attempt to review for more than one category at a time! • As you complete each review step, check off that item in the box at the right. • Complete the checklist for one program or program unit before reviewing the next.

Complete	Verify that the design covers all of the applicable requirements. • All specified outputs are produced. • All needed inputs are furnished. • All required includes are stated.				
External Limits	Where the design assumes or relies upon external limits, determine if behavior is correct at nominal values, at limits, and beyond limits.				

Logic	• Verify that program sequencing is proper.
	    • Stacks, lists, and so on are in the proper order.
	    • Recursion unwinds properly.
	• Verify that all loops are properly initiated, incremented, and terminated.
	• Examine each conditional statement and verify all cases.				

Internal Limits	Where the design assumes or relies upon internal limits, determine if behavior is correct at nominal values, at limits, and beyond limits.				
Special Cases	• Check all special cases. • Ensure proper operation with empty, full, minimum, maximum, negative, zero values for all variables. • Protect against out-of-limits, overflow, underflow conditions. • Ensure "impossible" conditions are absolutely impossible. • Handle all possible incorrect or error conditions.				
Functional Use	• Verify that all functions, procedures, or methods are fully understood and properly used. • Verify that all externally referenced abstractions are precisely defined.				
System Considerations	• Verify that the program does not cause system limits to be exceeded. • Verify that all security-sensitive data are from trusted sources. • Verify that all safety conditions conform to the safety specifications.				
Names	Verify that • all special names are clear, defined, and authenticated • the scopes of all variables and parameters are self-evident or defined • all named items are used within their declared scopes				
Standards	Ensure that the design conforms to all applicable design standards.				

Produce Designs That Can Be Reviewed

If you are the only person who will review or use your design, then reviewability is not as great a concern. However, if other people will review your design or use it to do the implementation, make repairs, or develop enhancements, the design must be clear and understandable. I have even found that a clear and understandable design is important when reusing or enhancing my own programs. It is almost impossible to pick up a poorly documented design and review it. Not only are there issues about the design's objectives, but also there are questions about its relationship with other programs, the assumptions the designer made, and the various system standards and conventions. To minimize these problems, consider review issues when producing a design. The goal should be to produce a design that is complete, correct, and reviewable.

For a design to be reviewable, its purpose and function must be clearly stated, including an explicit list of the constraints and conditions it must satisfy. When working in a development organization, you will probably have design standards or system conventions. You should also have personal design standards. Without these standards, you will have a poor basis for doing a design review. The design description must also be complete and precise. Without a well-documented and complete design, it is impossible to do a competent design review. In Chapter 11, the design templates introduced with PSP2.1 satisfy the PSP design-completeness criteria.

Follow an Explicit Design Review Strategy

The review strategy specifies the order to follow in reviewing the various parts of the design. Because this order depends on the structure of the product, the review strategy should be part of your development strategy. The strategy of the Design Review Checklist in Table 9.7 is to start with the big picture and gradually get more detailed. You will want to review each design in conjunction with other related designs. Doing this will help you to build a review context and improve your ability to see coupling and interdependency issues. Plan the order of your design work to provide a logical and coherent order for the reviews. Although you need not review in the order you design, you do need to provide a review context for every design you review.

Review the Design in Stages

A reviewable design should be built in segments that encapsulate closely related logical elements. That is, it must suit a review strategy that covers one limited design segment at a time. During the review, you must build a mental picture of the entire design. My rule of thumb is to limit the design review material to about one to three pages of text if possible. Although this is not always practical, good designs are usually structured into sections that are compact and easy to understand. Complex designs tend to be redundant, poorly structured, and hard to decipher.

By reviewing only relatively small and self-contained portions of the design at one time, you are more likely to do a thorough review. Then, unless you make changes, the code review should ensure only that the design was implemented properly. However, if the design has been changed after the design review, you must review these changes during the code review. Rather than debate the amount of design material to review at one time, gather data and see what review approach works best for you. We all have limitations on what we can visualize, and individual abilities vary enormously. If your design reviews have high yields, even up to several pages of logic, then feel free to review such designs. I suspect, however, that there is some size beyond which you will start missing design problems. Until you have a sense for that size limit, I suggest that you start with one to three pages.

If the Design Is Incomplete, Review the Code

If you did not produce a precise design or the design has changed, do a design review of the source code before doing the code review. Although such reviews have all of the problems described in the preceding section, it is still important to find and fix all design defects before testing. Furthermore, if you wait and try to do the design review as part of the code review, you run the risk of not doing either review properly. In addition, you will not have the benefit of a full code review for all of the design fixes you made as a result of the design review.

Verify That the Logic Correctly Implements the Requirements

Verifying that the logic correctly implements the requirements is simple in principle but it can involve considerable work. You must review every requirement and verify that it is completely covered by the design. Oversights and omissions are important defect categories that can be handled almost completely by a careful review of the design against the requirements. However, such oversights are extremely hard to find either in code reviews or in testing. Don't forget to check the use of names and parameters. Some programmers feel that the compiler handles name and type checks so efficiently that they should not bother to do them. This would be reasonable if their data showed that they never had such problems. My preference is to check all of the globally declared and state-controlling parameters and all of the specially declared types during the design review. I then defer the more local name and type checks until the code review.

The design review is also the best time to check overall product structure. A possible symptom of design problems is the passing of parameters through multiple classes or methods. Although well-designed programs often do this, it can also indicate that the original design concept did not neatly fit the problem being solved or that the design was poorly structured. This condition is easy to check during the design review and provides an early indication of possible design problems.

Check for Safety and Security Issues

The principal security checks concern overflow and exception handling and name verification and authorization. You can prevent most security problems by ensuring that *all* attempts to access or modify the system or its contents are properly authorized beforehand and that *all* possible overflow and exception conditions are properly handled. You should also follow your organization's security guidelines.

For safety, the guidelines are similar: verify that the design conforms to all of the design specifications and that all safety standards and requirements are met. The design must ensure that a safe state is always maintained, both internally and in the external environment, and potentially hazardous states must be either prevented or mitigated by the design. To the extent possible, the system should also tolerate failures, either with fail-safe modes or with degraded but safe performance in the event of failure. Safe design requires a continuous focus on quality, as defective systems cannot be safe.

9.8   Review Measures

By measuring your reviews, you get the data needed to improve their quality. A high-quality review is one that efficiently finds the greatest number of defects. To assess review quality, measure the time spent on each review and track all of the defects that you find and miss. With these data, you will see where and how to improve your reviews. Like other skills, however, reviewing takes time to learn and to master, so give yourself time to improve. The standard PSP process measures provide the data needed to evaluate and improve your reviews:

- □ Size of the program being reviewed
- □ Review time in minutes
- □ Number of defects found
- □ Number of defects in the program that were later found (the **escapes**)

The following discussion uses LOC to describe some example code review measures. However, for design reviews, no size measure is available at review time, so use text lines, pages of design, or estimated program size. For other products, use the size measures used to plan and track the work. From the basic size, time, and defect measures, you can derive several other useful measures. The most important ones are as follows:

□ **Review yield:** The percentage of defects in the program that were found during the review

□ **Defect density:** The defects found per volume of design or code reviewed

□ **Defect rate:** The defects found per hour of review time

□ **Review rate:** The size of the product reviewed per hour

These measures are discussed in the following sections.

Review Yield

Review yield was discussed in Chapter 8. It refers to the percentage of the defects in the product at the time of the review that were found by that review. The yield cannot be precisely calculated until after the product has been thoroughly tested and extensively used, but you can make fairly accurate early yield approximations. For example, if you find 8 defects in the code review and 6 while compiling, you know that you found only 8 of the 14 defects known after compilation. As shown in Table 9.8, this would result in an initial review yield estimate of 57.1%.

The essential data for the yield calculations are shown in Table 9.9. These data are available from the defect log. The yield calculations are shown in Tables 9.8 and 9.10. To produce the yield table, find in the defect log the number of defects injected and removed in each phase and enter the totals in the proper spaces. The *Cum. Injected* and *Cum. Removed* columns are the cumulative sums of the *Injected* and *Removed* columns for each phase. Note that at compile time, you would know

TABLE 9.8 YIELD CALCULATIONS (AFTER COMPILE)

Phase	Injected	Removed	Cum. Injected	Cum. Removed	Escapes	Defect Objective	Yield %
Detailed Design	5	0	5	0	5	5	0
Design Review	0	3	5	3	2	5	60.0
Code	13	1	18	4	14	15	5.5
Code Review	0	8	18	12	6	14	57.1
Compile	0	6	18	18	0	6	100.0

TABLE 9.9 DEFECT DATA

Defect #	Phase Injected	Phase Removed
1	Design	Design Review
2	Design	Design Review
3	Design	Design Review
4	Design	Code
5	Code	Code Review
6	Code	Code Review
7	Design	Code Review
8	Code	Code Review
9	Code	Code Review
10	Code	Code Review
11	Code	Code Review
12	Code	Code Review
13	Code	Compile
14	Code	Compile
15	Code	Compile
16	Code	Compile
17	Code	Compile
18	Code	Compile
19	Code	Test
20	Code	Test
21	Design	Test

about the defects found through compiling, but not the ones found in unit testing or later.

The escapes are those defects injected before or during a phase that were not found until after that phase. These escapes can be calculated for each phase by subtracting each entry in the *Cum. Removed* column from the corresponding entry in the *Cum. Injected* column. The column called *Defect Objective* holds the sum of the escapes from the previous phase and the defects injected in this phase. This is the total number of defects that could be removed in the phase. For example, in Table 9.10, there are 21 − 12 = 9 escapes from the code review.

TABLE 9.10 YIELD CALCULATIONS (AFTER UNIT TEST)

Phase	Injected	Removed	Cum. Injected	Cum. Removed	Escapes	Defect Objective	Yield %
Detailed Design	6	0	6	0	6	6	0
Design Review	0	3	6	3	3	6	50.0
Code	15	1	21	4	17	18	5.5
Code Review	0	8	21	12	9	17	47.1
Compile	0	6	21	18	3	9	66.7
Unit Test	0	3	21	21	0	3	100.0

The yield for any phase is the number of defects removed as a percentage of the defect objective. For the code review, the defect objective was the escapes from coding (17) plus those injected in the code review (0), so the yield is 100*8/17 = 47.1%. As you get the defect data from subsequent phases, you will have to recalculate the yield. Many TSP and PSP support tools calculate these figures for you. After unit testing, the yield table would look like the one shown in Table 9.10.

A high yield is good; a low yield is poor. The yield goal should be 100%. The PSP goal is to find and fix all defects before the first compile or test. By doing design and code reviews before first compiling or testing the program, you will find many defects that compiling and testing would also have caught. You are also likely to miss several. When developers start doing reviews, their PSP data show that they find only about one-third to one-half of the defects present.

By analyzing your review data and updating the Code Review Checklist, you can significantly improve review yields. With care and practice, many developers can catch 80% or more of their defects before compiling or testing. A significant number achieve one or more 100% process yield reviews during the PSP course. That is, they find all of the defects in a program before they first compile or test it. Having a program compile correctly the first time and then run all of the test cases without a single error is a marvelous experience. Data on the yields achieved by 810 developers in PSP courses are shown in Figure 9.9.

Yield Estimates

To make a yield estimate for any phase, you must assume a yield for the last completed defect-removal phase. For the data in Table 9.10, you might estimate that the unit test yield was 50%. That would mean that, after unit testing, three more defects would remain to be found. Next, assume that these defects were injected in the same proportion as those found to date. In this case, 3*6/21 = 0.857 of these undis-

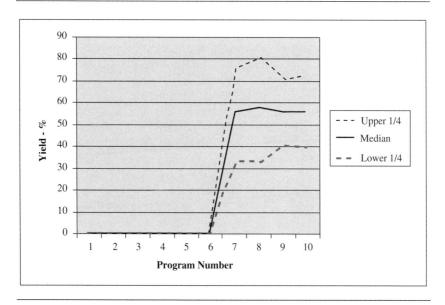

FIGURE 9.9 YIELDS FOR 810 DEVELOPERS (UPPER, MEDIAN, AND LOWER QUARTILES)

covered defects would then have been injected in detailed design, and 3*15/21 = 2.143 during coding. After system testing, you would then assume a yield of 50% for system testing and calculate the yields of all the previous phases, including unit testing. Of course, after you have historical data on the yields of these phases, you can use those numbers instead of making the 50% assumption.

Defect Density

Although the yield measure provides the best guide to review quality, it cannot be accurately calculated until well after the review is completed. Thus, to manage the quality of the reviews while you do them, you need current or instant measures that correlate with yield. That is, if you generally had high yields when you reviewed 100 or fewer LOC in an hour, and generally had low yields when you reviewed more than 300 LOC in an hour, LOC/hour would be a useful instant measure. Although defects per KLOC is also an instant measure, a low defect rate could mean either that the review was superficial or that the program had few defects. This would not be a useful measure for managing review quality. Defects per hour is also an instant measure, but it indicates only the speed with which you find defects, not how many you find or the review's effectiveness.

Review Rate

As discussed in Chapter 8 (see p. 146), the review rate measure provides useful guidance on review quality. In Figure 8.9 for example, the lowest review rates are at the front of the figure and the highest ones are at the back. By looking at the trends for 0% yield at the left and 100% yield at the right, it is clear that the lower review rates are much more effective than the higher ones.

The yield-rate relationship is often clearer for individual developers. Figure 9.10 shows review data for one developer who wrote 10 PSP exercises, and Figure 9.11 shows the results for 25 of my C++ programs. In both of these cases, reviews above about 200 LOC per hour did not generally have high yields. Similarly, although low review rates were more likely to have higher yields, that was not guaranteed. This result is consistent with the findings on review rates for code inspections, where 300 LOC per hour is considered an upper limit (Fagan 1986; Gilb and Graham 1993; Humphrey 1989). Achieving high review yield is obviously a personal skill. Lower review rates will generally improve yield, whereas an excessively fast review is likely to be a waste of time.

Defect-Removal Leverage

Defect-removal leverage (DRL) measures the relative effectiveness of defect-removal methods. It is the ratio of the defects removed per hour in any two phases, and it is useful for comparing review phases with one of the test phases, such as

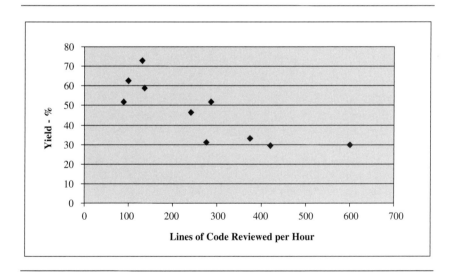

FIGURE 9.10 REVIEW YIELD VERSUS REVIEW RATE IN LOC/HOUR (STUDENT 12)

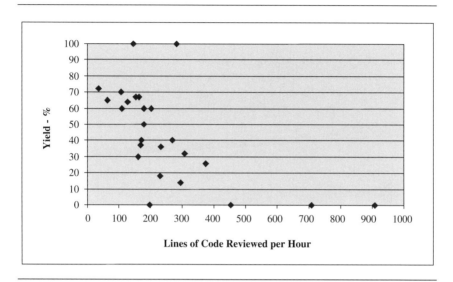

FIGURE 9.11   REVIEW YIELD VERSUS REVIEW RATE IN LOC/HOUR
(25 C++ PROGRAMS)

unit testing. For example, Table 9.11 shows the average of the design and code review DRLs versus unit testing for 810 developers on PSP Programs 7 through 10. Although there is wide variation among developers, design reviews are about as fast as testing for finding and fixing defects, and code reviews are much more efficient than testing. For every 10 hours you now spend finding and fixing defects in testing, a code review would take $10/2.08 = 4.8$ hours. By spending a few hours on a review, you would save 5.2 hours (less review time) and have higher-quality code. The improved program quality would then save you even more time in the integration, system, and acceptance testing to come.

TABLE 9.11   DEFECTS PER HOUR AND DRL
(PROGRAMS 7 THROUGH 10)

Phase	Defects/Hour	DRL vs. UT
Design Review	3.22	0.97
Code Review	6.90	2.08
Unit Test	3.31	1.00

9.9   Review Issues

Thousands of PSP exercise programs have now been written by experienced developers, and the data show that personal reviews are the most cost-effective and efficient way to remove defects. However, to get the maximum benefit from personal reviews, you must do them properly. The following sections discuss some of the most common review issues.

Review Practices

By consistently following five review practices, your reviews will be most effective and efficient:

1. **Take a break after coding.** By taking even a brief break before you start the review, you will be more rested and more likely to see problems.
2. **Print and use a program listing for the review.** Trying to review a program on the screen is often a complete waste of time. If you don't believe me, do several reviews each way and see what your data tell you.
3. As you do the review, check off each checklist item as you complete it. When you do, treat the check as your certification that the program has no remaining defects of that type.
4. Periodically update the Design and Code Review checklists to reflect your latest data.
5. Develop and use a different checklist for each programming language.

Reviewing on the Screen

Many developers, when they first do code reviews, want to do the review on the screen. However, if you do this, you will find that the screen focuses your attention on a very small portion of the program. This narrow view makes it hard to see the relationships between your program and any other programs or to examine overall structure, security, performance, or any other larger-scale program properties. With a little experience, you will see that reviewing a listing is actually faster than reviewing on the screen, and you will find many more of the program's defects.

Review Economics

If there were only one or two defects in a one-KLOC program, you might question the wisdom of studying every line to ensure its correctness. Furthermore, your willingness to study every line will depend on how important it is to you to produce a defect-free program. PSP data show, however, that even experienced developers typically inject about 100 defects per KLOC. The defect-injection rates for 810 experienced developers who wrote ten PSP programs are shown in Figure 9.7 (see p. 173). At the beginning of PSP training, the average defect-injection rate was 120 defects per KLOC, and 25% of the developers injected 150 or more defects per KLOC.

Before PSP training, developers typically find about half of their defects in compiling and about half of the rest in unit testing. The ones they don't find, of course, are left for integration testing, system testing, or the users. By the end of the PSP course, the average defect-injection rate is reduced to 54 defects per KLOC, a 55% reduction. Although some of this improvement is due to the PSP design methods discussed in the next three chapters, these methods are not introduced until the defect-reduction rate has fallen by about 30% to 40%. The principal reason for this initial improvement is that the developers have been recording data on their defects, so they are more aware of their personal mistakes and are both more motivated and better able to prevent them. This improvement is largely due to defect recording and defect analysis.

Because of the large numbers of defects, the major quality-management issue is not how long it takes to find a rare defect, but how to best find, fix, and prevent a lot of defects. The principal lesson from the PSP is that finding defects in personal reviews is much more efficient than finding them during testing. Of course, preventing them in the first place is even more efficient. As shown in Chapter 8, the enormous schedule impact of finding and fixing numerous defects in system testing justifies almost any time developers spend doing thorough design and code reviews.

Review Efficiency

Code reviews are inherently more efficient than testing. In a review, you find the defects directly; in testing, however, you only get symptoms. The time required to get from symptoms to defects is called debugging. **Debugging** is the process of finding the defective code that caused the program to behave improperly. Sometimes trivial defects can produce unbelievably complex system behavior and require a great deal of time to figure out what caused the weird symptoms. The amount of debugging time generally bears little relationship to the sophistication of the defect.

It might seem surprising that the difference in defect fix time between reviews and testing could be so large. When reviewing a program, you know where you are and can see the results that the logic is supposed to produce. As you work through the design or code, you establish logical relationships and gradually construct a mental context of the program's behavior. When you see something that you don't understand, it is often because the program doesn't do what you thought it would. With deeper study, you sometimes find that the program is correct, but you sometimes conclude that it is not. You thus start with a potential problem and try to find its consequences. With experience, you learn to make such searches quite directly and logically. You don't need to stumble into a lot of blind alleys to figure out what could have caused the unexpected behavior. You are also in a better position to correctly fix any problems you find because the review helps you to build a mental picture of what the program does and why.

In debugging, the situation is quite different. You start with some unexpected system behavior. For example, the screen could go blank, or the system may just hang, produce an incorrect result, or print out gibberish on the eighty-seventh iteration of a loop. Some confirmed debuggers will argue that they can find defects more efficiently with a debugging tool than they can by inspecting the design or the code. Although it is true that some defects can be traced quite quickly, others can be extraordinarily hard to find. In one operating system example, three experienced developers worked for three months to find a subtle system defect that was causing persistent customer complaints. At the time they found the defect, the same code was being inspected by a different team of five developers. As an experiment, the inspection team was not told about the defect. Within two hours, this team had found not only this defect, but 71 others! Once found, the original defect was trivial to fix. Interestingly, no one on the inspection team thought that it would take more than an hour or two to find this defect during testing.

The debugger's principal advantage is that it helps you to step through the program logic and to check the important parameter values. However, this process is effective only if you know what the parameter values are supposed to be. Therefore, you must have already worked through the program's logic. If you must go to all that trouble anyway, why not be a little more thorough and check the accuracy of the logic? In complex cases, you should also use the debugger to check your review results.

Reviewing before or after Compiling

Although a growing number of development environments no longer require compiling, some still do. With a newer environment, you could turn off the automated checking until after doing the code review. However, I have not found that useful. The best practice is to use all of the available tools to produce the code but then to do a high-yield review before using any automated checking, formatting, compiling, or testing tools. Again, the best guideline is to try various techniques and see what your data tell you.

For those who still use compilers, one of the more contentious issues is whether to review the code before or after compiling it. Some programmers refuse to consider reviewing their code before they do a first compile. They feel that the compiler is designed to find simple syntax errors and that trying to find them by hand is a waste of time. However, the data show that this is not true. The compiler is not designed to find errors; its job is to produce code. If it can produce code from the erroneous source you give it, it will. The compiler flags defects only when it can't figure out how to generate code from whatever you wrote.

The issue of reviewing before or after compiling is related to tool effectiveness. For example, if you had a tool that would reliably find 100% of a class of your programming mistakes, then you would not have to worry about any of them. However, if the tool identified 99.9% of these mistakes, then you would have to find the other 1-in-1,000 error yourself. Now the question concerns the importance of finding that 1-in-1,000 defect. If it might cause a little user inconvenience, you could ignore it; but if it could result in a user's death, you would want to find it.

Assuming that you planned to use code reviews to find and fix these rare defects, you must decide whether to run the tool before the review or afterwards. By running the tool first, you would find practically none of these defect types. Then you would have no way to judge the quality of your review. However, if you reviewed the code first and then ran the tool, a comparison of the number of defects you found with those found by the tool would indicate the quality of your review.

If the compiler caught 100% of all your syntaxlike mistakes, you would not have to search for them in a code review. My data on 2,041 defects show that 8.7% of my Pascal syntaxlike mistakes and 9.3% of my C++ syntaxlike mistakes were not caught by the compiler. This does not mean that the compiler was faulty, but that random coding and typing mistakes occasionally produce valid syntax. The code, however, does not do what was intended. The defect types that were caught and missed by the C++ compiler are shown in Figure 9.12. Here, the 9.3% syntaxlike defects that were missed by the compiler were of defect types 20, 21, 22, 41, and 51. These defect types are shown in Table 9.5 (see p. 178). Compilers can be very effective at finding syntax, naming, and referencing defects, but you cannot rely on them to find all of even these defect types.

The arguments for compiling before doing a code review are the following:

☐ For some defect types, compiling will find defects about twice as fast as code reviews.

☐ The compiler will find about 90% of the coding and typing mistakes.

☐ In spite of your best efforts, your reviews will likely miss between 20% and 50% of the syntax defects. This result is highly individual, however, as some reviewers can catch most syntax problems while others catch very few.

☐ The syntaxlike defects missed by the compiler are generally not difficult to find during testing.

☐ Some development environments, such as Java and VB.NET, highlight the defects so that they can be fixed directly.

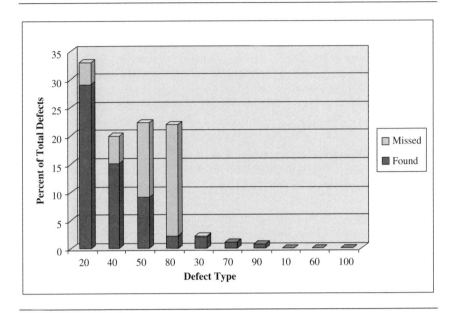

FIGURE 9.12 C++ DEFECTS FOUND AND MISSED BY THE COMPILER

The points that favor reviewing before compiling are as follows:

☐ Because the compiler will miss about 9% of your syntaxlike mistakes, you will have to review for them anyway.

☐ Doing the review first will cut your compile time from about 6% to 16% of development to about 2% (as shown in Figure 9.2 on p. 166).

☐ On average, it takes several times longer to fix syntax defects in testing than it does in the code review. In testing, you will quickly find most of the syntax defects the compiler misses, but some will occasionally take much longer.

☐ Unit testing typically finds about half of a program's defects. If you count on the compiler to find all of the syntaxlike mistakes, about 4% of them will likely escape both the compiler and unit testing and will have to be caught by integration testing, system testing, or the users. One such defect could cost you or your teammates many hours.

☐ Typically, subsequent test phases have even lower yields than unit testing (Thayer et al. 1978).

☐ If you are going to review the code anyway to find syntaxlike defects, you won't save time by compiling first. However, you will save time by reviewing first.

□ Because you know that the compiler will find nearly all of the syntaxlike defects, you can treat them like seeded defects (Knight and Ammann 1985). That is, you can use the compiler to evaluate the thoroughness of your reviews. If you found 80% of the syntax defects, you probably also found about 80% of the other coding defects and many of the design defects. Of course, some design defects cannot be found by a typical code review.

□ You will likely get great satisfaction from a clean first compile.

□ Reviewing before compiling is more rewarding and more effective. If you don't review before compiling, your reviews of the compiled code will find only about one-tenth as many syntax and naming defects. Reviewing would then seem like a waste of time and you could easily get discouraged and do a poor review. After a while, you would likely stop doing code reviews entirely.

Review Objectives

If your objective is to get into testing as quickly as possible, there is probably no way to convince you to do a review before compiling. This attitude, however, confuses speed with progress. Although getting to testing would seem like progress, the testing time for defective code is highly unpredictable, and for large programs it can take many weeks or months. If you measure your overall performance both with reviews and without, you will find that by reviewing first, you may take a little longer to get into testing but the testing time will be much less.

Conversely, if your goal is to remove the maximum number of defects, you will want to do the code reviews when they are most effective. The compiler is equally effective before or after the review, so if you find any of the defects it would miss, you are ahead. My preference is to review the code before compiling and then use the compiler as a check on the quality of my code review. If the compiler finds more than a very few defects, I probably have a quality problem and need to reexamine my review practices. This is also a good guide for when to update your Code Review Checklist.

The Relationship between Reviews and Inspections

In a review, you personally review your own program. An inspection is a team review of a program. After personal reviews, inspections are the most valuable quality technique a software team can use (Fagan 1976; Gilb and Graham 1993; Humphrey 2000). If your objective is to achieve 100% process yield, incorporate inspections into your personal process. You could even use them for the exercises in this book. To do that, either change the process to include inspections or record your and your inspectors' times in your respective time logs. Then record all of the defects you and everyone else find in *your* defect log. Also note in the comments section of the time and defect logs that these data were for inspections. Then, record your and your inspectors' inspection data on your Process Improvement Proposal (PIP) form, both to have a personal record and to tell your PSP instructor what you did.

When using inspections, you must decide where in the process to put them. The principal questions are whether to review the code before the inspection and whether to compile and test the code before the inspection. The central issue here is one of personal standards. Would you ask someone to review the rough draft of a technical report? You would presumably read it first to eliminate the obvious mistakes. Programs are much the same. Most first-draft programs have obvious defects that are quickly found in even a cursory review. Do you want each of your reviewers to separately wade through these obvious defects just because you were too lazy to find and correct them first?

The people who inspect your code are taking their precious time to help you improve the quality of your product. To show your appreciation, treat their time as important and carefully review your code before the inspection. This is not just a question of courtesy; obvious defects are distracting. When there are many simple problems in the code, the reviewers are less likely to see the important issues. Because you can easily find most of the simple problems yourself, thoroughly review your designs and code and make them as clean as you can before having them inspected.

Whether or not you compile before the inspection is more debatable. The issue here concerns where you need help. While you are gaining fluency with a language, it might help to have associates inspect the code before you compile. Your objective, however, is to improve your reviewing skills so that you can later find most of the syntax mistakes yourself. Once you become more fluent with the language, it will be more effective to review and compile first and have the inspection focus on the more subtle requirements, design, and coding issues.

If the quality of the code entering an inspection is so important, why not also unit-test it first? This is a question of inspection psychology. When the inspectors know that the code has been tested, they are not as likely to do a thorough analysis. It would seem pointless, for example, to struggle through a complex while-loop verification when you know that it has already been tested. Even though most programmers understand that an initial unit test will not find all of the defects in a complex program, the fact that the program is known to run can be demotivating. I recommend that you not test your programs before the first code inspection. The inspection objective should be to have no defects found in testing. Your personal review goal, of course, is to have no defects found in compiling, inspections, or testing.

9.10 Summary

This chapter deals with personal design and code reviews. The purpose of a review is to efficiently produce a high-quality program. The principal kinds of reviews are inspections, walk-throughs, and personal reviews. Reviews should be done for the requirements, the design, the documentation, and all other product elements. Many software projects spend nearly half of their development time in testing. This is very inefficient. Design and code reviews are much more cost-effective for finding and fixing many defects. Reviews find defects directly, whereas tests only provide symptoms. When reviewing a program, you will know where you are and what the logic is supposed to do. Your fixes are therefore likely to be complete and correct. In testing, you must figure out the source of the problem. However, because you will almost certainly be rushed, there is a good chance that you will introduce new defects when correcting an existing one.

Reviews provide a greater return on your personal time than any other single thing you can do. Read each program, study it, and understand it. Then fix the defects, the logic, the structure, and the clarity. In addition, learn to rewrite programs. When areas are unclear or confusing, add comments, or better yet, do a complete rewrite. Make it easy to read and to understand. Produce something that you would be proud to publish or to show to friends and associates. The basic principles of personal reviews are to establish review goals, follow disciplined methods, and measure and improve the review process.

Your decision to do reviews is driven by your desire to be productive and to create quality products. To determine whether your reviews are helping to achieve these goals, measure them. Use a Pareto distribution to establish review priorities and to develop a review checklist. Reexamine this Pareto distribution periodically to ensure that you are still focusing on the most significant defects.

Although yield provides the best measure of review quality, you cannot calculate yield until after you have completed development and testing. To manage your personal reviews, you need current or instant measures that correlate with yield, such as LOC reviewed per hour. You can then use the review rate data to improve the quality of your reviews. A review rate of under 200 LOC per hour is generally required for high-yield reviews.

One of the more contentious PSP issues is whether to review code before or after compiling it. Although there are valid arguments for both options, my preference is to review the code before compiling. I then use the compiler as a statistical check on the quality of my review. If the compiler finds more than a very few defects, there is likely to be a quality problem.

9.11   Exercises

The assignment for this chapter is to use PSP2 to write one or two programs. If you produced a Code Review Checklist while writing the R4 report, use it. If not, before writing these programs, use your defect data to produce one. The PSP2 process and the program specifications are given in the assignment kits, which you can get from your instructor or at **www.sei.cmu.edu/tsp/**. The kit contains the assignment specifications, an example of the calculations, and the PSP2 process scripts. In completing this assignment, follow the PSP2 process, record all required data, and produce the program reports according to the specifications in the assignment kits.

References

Fagan, M. "Design and Code Inspections to Reduce Errors in Program Development." *IBM Systems Journal* 15, no. 3 (1976).

————. "Advances in Software Inspections." *IEEE Transactions on Software Engineering,* vol. SE-12, no. 7 (July 1986).

Gilb, T., and D. Graham. *Software Inspections.* Reading, MA: Addison-Wesley, 1993.

Humphrey, W. S. *Managing the Software Process.* Reading, MA: Addison-Wesley, 1989.

————. *Introduction to the Team Software Process.* Boston: Addison-Wesley, 2000.

Knight, J. C., and P. E. Ammann. "An Experimental Evaluation of Simple Methods for Seeding Program Errors." *Proceedings of the Eighth International Conference on Software Engineering,* August 28–30, 1985, Imperial College, London.

Thayer, T. A., M. Lipow, and E. C. Nelson. *Software Reliability: A Study of Large Project Reality.* TRW Series of Software Technology 2 (Amsterdam: North-Holland, 1978).

10

Software Design

Now that you have mastered the mechanics of developing quality products on predictable schedules, it is time to address more advanced topics. The first of these is design. Software design is important because good design is the key to scalability, and scalability is the key to producing cost-effective and high-quality systems. To appreciate the impact of scalability on software development, consider building a boat. A competent amateur could probably build a 10-foot rowboat in his or her garage. However, building a 1,000-foot ship would be a totally different matter. Scaling up a boatbuilding job by 100 times changes almost every aspect of the job. With software, however, we attempt to build million-LOC systems with the same design methods we used for 10,000-LOC programs. And for these 10,000-LOC programs, we often even use the same methods we used for 100-LOC programs.

If our small-scale methods were scalable, large-system development would not be such a serious problem. To be scalable, our design methods must start with a solid foundation and they must produce precise, complete, and correct design artifacts. We all make mistakes, so our development process must include thorough design reviews and analyses, and it must find and fix as many of the design defects as possible. The top priority must be design quality, not development speed. If our small program parts do not all have flawless designs, our large system projects will be troubled and possible even fatally flawed.

Because the design methods that work best for you depend on the kind of work you do as well as on your skill and experience, the PSP does not specify any particular design method. It concentrates instead on producing a precise design representation. This chapter discusses the need for good design practices. It also covers the concepts and strategies to consider in producing designs, as well as some common ways to address scalability problems when developing large software systems. Chapter 11 describes the design templates the PSP uses to ensure design completeness and precision, and Chapter 12 addresses design analysis and design verification.

10.1   What Is Design?

Physicists and engineers make approximations to simplify their work. These approximations are based on known physical laws and verified engineering principles. The software engineer has no Kirchhoff's law or Ohm's law and no grand concepts like Newtonian mechanics or the theory of relativity. We lack basic structural guidelines like strengths of materials or coefficients of friction. We can, of course, defer rarely used functions or temporarily ignore error and recovery procedures, but we cannot separate software procedures by their likely impact on the system's performance. With hardware, you can often determine that the performance of some elements will have a 10% impact on the system, whereas others will have less than a 1% impact. In the software business, minor details often make the difference between a convenient and functioning product and an unusable one. Because of the very nature of software, we cannot generally reduce the complexity of our products by making approximations.

The Power of Abstractions

We do, however, have some powerful tools at our disposal. We can create abstractions and arbitrarily combine them into larger abstractions. Even when we know nothing about the internal structure of these abstractions, we can name and use them as long as we know all of their important external specifications. Hence, we have the opportunity to essentially write our own rules. If we conform to the capacities and capabilities of the systems we support, we can create whatever logical structures we choose.

This freedom, however, has its price. We do not face the physical constraints of physicists and hardware engineers, but we do face intellectual ones. As our products become more complex, we are often unable to grasp all of their critical details. Although we are not constrained by the physical laws of nature, we do need consistent rules and concepts. Because of human fallibility, however, our rules and concepts are often flawed, incomplete, or inconsistent. That is why design and quality management are such important issues for software engineering.

The Problem with Abstractions

Because the fundamental software development problem is scale, it is worthwhile to consider the various ways to address scalability. The most common approach is to subdivide the overall system into parts. However, depending on how you do this, you might still not have usefully partitioned the work. Suppose, for example, you defined a family of general-purpose, reusable parts that could implement an entire system. Although this would likely be helpful, the degree of help would depend on the size and nature of the parts. If the system were to have 1,000,000 LOC and you created 500 part types that each averaged 10 LOC, then the system design task would have been reduced to designing a system of 100,000 parts. Although this would seem to be a big help, it would probably not solve the system design problem. In fact it could even make it worse. The designers would now have to learn and become fluent with each of these 500 part types. They would have to both design and develop the parts and then design the system to effectively use them. Essentially, you would have designed a new programming language, rather than addressing the system scalability problem. Designers have limitations, and they cannot effectively use large numbers of unfamiliar parts. Merely devising a richer language may help, but doing this does not address the essential problem of scalability.

Object-oriented designers can encounter this same part-multiplicity problem unless they are careful. Once they define a comprehensive family of elemental system classes, they might then expect to just put these classes together to form the system. Although having such classes could help, part definition does not replace the need for system design. To have useful scalability, you must not only meet the requirements of physical scalability, but also capture significant system function in the parts.

Solving the Abstraction Problem

Another way to solve this abstraction problem is to follow the divide-and-conquer rule. That is, divide the overall system into ten or more smaller parts that, we hope, can each be viewed as a coherent subsystem or component. If we do this properly, we will then have reduced the overall problem by a factor of ten or more. Doing this properly, however, is a challenging task, and it is called design.

A good software design transforms an often ill-defined requirement into a precise and implementable design specification. For any but the simplest programs, it is nearly impossible to produce a high-quality implementation from a poor-quality design. Design quality has two parts: the quality of the design concept and the quality of the design representation. Although you might view representation as the less important of the two, in many ways it is more important. Designs that are badly represented will almost always be poorly implemented, almost regardless of the quality of the design concept. A poor representation can also make the design so hard to understand that you won't recognize its conceptual problems until you implement it or even later.

10.2   Why Design?

One of the reasons why software quality and security problems are so common is that few software developers take the time to produce thorough designs before they start coding. Although there are many reasons for this, the principal one is that when they spend much time on design, it takes them longer to develop programs. As you can see from Figure 10.1, the fastest programmers spent the least amount of time on design work.

   If all you had to do was write small programs, and if these programs didn't have to work flawlessly in some large system, then design practices might not

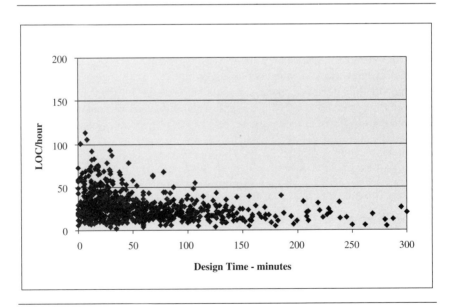

FIGURE 10.1 DESIGN TIME VERSUS PRODUCTIVITY (810 DEVELOPERS, PSP PROGRAM 6)

seem important to you. However, the need for safe and secure software systems is increasing daily, and safety and security cannot be assured without a sound design and disciplined quality management. Furthermore, if you don't practice sound design methods with module-size programs like the PSP exercises, you won't have the skill and experience to do a quality job when you really must produce a design.

The PSP strategy is to write every program as if its quality were critical. To do this, you must measure your work, produce thorough designs, and follow the quality-management practices described in Chapters 8 and 9. This is important because design quality is a trade-off. Producing a clear, complete, and defect-free design will slow you down as an individual developer. However, if you and your teammates all produce clear, complete, and defect-free designs, it will accelerate the team's work.

10.3   The Design Process

Software design is a creative process that cannot be reduced to a routine procedure. This process, however, need not be totally unstructured. Design work generally starts by reviewing the product's purpose, gathering relevant data, producing an overview design, and then filling in the details. These steps are not isolated sequential tasks, however, but are often highly iterative parallel activities. Design involves discovery and invention, and it frequently requires intuitive leaps from one abstraction level to another.

For complex designs, good designers follow a dynamic process. They work at a conceptual level for a period and then delve deeply into a particular issue. When they are unsure how to proceed, they write some code. Curtis, a well-known expert on software development practices, found that this behavior is normal and that it produces the insights needed for high-quality designs (Curtis et al. 1988). This dynamism was a trait of all the best designers he studied.

At the outset, no one will really understand the requirements, the design, or the implementation. As each area is refined, it sheds further light on the others. This is particularly true once development reaches the point where users can try early product versions. Each such exposure leads to new knowledge, new ideas, and more changes. The most sensitive development decision concerns the precise time to truncate this learning process to produce a suitable product on a reasonable schedule and at an affordable cost.

Requirements Uncertainty

For any but the simplest programs, the design process can be quite complex. Figure 10.2 shows some of the more important elements of this process and one way

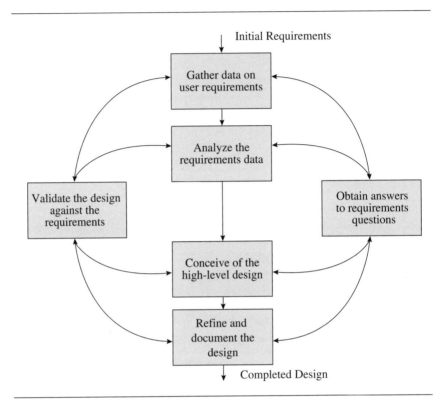

Initial Requirements

FIGURE 10.2 THE DESIGN FRAMEWORK

to relate them. In the simplest case, assuming the requirements information is current and properly communicated, this process can proceed directly from top to bottom. Of course, this assumes there are no false starts or changes. However, in the real world, misunderstandings, errors, and omissions are common, and properly handling the resulting changes takes many feedback loops and iterative cycles.

This creative design process is complicated by the generally poor state of most requirements descriptions. This is normal for new software systems because of what I call the **requirements uncertainty principle**: the requirements will not be completely known until after the users have used the finished product. The users' jobs will then have changed, as will their needs and requirements. Therefore, the true role of design is to create a workable solution to an ill-defined problem. Although there is no procedural way to address this task, it is important that the designers treat design as a discovery process and be alert for any new information that might impact their initial design approach.

Projects rarely get into trouble because of the occasional massive requirements change. Such large changes are typically recognized and properly reviewed. The most dangerous ones are the many seemingly trivial enhancements that can nibble you to death. If you do not have the knowledge, skill, and discipline to analyze the impact of every small change, the scope of the job can quickly double or triple. The PSP process will help you to control this change spiral. It enables you to make accurate plans and to estimate the probable impact of even the smallest change. These plans provide you, your teammates, and your managers with a rational basis for deciding when to freeze and build and when to make further changes.

Design as a Learning Process

Once you have a reasonably clear understanding of the high-level requirements, you will probably know enough to produce a high-level design. At this point, the requirements data-gathering process changes. You now seek information that will either validate this initial design approach or at least define its scope and limits. What are the performance specifications and size limits? Are there special peak demands or unusual response needs? What must the users know, and what are their likely skills? What is the best way to handle the security, privacy, and safety issues?

To keep from getting lost in a mass of detail, "walk around" the problem and look at it from every angle you can imagine. Think like a user and visualize the likely scenarios. Then walk through these scenarios to ensure that the high-level design handles them naturally and smoothly. If you identify too many exception conditions, this design may not be a natural fit to the problem. Once you have corrected and validated the high-level design, it provides the framework for cataloguing the more detailed knowledge you gain throughout the development process.

Even though the design process is dynamic, it is still helpful to think of it in process terms. This is not to constrain design behavior but to help define the design products and provide guidance in producing those products. A structured design process also helps manage the dynamics of the work. While mentally jumping from one artifact to another and simultaneously considering several design levels, a process framework helps to maintain control of what you are doing. The process also helps you track design status.

Prototyping

Although complex problems often have complex solutions, that is not always the case. The principal exception is when you can identify elements of the problem that have been solved before. In this case, you may be able to reuse part of that previous solution. Similarly, simple problems do not always have simple solutions. Often, the simplest requirements cause the most problems. Application functions that are very simple for people to conceptualize are often extraordinarily hard to design and implement.

This is why, as we design any but the simplest products, we should regularly consider the following five points:

1. Do I need to refine this design further?
2. If I do, do I need to do it now?
3. If I need to make the refinement now, do I know enough to do so?
4. If I don't need to do the refinement now, am I confident I will be able to do so when I need to?
5. If I don't know enough to refine the design, I must address that problem now.

If you don't know enough to refine your design, consider developing a prototype of the potentially troublesome functions before proceeding. If your design is based on functions that you might not be able to implement, resolve that uncertainty as soon as you can. If you don't, there is a good chance that you will waste much of your subsequent design work. That is a principal reason for developing prototypes. Occasionally, you will not be able to even specify a function until you have designed and possibly built and tested it. In these cases, develop prototypes for these functions before completing the design.

Prototyping is a powerful tool that can be used in many ways. You may want to experiment with reusable program elements to verify that they work the way you want them to work. You might need to understand a program's real-time response capability, minimize memory usage, or demonstrate some function to a potential user. One useful quality practice is to build a prototype every time you use a new or unfamiliar library function. These small throwaway programs are intended only to answer questions; they will not be part of the finished product.

Before developing a prototype, specify its purpose and define the questions it is to answer. In the PSP, prototype work is part of design. If you later want to use the prototype code in the product, then all of the design and coding work required to bring the prototype design and code up to product standard is tracked as a normal part of development. If the prototype code is not to be part of the product, there is no need to measure its size or track the defects you found while developing it. Of course, the prototype development time is recorded as design time.

10.4   Design Levels

Unfortunately, there is no standard nomenclature for levels of design. In this book, I discuss the following five design levels:

1. **The conceptual design:** This is not really a design level but more of a planning concept to help you estimate a product's size.

2. **System-level design (SLD):** This is the overall design for the highest-level view of the entire hardware-software product. One way to define the system level is that level above wherever you work. For example, if you worked on automobile engines or brakes, the system level would be the car, but if you worked on pistons or carburetors, the system level would be the engine.

3. **High-level design (HLD):** This design level spans the range from immediately below the system-level design to immediately above the detailed-level design. The role of HLD is to divide whatever product level you are currently addressing into smaller parts.

4. **Detailed-level design (DLD):** The DLD level starts with the lowest-level parts specified by the HLD and defines how to build them.

5. **Implementation-level design (ILD):** The implementation takes the DLD and refines it into a form from which the product can be automatically constructed.

It helps to think of the design process as an inverted pyramid (see Figure 10.3). Each level provides a foundation for the next. During high-level design, you deal with structural, performance, security, safety, and functional decisions. If you do not make and document all of the necessary high-level design decisions in high-level design, you will have to reconstruct them again during detailed design. If you don't

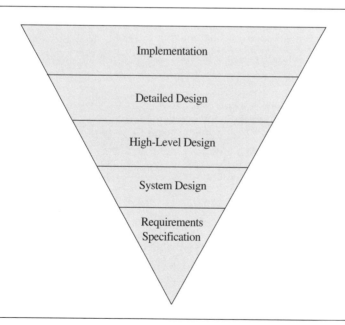

FIGURE 10.3 THE DESIGN PYRAMID

make and document all of the detailed-design decisions in detailed design, you will have to reconstruct them during implementation. Even when you are the implementer, reconstructing the reasons for and content of all of your mentally completed but undocumented designs is both time-consuming and error-prone. During implementation, you think at an implementation level. Without considerable effort and a complete change of mind-set, you will have trouble reconstructing the relevant high-level and detailed-level design information you need to produce a quality implementation. This is when design errors are most likely.

Design level is a concern during every process phase. For example, when you resolve requirements issues during high-level design, or high-level design issues during detailed design, you will also likely make mistakes. The typical requirements-specification-design process for large projects is shown in Figure 10.4.

Briefly, the design steps called for in this figure are as follows:

1. Define the need (requirements definition).
2. Define the solution (system specification).
3. Conceptualize the solution (system high-level design, or HLD).
4. Subdivide the work (product specifications).
5. Define the product design (product HLD).
6. Subdivide the products into components (component specifications).
7. Define the component design (component HLD).
8. Subdivide the components into modules (module specifications).
9. Detail the solution (module detailed design, or DLD).
10. Implement the solution (module implementation and test).

The specifications and high-level designs are progressively refined until you reach the detailed-design and implementation levels. Only then are you ready for implementation. Again, however, this is not an orderly top-down process. Depending on the nature of the problems, the first step in high-level design could be to implement some critical but poorly understood module.

Requirements Definition

Even when a systems engineering or requirements group is charged with documenting the requirements, what they produce will rarely be adequate for your needs. To produce a competent design, you must have accurate and complete requirements and you must understand them. You could argue that you should have complete requirements before starting the work, but that is rarely possible, for several reasons:

☐ Requirements specification is a specialized skill, and one for which few people have the requisite knowledge and experience.

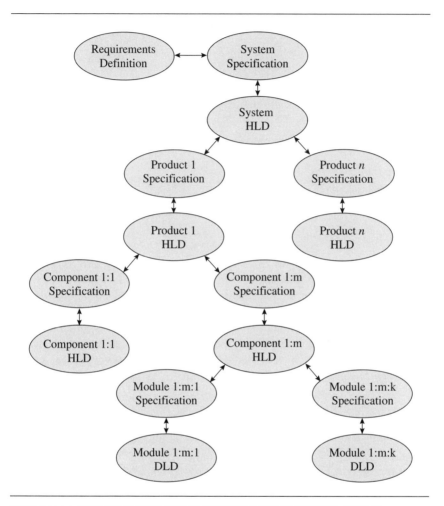

FIGURE 10.4 THE REQUIREMENTS-SPECIFICATION-DESIGN CYCLE

☐ Requirements change. As your design progresses, you will ask questions that cause the system engineers and/or customers to think more deeply about their needs. This will generate new ideas. Even if you do not stimulate this process with probing questions, the longer you take to produce the design, the more likely they are to think of new or changed needs.

☐ The solution you develop will often change the problem. Because many computer applications concern new services, using the product changes how people work, which probably changes their needs. These changes then impact the requirements.

The third reason is the requirements-uncertainty principle and it has major implications for the development process. Although you can often hold the customers (or system engineers) responsible for the requirements they produce, your principal concern is to produce a quality design, not to assign blame for requirements oversights and errors. Therefore, you must learn as much as you can about the requirements. Once you have a clear and complete requirements definition, you can proceed with confidence to specify the design. If the answers you get are confused or incomplete, focus on helping the users (or system engineers) produce a complete and precise requirements statement. Do not produce the requirements statement for them, but propose design solutions, postulate test scenarios, or build prototypes or initial product versions to help them better understand their own needs.

The Design Specification

The design specification should be a complete and precise statement of what the program must do. Although using spoken language can produce reasonably clear specifications, a truly precise specification must be written in a truly precise language such as Z (Jacky 1996). The requirements can be viewed as a problem statement without a solution. In fact, if the requirements are properly produced, they should not imply a design. The specifications, however, postulate the existence of a solution and state its constraints and invariants. For small products, the specifications can often be a simple extension of the requirements. However, for larger products, the specifications should be completely separate from the requirements.

As shown in Figure 10.4, the requirements definition and system specification are developed at the highest level. As development proceeds, you divide the system into major products, each of which must be specified and designed. These products, in turn, may be composed of several components that must also be specified and designed. Thus, the specification must be refined for each product level.

The system specification is inextricably linked with the requirements definition. It takes considerable effort to subdivide the system's functions into coherent products and components and to specify their relationships. If these design decisions are not precisely recorded when made, they must be re-created later. For example, this will be necessary whenever there are system-level questions on safety, security, or performance. Trying to document these decisions later is difficult, error-prone, and time-consuming. Once you have clarified some aspect of the requirements, promptly reduce it to a rigorous specification. Then address and specify the next system aspect. If this specification conflicts with previously completed specifications, make the needed changes as soon as possible. Any delay will likely either delay the design work or cause errors.

The more precise the specifications, the more likely you are to identify requirements mistakes, omissions, and inconsistencies. The precision of the specification is much like the resolving power of a lens. An imprecise specification provides a vague and out-of-focus view of the system, whereas a precise specification brings requirements mistakes and uncertainties into clear focus. In resolving these issues, you will often have to retrace some of your earlier decisions, so it is helpful to include specification notes that explain why you made each key choice.

Although this may sound like a sequential process, it is not. Every specification question can force a requirements change and every design question can impact the specifications. These phases must be dynamic so specification issues can be resolved rapidly. With a clear and explicit specification, you can confidently proceed with the design.

High-Level Design (HLD)

In the high-level design phase, you create the overall design. This involves decisions about reusing existing components, defining classes, and specifying class relationships. The high-level design must consider two different systems: the application system and the reusable component library. Any potentially reusable functions should be designed to be part of the reusable component library, and the application-specific functions should be tailored to the unique needs of the product. Because reuse can save a great deal of time and effort, capitalize on the reuse library during every development phase, starting with HLD.

HLD is also where you make trade-offs between product content, development cost, and the schedule. An elegant design must balance development economics, application needs, and technology. By properly relating these three dimensions, you can balance the feasible with the desirable and the affordable. Although you may not produce a product that does everything the users want, you should aim to provide one that neatly and cleanly does what they need and can afford.

During HLD, many questions arise and many redesigns must be considered. You, the customers, and the system engineers must be in close and continuous contact. During the HLD and requirements work, these trade-offs are generally easy to make but are largely a matter of guesswork and judgment. However, some functions can be very expensive, and their inclusion could jeopardize the project. This is why you must give the users credible estimates for the cost and schedule impact of each change. Cost and schedule are important design considerations, and when users do not appreciate the business consequences of their requests, development disasters are most likely. By precisely describing the costs of a proposed change, you can help the users and system designers make logical and businesslike decisions about what they really need and can afford.

Detailed-Level Design (DLD)

The next design phase is detailed design. Here, you reduce the HLD to implementable form by detailing the functions, specifying the class state machines, and producing the finished design. Some of the HLD concepts might be unimplementable, while others could be unsound. You could see reuse opportunities, have performance insights, and think of integration and system testing issues. Because these changes can impact the requirements and HLD, neither the requirements nor the HLD can be considered firm until you have completed the DLD.

Implementation-Level Design (ILD)

The final design phase is implementation. Although writing code is not usually considered design, it does involve design issues. Not only will low-level design choices remain after DLD, but as you address implementation issues, you will generate questions about the design. Some of these will require design changes, some may lead to design improvements, and some may even cause requirements changes. In a sense, then, the actual code-writing process is the first real test of the design.

10.5   Design and Development Strategies

Your design approach must be closely coupled to your development strategy. In essence, design by abstraction consists of successive disintegrations of the system into manageable pieces. Implementation consists of building and integrating these pieces into a coherent whole. If the design strategy is a poor fit to the problem, you can waste time constructing special test drivers and making multiple program modifications. A poor development strategy is also likely to produce a confused, hard-to-understand, and hard-to-modify design that has quality, usability, security, safety, or performance problems. Because the development strategy must reflect the product's unique needs, there is no best strategy for all systems.

With the PSP exercises, you can use a simple development strategy. However, on a TSP project, you and your team will define your own design and development strategy and process for each project. Before defining them, however, consider the design levels needed for that project and the proper way to address them.

Strategy Guidelines

In designing large programs, you will often be unable to specify all of the program's highest-level functions until you know more about some of the functions at a lower level. You might leave some higher-level specifications incomplete until you have done some lower-level design work. Starting at the top, you would proceed until you hit an unknown abstraction. Then, if this abstraction were particularly difficult or critical, you might design it before proceeding. This abstraction in turn might call others that appear equally critical, and those could lead to others. You could find yourself delving deeply into the system before you complete the highest-level design. On occasion, you may even find it desirable to work from the bottom up or in some other order. Although this sequence would seem quite logical to you, it could look to an uninformed observer like a random series of disconnected partial design steps.

When following a dynamic development strategy, consider the following guidelines:

□ Where practical, complete the highest-level designs first.

□ Do not consider the design of a program or a major program element complete until the specifications for all of the abstractions it uses are complete.

□ Do not consider the design of a program element complete until the specifications for all of the program elements that depend on this element are also complete.

□ Log the assumptions you make so you can later check to ensure that they are valid. It is good engineering practice to maintain an issue tracking log to record outstanding issues, questions, or problems.

□ Make a practice of writing design notes that explain the logic for your design choices. Make these notes either in the design documentation itself or in your personal engineering notebook.

□ Resolve the uncertainties that prevent you from specifying an abstraction before you attempt to design it. It may be helpful to use prototype experiments to do this.

□ Penetrate as many design levels as needed to resolve specification uncertainties.

□ Defer resolving lower-level design uncertainties if there are no feasibility concerns and these lower-level designs do not impact other system elements.

The development strategy provides the framework for disintegrating and reintegrating the product. A well-founded strategy must consider the logical structure of the ultimate product. By producing a strategy that naturally fits the product's structure, you can usually simplify the design job and accelerate development.

Example Development Strategies

Suppose you were developing a product with a central control element and a family of application classes. Suppose further that each class used additional classes, which in turn used others. You could visualize all of these classes as a tree, with the control element at the top calling those classes immediately below, and so on. Classes that are used in several places would appear in multiple places on the tree.

After dividing this total tree into PSP-implementable elements, you must decide on the order for developing and integrating these elements. One approach would start with the top element and work toward the bottom of the tree. Another approach would start at the bottom and work up. Obviously, a third approach would be to start somewhere in the middle and work in both directions. You could also use hybrid strategies, such as developing multiple top-to-bottom threads or slices of the entire system.

These approaches each have advantages and disadvantages. A top-down strategy ensures that each cycle has a clear operational context and well-defined requirements. The reviews and tests can then realistically address operational issues. The principal problem with the top-down approach is that the lower-level abstractions must be stubbed or bypassed. Now, because some of these functions may be incompletely defined, the higher-level functions may misuse them.

Starting from the bottom and working up has the advantage of working with a solid foundation. You first develop those leaf elements that use no undeveloped abstractions. As you add layers, you are building on proven designs and are less likely to run into problems with overlooked details. The principal disadvantage of the bottom-up strategy is that you are implementing component specifications that may not do precisely what the system requires. You may, for example, develop a function and then later discover that it was improperly specified. Another potential problem is the lack of test drivers. With the bottom-up strategy, the lower-level abstractions will not typically form a coherent system. Such a strategy will not provide a natural test environment for most of the abstractions.

The third approach—starting in the middle—could be advantageous when a critical function determines the success of the entire program. An initial focus on that function could be appropriate if it is unusually complex or if you suspect it presents special problems.

The example strategies described in the following sections are the **progressive**, **functional-enhancement**, **fast-path**, and **dummy** strategies.

The Progressive Strategy

The progressive strategy is a natural way to develop systems that consist of sequentially executing functions. You first develop and test the operations that are performed first, then add and test the next functions, then the next, and so forth. If there is some central control structure, you can develop it in gradually widening vertical slices. The classes that support each slice are then implemented from top to bottom in a complete development iteration or cycle. As each cycle is designed, implemented, and tested, the pipeline is gradually lengthened to include additional functions.

This strategy has the principal advantage of being easy to define and to implement. It needs test scaffolding only for special cases, and there is little to rebuild or redesign between cycles. One disadvantage is that there may be no easy way to exhaustively test the behavior of each slice. You thus may need special scaffolding to test functions that are not directly visible to users. However, this would likely be a problem for such functions with almost any development strategy.

The Functional-Enhancement Strategy

The functional-enhancement strategy defines an initial stripped-down system version, or kernel, and adds enhancements. This is the common strategy for follow-on enhancements to large systems. A base system kernel is initially defined that need not be functionally useful. The only requirement is that it provide an operational context for subsequent enhancements. This kernel should be as small as possible and it must be carefully reviewed and tested. The added functions are then incorporated in small steps.

The functional-enhancement strategy builds a working system at the earliest point. Because its initial focus is getting a working system, it often leads to earlier identification of overall system problems. It also provides an early base for safety, security, and performance testing and for preliminary user trials. This strategy is also the natural backup case for most large-system development projects. When developers attempt to deliver too much function with the first release, they usually end up paring functions and shipping a minimum initial system. The principal debates with this strategy concern the functions to ship with each release. The principal problem with this strategy is that the first step is often quite large.

The Fast-Path Enhancement Strategy

The fast-path strategy is much like functional enhancement except that the initial system kernel is designed to demonstrate fast-path performance. The critical timing issues are identified and the basic real-time control cycle is implemented. The focus is on performance, so this initial fast-path kernel should contain only the minimum logic needed to control the performance-sensitive functions.

The principal advantage of fast-path enhancement is that it exposes timing problems at the earliest point. Although the first system kernel may provide no recognizable external functions, performance can be measured and overall system performance estimated. After the kernel's fast-path performance is demonstrated, functional enhancements can be added incrementally. System performance can be measured with each enhancement and steps taken to ensure that it does not deteriorate. You will know early on if kernel performance does not meet the performance requirements, and have the maximum amount of time to fix the problems. For time-critical systems or for the initial release of an operating system, this can be a very attractive development strategy.

Its principal disadvantage is also size of the first step. Although this kernel could be smaller than for the functional-enhancement strategy, it could still be too large to conveniently handle with a single development team.

The Dummy Strategy

The dummy strategy follows a top-down sequence. It starts with high-level system functions and dummies the rest with stubs that provide predefined returns. After the highest-level functions are tested, succeeding cycles gradually replace the stubs with implemented functions. This is an appropriate strategy for layered systems or for the kernel portion of fast-path or functional-enhancement systems. This strategy has the advantage of building the system in small steps and it provides considerable flexibility in ordering the functional implementation. In building the kernel for a fast-path development strategy, for example, the initial control loop would probably need multiple stubbed dummy functions. Each of these functions could then be more or less independently developed and incorporated in the growing system.

The principal disadvantage of the dummy strategy is that useful system behavior is often not visible until late in development. This could make it difficult to do early testing of critical system functions.

Selecting a Development Strategy

One potential problem with any strategy is that some critical function may not be developed until the later development cycles. This would delay exposing key project risks and possibly result in initially testing some complex system function in the full system. If the system has many defects, this could greatly delay and complicate testing. It is generally wise to test the most difficult components with the smallest amount of untested code. The defects are then more easily identified and fixed.

There is no one best strategy. You must examine the system structure, assess the principal development risks, and select a strategy to fit each situation. The goal is to have the strategy naturally fit the system structure and to expose the principal risks as quickly as possible.

10.6   Design Quality

The software design should contain a sufficiently complete, accurate, and precise solution to a problem to ensure its quality implementation. Because a design has many potential users, the following sections discuss these issues from the perspective of the design's users.

Design Precision

The lack of a precise design is the source of many implementation errors. By examining your PSP data, you will likely find that many of your design defects were caused by simple errors. The reasons will vary, but a common cause is the lack of a properly specified design. In some cases, you may have completed the design but not documented it. At other times, you may not even have produced a complete design. If you don't have a precise specification for what the design must contain, your decisions about where to stop will generally be ad hoc and inconsistent. Often, in fact, you will think, "Anyone would know how to do this," and not bother to document it. However, without a precisely documented design, you or any other implementer must finish the design during implementation, which is highly error-prone.

Design Completeness

You can waste time overspecifying the design, but an underspecified design can be expensive and error-prone. The complete specification of a software design requires a great deal of information: defining classes and their relationships, identifying class interactions, defining required data, specifying system states and transitions, and specifying inputs and outputs. The complete and unambiguous definition of all of this material generally requires significantly more documentation than the source listing of the finished program. The source code must include all of the design decisions but in very terse form. A program's uncommented source code is very dense, has little redundancy, and precisely defines the product's behavior. With the possible exception of the object code, the source code is the most compact way to completely define a program's design. Unfortunately, unless the source code is extensively commented, it is almost unintelligible to anyone but the designers and implementers, and even they can have trouble deciphering it. The key question is, how much detail must the designers provide to the implementers and other design users?

A fully defined design is expensive, and much of its content is not needed by experienced implementers. In addition, particularly if you are both the designer and the implementer, overspecifying the design will waste time. To be most efficient, make an explicit design-content trade-off. This requires a specification of design completeness. Such a specification will help you to produce a quality design and will guide your design reviews. As long as you meet the design exit criteria, you can use whatever design methods and notations you prefer.

The Users' Needs

To properly specify the products of the design phase, consider the needs of the people who will use the design. The principal users are the implementers, the design and code reviewers, the documenters, the test developers, the testers, the maintainers, and the enhancers. With the TSP, you are the principal user of the design, but not the only one. However, for the PSP exercises in this book, you are the only user of your designs.

On a TSP project, everyone you work with will need access to all of your design information. Although the design materials must be generally available, they must also be controlled. Each design product must have an author and an owner. The owner should be the only person who can change the design. The following sections describe the various categories of owners and the design products they should control.

System or Product Management
The items that should be owned, tracked, and controlled by system or product management are as follows:

- **Issue tracking log:** A running list of open issues and questions that must be resolved as the design progresses. These are like defect reports: anyone can submit one, resolution responsibility must be centrally assigned, the open issues should be tracked, and the resolution must be recorded and communicated.
- **Specification of any implementation constraints:** Coding specifications and configuration management standards and procedures.
- **A precise description of the program's intended function.**
- **Application notes:** Descriptions of how the product or system is to be used. These include a statement of how the user will use the products, including explanations of special conditions, constraints, or options.
- **System-level user scenarios:** Example usage scenarios.
- **System constraints:** Timing, size, packaging, error-handling, security, and hardware and system interface specifications.

System Engineers
Depending on the particular way the design was handled, the following items could be produced and owned at either the system or the product-design level:

- **A description of all relevant data and files:** The precise specification of the data to be provided and their structure
- **A description of system messages:** In a communication system, the specification of all message types, including formats, routings, and any relevant performance, security, or integrity specifications
- **Any special error checks or conditions**
- **Reasons why the system design choices were made**

Software Designers
The following basic design information is the sole responsibility of the software designers:

- □ **A picture of where the program fits into the system**
- □ **A logical picture of the program itself**
- □ **A list of all related classes, components, or parts:** Scope, class structure, functions provided, where initialized, where terminated
- □ **A list of all external variables:** Includes, scope, limits, constraints, where declared, where initialized
- □ **A precise description of all external calls and references**
- □ **A clear statement of the program's logic (pseudocode)**

A complete and comprehensive set of design products that meet these needs would be large, unwieldy, and confusing. They could also be a major source of error unless there were some automated way to ensure their self-consistency. Any reasonably large system includes many design changes. Thus, with inadequate change control, design changes will not be completely reflected in all of the design records. These design records will then become inconsistent, and anyone who uses them could be misled. This change control problem is vastly complicated whenever you record the same information in multiple places. It is therefore essential to specify the absolute minimum of required design information and to ensure that it is always kept up to date.

Although these design materials must be produced in some form, their content and format will vary considerably depending on the size of the system, the application domain, and the product standards. For the PSP, however, some design elements can be more or less standardized—those listed as the software designers' sole responsibility. They form the base for the PSP design process. The PSP thus concentrates on defining standards for this basic design subset. These standards and a defined way to meet them are covered in Chapter 11.

10.7 Summary

The size of software projects has increased rapidly for over 30 years. The products you develop in the future are thus likely to be much larger than today's. Because a process that is optimum for a small program will not likely be optimum for one that is 5, 100, or even 10,000 times larger, you will almost certainly have to change your development process and probably keep changing it for as long as you do software development work.

Many of software development's historic problems have stemmed from a misplaced expectation that development should start with firm and complete requirements. History demonstrates, however, that for a new software system, the requirements will not be completely known until after you have a working product, and possibly not even then. In defining the design process, you must therefore recognize that the requirements will likely change—and take steps to identify and resolve requirements uncertainties as early in development as possible.

The design phase of large-scale software systems typically starts with a high-level system design effort that subdivides the product into components. These components are separately developed and then the system is integrated. Because these components are much smaller than the total system, they can presumably be developed with smaller-scale methods.

A well-founded development strategy is built on the natural structure of the planned product. Although there are many possible development strategies, they are all different forms of divide-and-conquer: disintegrate the system into multiple parts, develop the parts, and then integrate the parts back into the finished system. The strategy concerns the particular way to do this integration and disintegration.

There are two different aspects to software design: how to produce the design and how to represent that design once it is produced. Although the PSP does not specify a particular design method, it does define the exit criteria for the design phase. These exit criteria are based on a standard that defines the contents of a completed design.

References

Curtis, B., H. Krasner, and N. Iscoe. "A Field Study of the Software Design Process for Large Systems." *Communications of the ACM* 31, no. 11 (November 1988).

Jacky, J. *The Way of Z: Practical Programming with Formal Methods.* Cambridge, UK: Cambridge University Press, 1996.

11

The PSP Design Templates

At this point in learning the PSP, you are probably making fewer coding mistakes than at the beginning of the course. However, this reduction is not an accident; it is the result of the increased awareness caused by gathering defect data. The quality impact of gathering defect data is illustrated in Figure 11.1, which shows data for 810 developers who wrote ten programs with the original PSP course. In that course, the completed defect analysis after the third program. Not surprisingly, the big defect reduction in Figure 11.1 happens after program three. That is when developers became aware of the kinds of mistakes they typically make during program development. After seeing how many mistakes they make, most developers substantially reduce the number of defects they inject. Since PSP courses based on this current text may have a different number of exercises, the defect analysis may be made as part of report R4, which comes after three to six of the programs.

Avoiding design defects requires more than just awareness and care. It requires better designs. The PSP addresses design issues from a defect prevention point of view. The objective is better and more precise designs. This chapter describes how the PSP design templates address this need and how to use them.

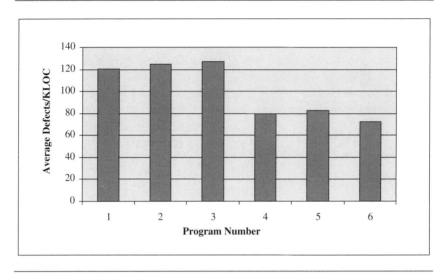

FIGURE 11.1 AVERAGE DEFECTS/KLOC (810 DEVELOPERS,
PSP PROGRAMS 1 THROUGH 6)

11.1   Design Representation

The Unified Modeling Language (UML) provides a comprehensive framework for representing designs (Booch et al. 1999). Rather than require that all developers who use the PSP also learn UML, this book provides a simplified set of generalized design templates for precisely recording relatively simple designs. These PSP design templates complement UML and other design methods by providing a simple summary format for documenting small program designs.

The lack of a precise design is the source of many implementation errors. If you reviewed your design defect data, you would likely find that many of these defects were caused by simple errors. The reasons for these errors would vary, but a frequent cause would likely be the lack of a properly specified design. A principal objective of a software design is to provide a concise and precise statement of exactly what the program is to do and how it is to do it. Doing this requires three things: producing a sound design, recording all of the required design information, and recording it in a precise and understandable way. Then, of course, you must faithfully implement that design.

Precise Logic Notation

Once you have created the design, you must analyze it for correctness, completeness, and consistency. This requires that the design be precisely documented. With spoken languages and pictures, it is often hard to be sufficiently precise in describing exactly what a program is to do and how it is to be constructed. Both language and pictures should be used to communicate designs, but the design must be recorded in a concise and precise notation that completely and accurately defines it for the implementation work to follow. This notation should meet the following criteria:

- □ It should be capable of precisely and completely representing the design.
- □ It must be understood and used by the people who use the design.
- □ It should help you to verify that the design does precisely what you intend.

This chapter describes how to represent designs with a set of templates and a precise logic notation. This notation is based on propositional logic and uses a simplified version of the Z notation that is easy to learn and to use (Jacky 1996). If you are not familiar with propositional logic, Table 11.1 provides a brief summary of the key terms, and the following paragraphs present a simple example of their use. Additional examples of this notation are given with some of the template descriptions in this and the next chapter.

Although you may choose not to use this notation after PSP training, you should use it for documenting the designs of the remaining PSP exercise programs. The design method is your servant. If, after using it in the PSP course, it does not help you to produce clearer designs, it is probably not right for you, at least not at this time.

Using the Logic Notation

Although this notation may seem new and unfamiliar, it is easy to use and very concise and expressive. Suppose, for example, you had a large volume of PSP data that you wanted to analyze. Suppose also that in order to do this analysis, you wanted a list of the names of all the developers of the PSP programs. One way to define a NameList that contains the names of all the developers of the PSPData would be as follows:

$\forall$ dname : DeveloperName | dname $\in$ NameList • $\exists$ pdata : PSPData
• pdata.Name = dname

This statement says that for all developer names (dname) in the list DeveloperName, where dname is a member of NameList, there exists a pdata in PSPData such that the name field of pdata equals dname.

TABLE 11.1 LOGIC NOTATION

Symbol	Function	Example
:=	assignment	A := B – Assign the value B to variable A.
!	not	!A
=	equal	A = B
≠	not equal	A ≠ B
>=	greater than or equal	A >= B
<=	less than or equal	A <= B
>	greater than	A > B
<	less than	A < B
∈	member of	d ∈ CData – d is a member of CData.
∉	not a member of	d ∉ CData – d is not a member of CData.
true	true	
false	false	
•	it is true that	If A = x • B = C – If A = x, it is true that B = C.
∀	for all	∀ a : A • a ∈ CData – Every member a in set A is a member of CData.
∃	there exists	∃ a : A • a ∈ CData – At least one member a of set A is a member of CData.
∧	intersection, logical and	A ∧ B – A and B
∨	union, logical or	A ∨ B – A or B
A → B	guarded command	If A = x → B := C – A = x causes B to be set equal to C.
;	sequence	A; B; C – A followed by B followed by C

In this case, it would have been easier to just say you want to ensure that all names in NameList also have at least one entry in PSPData. However, in many cases the relationships are much more complex, and the language description would become so convoluted that it would be almost impossible to understand. After a little practice using this notation with a few simple cases, you will likely get the hang of it and find it very convenient.

11.2   The Design Templates

The design representation described in the remainder of this chapter uses four templates to represent a program's design. These templates are used to describe the essential properties and structure of module-size programs. The PSP templates also help to minimize duplication. Each item is recorded in only one place and its location is referenced when needed. This saves time, reduces the likelihood of error, and provides reliable references. A good design should have minimum redundancy.

The PSP templates are designed to provide a complete and precise design representation for the basic program building blocks of software products and systems. Although many of the large-scale properties of software systems are not covered by the templates, these larger-scale properties must ultimately be reflected in the design and code of one or more of the program's modules. These templates help to ensure that these larger properties are completely and properly implemented at the module level. As with all PSP elements, you should modify these templates to suit your needs, and augment them with whatever other design tool, method, or graphical aid you find helpful.

The elements of a complete design can be visualized with the two-dimensional specification structure shown in Figure 11.2 (de Champeaux et al. 1993). Here, the elements of the module's design are divided into four categories:

1. **External-static:** This category defines the static relationships of this part to other parts or system elements. Examples are the call-return behavior and the inheritance hierarchy.

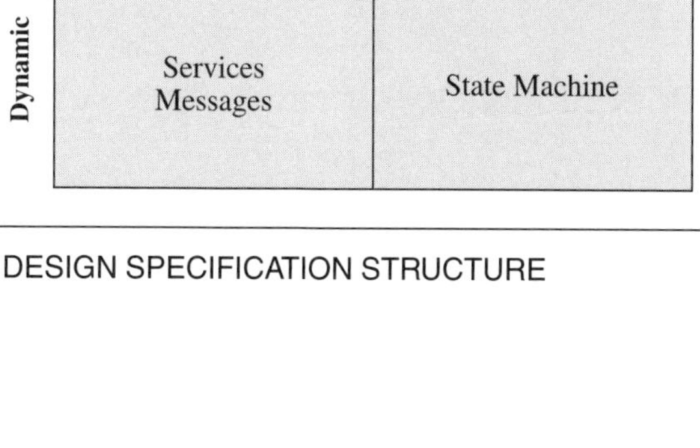

	External	Internal
Static	Inheritance Class Structure	Attributes Program Structure Logic
Dynamic	Services Messages	State Machine

FIGURE 11.2 DESIGN SPECIFICATION STRUCTURE

	External	Internal
Static	Functional Specification Template (Inheritance, Class Structure)	Logic Specification Template
Dynamic	Functional Specification Template (Interactions) Operational Specification Template	State Specification Template

FIGURE 11.3 PSP TEMPLATE STRUCTURE

2. **External-dynamic:** This category defines the interactions of this part with other parts or system elements. Examples would be user scenarios, system- or regression-testing scripts, or real-time interrupt-response behavior.

3. **Internal-static:** This category contains a static description of a module or part, such as its detailed logical structure.

4. **Internal-dynamic:** This category defines the part's dynamic characteristics. Examples of internal-dynamic behavior are state machines, response-time specifications, and interrupt-handling performance.

With the four templates described in the following sections, you can precisely specify the design of just about any small program. The four PSP design templates roughly correspond to de Champeaux's four quadrants as shown in Figure 11.3. These templates and the information that they contain are described in the following sections, together with examples of how they are used.

11.3   The Operational Specification Template (OST)

The example Operational Specification Template (OST) and the OST Instructions are shown in Tables 11.2 and 11.3. The OST is a simplified form of use case that is used to describe a program's operational behavior (Schneider and Winters 1998). The OST helps you to visualize how the program is supposed to react under various usage scenarios. When faced with a design decision that involves an actor, produce a trial scenario to see how each action would appear to the actor. This will help you to visualize the program's behavior and to make proper design choices. Although no set of scenarios can cover all usage combinations for even a moderately complex system, include examples of the key functions and exception conditions. With careful planning, you can often cover most important use cases with just a few scenarios. In addition to aiding in program design, these scenarios also provide a sound basis for test design and development. If you don't construct and test such scenarios, you are likely to overlook some key program actions.

The OST provides a space for the scenario number at the top. Numbering the scenarios helps when you use several scenarios for one program. In the next space, *User Objective,* briefly describe the user's expected purpose for the scenario. It is often hard for program designers to see the product from the user's perspective. By writing a brief statement of what the user is trying to accomplish with the scenario, you can better visualize the user's viewpoint. Next, enter a brief statement of your objective in constructing the scenario in the *Scenario Objective* space. Examples would be to illustrate error behavior or to define overflow exception handling. In the *Source* column, enter the originator of each action; in *Step,* enter the action

TABLE 11.2 EXAMPLE OPERATIONAL SPECIFICATION TEMPLATE (OST)

Student ___J. Developer_____ Date ____10/26_____

Program ___LogIn_____ Program # _____

Instructor ___Humphrey_____ Language __C++_____

Scenario Number	1	User Objective	To log onto the system
Scenario Objective		To illustrate normal LogIn operation	
Source	**Step**	**Action**	**Comments**
User	1	Call the system	
System	2	Request UserId	Check for timeout
User	3	Supplies UserId	Check for data errors
System	4	Check UserId	Check the user's ID
CheckId	5	UserId is proper	Also check error case
System	6	Request UserPW	Check for timeout
User	7	Supplies UserPW	Check for data errors
System	8	CheckPW	Check the user's PW
CheckPW	9	PW is proper	Also check error case
System	10	LogInUser	Log user onto system, stop

TABLE 11.3 OPERATIONAL SPECIFICATION TEMPLATE (OST) INSTRUCTIONS

Purpose	• To hold descriptions of the likely operational scenarios followed during program use • To ensure that all significant usage issues are considered during program design • To specify test scenarios
General	• Use this template for complete programs, subsystems, or systems. • Group multiple small scenarios on a single template, as long as they are clearly distinguished and have related objectives. • List the major scenarios and reference other exception, error, or special cases under comments. • Use this template to document the operational specifications during planning, design, test development, implementation, and test. • After implementation and testing, update the template to reflect the actual implemented product.
Header	• Enter your name and the date. • Enter the program name and number. • Enter the instructor's name and the programming language you are using.
Scenario Number	Where several scenarios are involved, reference numbers are needed.
User Objective	List the users' likely purpose for the scenario, for example, to log onto the system or to handle an error condition.
Scenario Objective	List the designer's purpose for the scenario, for example, to define common user errors or to detail a test scenario.
Source	• Enter the source of the scenario action. • Example sources could be user, program, and system.
Step	Provide sequence numbers for the scenario steps. These facilitate reviews and inspections.
Action	Describe the action taken, such as • Enter incorrect mode selection. • Provide error message.
Comments	List significant information relating to the action, such as • User enters an incorrect value. • An error is possible with this action.

sequence number; in *Action*, describe the action taken; and in *Comments*, note results, exception conditions, or other useful information.

The OST example in Table 11.2 is for a simple LogIn routine. It shows the user and system actions to verify the user's ID and password (PW). OSTs should also be completed to define how the error conditions shown in OST #1 are handled: timeout errors where the user fails to respond within a specified time, data errors where the password or user ID strings have an unacceptable format, or incorrect IDs or passwords. An unacceptable string might be excessively long or it could contain improper characters. Such strings are the source of over half of the security vulnerabilities on the Internet. All input character strings should be checked for security problems before being passed to the LogIn class or any of its methods. Such checks should be made for every publicly exposed input on any Internet-connected system.

One OST should describe the program's normal flow, noting all possible error or other abnormal cases. OSTs should also define the tests needed to verify the program's normal and abnormal operation. Complete this portion of test development during program design. When you design the tests for a program while you are designing it, you will often find design problems. For larger systems, it is also desirable to define the external behavior of the lower-level subsystems and components with OSTs.

11.4   The Functional Specification Template (FST)

The Functional Specification Template (FST) provides a simple way to document much of the material in a UML class diagram. An example FST and its instructions are shown in Tables 11.4 and 11.5. The FST describes a part, including its methods, its relationships, and its constraints. The part could be a class, a program module, or even a large program or system. As shown in Table 11.4, the part or class name is listed at the top, together with the classes or other parts from which it directly descends. The attributes are listed next, with their declarations and descriptions. The third section lists the part's methods or items, with their declarations, descriptions, and returns.

The *Attributes* section is also where you list the relationships of this class or part with other classes or parts. A suggested simple attribute notation is as follows (Rumbaugh et al. 1999):

Name[multiplicity] : type = initial-value {constraint}

where

☐ **Name** is the name of the attribute.

☐ **Multiplicity** indicates the number or range of occurrences.

☐ **Type** is a standard type or class, with normal font for a standard type and italics for a class.

☐ **Initial value** is the value assigned when the attribute is created.

☐ **Constraint** defines any constraints on the class.

For example, a UserClass with 0 to n instances might be listed as UserClass[0..n] : *UserClass*. The italicized type indicates that this attribute concerns a

TABLE 11.4 EXAMPLE FUNCTIONAL SPECIFICATION TEMPLATE (FST)

Student	J. Developer	Date	10/26
Program	LogIn	Program #	
Instructor	Humphrey	Language	C++

Class Name	LogIn
Parent Class	

Attributes

Declaration	Description
MaxTime: Integer, minutes	Maximum time-out minutes - adjustable
n: Integer	Count of user ID and password errors
nMax: Integer	Maximum of n error count
ValidIdSet	Set of valid user IDs with passwords

Items

Declaration	Description
Void LogIn.Start(n: Int)	Initialize system Handle LogIn transaction, error count, and time-outs
Int LogIn.GetId(ID: String)	Get UserId and check it for problems. Return true for an acceptable string, false for timeout or an unacceptable string
Int LogIn.CheckId(ID: String)	UserId $\in$ ValidIdSet $\rightarrow$ Valid ID UserId $\notin$ ValidIdSet $\rightarrow$!Valid ID
Int LogIn.GetPW(PW: String)	Get password and check for problems. Return true for an acceptable string, false for timeout or an unacceptable string
Int LogIn.CheckPW(PW: String)	PW = UserId.PW $\rightarrow$ Valid PW PW $\neq$ UserId.PW $\rightarrow$!Valid PW
Void LogIn.LogInUser(ID: String, n: Int)	n >= nMax $\rightarrow$ Reject user, deactivate ID Valid ID $\wedge$ Valid PW $\rightarrow$ Log in user

class, rather than a standard type. The multiplicity could be [n], [n..i], [n..*], [*], etc., for example. Example attribute constraints would be n : integer {even} for an integer *n* that must have only even values. Similarly, you could list UserClass-Member : *UserClass* {UserClassMember.ID $\in$ UserIDList}, specifying that the members of the UserClass have IDs that are in the UserIDList. An example of some attribute categories is shown in Table 11.6.

The FST also defines the program's items, their calls, and their returns. For example, CheckId returns true when ID is a member of the ValidIdSet, so the ID is valid. If the return is false, the program should still request a PW even though the ID is incorrect. It is good security practice to get both the ID and PW before telling the user that one of them is incorrect. This makes it harder for intruders to identify valid user IDs and passwords.

The FST provides a concise description of the class's external appearance and actions. It also provides a central description of the class's attributes. However, it does not describe the internal workings of the class. The Logic Specification Template (LST) and the State Specification Template (SST) do that.

In the example FST, the Start item initializes the system and manages the LogIn activities. However, until you produce the SST and LST, you will not know precisely how the program works. Though it might seem desirable to include enough of a description on the FST to explain its internal behavior, that would duplicate the SST and LST. Then they would either be unnecessary or you would have to make duplicate updates whenever you changed the design. To the extent that you can, try to keep the OST and FST focused on what the program does, rather than how it works.

TABLE 11.5 FUNCTIONAL SPECIFICATION TEMPLATE (FST) INSTRUCTIONS

Purpose	• To hold a part's functional specifications • To describe classes, program modules, or entire programs
General	• Use this template for complete programs, subsystems, or systems. • Use this template to document the functional specifications during planning, design, test development, implementation, and test. • After implementation and testing, update the template to reflect the actual implemented product.
Header	• Enter your name and the date. • Enter the program name and number. • Enter the instructor's name and the programming language you are using.
Class Name	• Enter the part or class name and the classes from which it directly inherits. • List the class names starting with the most immediate. • Where practical, list the full inheritance hierarchy.
Attributes	• Provide the declaration and description for each global or externally visible variable or parameter, together with any constraints. • List pertinent relationships of this part with other parts together with the multiplicity and constraints.
Items	• Provide the declaration and description for each item. • Precisely describe the conditions that govern each item's return values. • Describe any initialization or other key item responsibilities.
Example Items	An item could be a class method, procedure, function, or database query, for example.

TABLE 11.6 EXAMPLE FST ATTRIBUTES

Class Name	User

Attributes	
Declaration	**Description**
UserID : string {unique}	A unique user ID
UserPassword : string	User's password
MemberOf[0..1] : *Group*	The group class this user is a member of

11.5   The State Specification Template (SST)

A state machine's behavior is defined by its current inputs and the system's state. The State Specification Template provides a simple way to precisely describe a part's state behavior. Programs with multiple states are called **state machines** and their behavior can be enormously complex. A typical state machine is a thermostat, automobile cruise control, or stopwatch. The actions of a state machine depend both on the input and on the current system state. Any system is a state machine if it has memory and its behavior depends on the contents of its memory.

In the programming world, state machines can be helpful in designing counters, sorts, interrupt handlers, security systems, web sites, and many other products. For example, every page on a web site can be viewed as a state, and the transitions among the web pages can be represented as state transitions. The growing importance of Internet security now requires that the transitions among web pages be controlled. It also means that the security authorization state of the user must be considered and authenticated on every web page. Without a clear understanding of states and state behavior, designing an effective security management system can be difficult, if not impossible.

In the PSP, state-machine behavior is described with the aid of the State Specification Template (SST). The state machine for the LogIn function is shown in Figure 11.4. The SST and its instructions are shown in Tables 11.7 and 11.8. This is the LogIn class described in the OST and FST templates in Tables 11.2 and 11.4.

A simple scenario illustrates how this state machine works. From Start, the system transitions to the CheckID state, sets n := 0, Fail := false, ID and PW to !Valid, and requests an ID from the user. From the CheckID state, whether the ID is valid or not, the system transitions to the CheckPW state and requests a PW from the user. If PW and ID are valid and Fail is false, the user is logged in. If PW

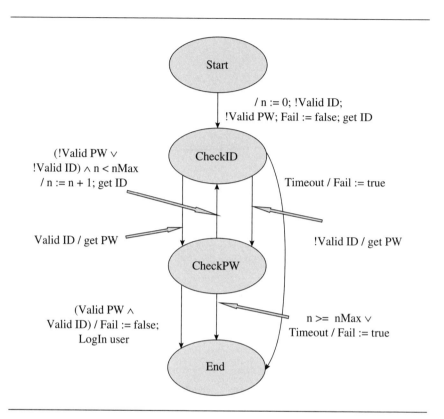

FIGURE 11.4 LOGIN STATE-MACHINE DIAGRAM

or ID is not valid, the system returns to CheckID, requesting an ID. The error count n is increased by 1, and if it reaches nMax, the system exists with Fail := true. Although this is a simple state machine, many are too complex to precisely describe in a figure. This complexity can easily be captured on the SST, as shown in Table 11.7. Note, however, that no design should be considered correct until it is verified.

The SST example in Table 11.7 shows all of the LogIn state-machine states and the transitions among them. These states are all listed at the top of the form followed by a section for each state and its next states. Each state should be briefly described, including the conditions that cause transition to each next state and the transition actions. Only the possible next states need be shown unless some impossible transition needs verification. If so, list the impossible transition and why it is impossible. It is then relatively easy to check these impossible conditions in a design review, inspection, or test.

TABLE 11.7 EXAMPLE STATE SPECIFICATION TEMPLATE (SST)

Student	J. Developer	Date	10/27
Program	LogIn	Program #	
Instructor	Humphrey	Language	C++

State Name	Description
Start	Start condition for system
CheckD	The state of the system after a user ID is requested
CheckPW	The state of the system after a user password is requested
End	The final state: LogIn either logs in or cuts off the user.

Function/Parameter	Description
ID	User identification: ID is Valid or !Valid
PW	User password: PW is Valid or !Valid
n	Integer count of ID and password errors
nMax	Maximum value of ID and password errors: n >= nMax is rejected.
Fail	Error count or timeout indicator: Fail = true is failure, Fail = false is ok.

States/Next States	Transition Condition	Action
Start		
Start	No transitions from Start to Start	
CheckID	True	Get ID, n := 0; ID and PW !Valid
CheckPW	No transitions from Start to CheckPW	
End	No transitions from Start to End	
CheckID		
Start	No transitions from CheckID to Start	
CheckID	No transitions from CheckID to CheckID	
CheckPW	Valid ID	Get password
CheckPW	!Valid ID	Get password
End	Timeout	Fail := true
CheckPW		
Start	No transitions from CheckPW to Start	
CheckID	$(!Valid\ PW \lor !Valid\ ID) \land n < nMax \land !Timeout$	Get ID, n := n + 1
CheckPW	No transitions from CheckPW to CheckPW	
End	Valid PW $\land$ Valid ID	Fail := false, login user
End	$n >= nMax \lor Timeout$	Fail := true, cut off user
End		
	No transitions from End to any state	

TABLE 11.8 STATE SPECIFICATION TEMPLATE INSTRUCTIONS

Purpose	• To hold the state and state transition specifications for a system, class, or program • To support state-machine analysis during design, design reviews, and design inspections
General	• This form shows each system, program, or routine state, the attributes of that state, and the transition conditions among the states. • Use this template to document the state specifications during planning, design, test development, implementation, and test. • After implementation and testing, update the template to reflect the actual implemented product.
Header	• Enter your name and the date. • Enter the program name and number. • Enter the instructor's name and the programming language you are using.
State Name	• Name all of the program's states. • Also enter each state name in the header space at the top of each *States/Next States* section of the template.
State Name Description	• Describe each state and any parameter values that characterize it. • For example, if a state is described by SetSize=10 and SetPosition=3, list SetSize=10 and SetPosition=3.
Function/ Parameter	• List the principal functions and parameters. • Include all key variables or methods used to define state transitions or actions.
Function/ Parameter Description	• For each function, provide its declaration, parameters, and returns. • For each parameter, define its type and significant values.
Next State	• For each state, list the names of all possible next states. • Include the state itself.
Transition Condition	List the conditions for transition to each next state. • Use a mathematical or otherwise precise notation. • If the transition is impossible, list "impossible," with a note saying why.
Action	List the actions taken with each state transition.

11.6   The Logic Specification Template (LST)

An example of the Logic Specification Template (LST) is shown in Table 11.9. It shows how to use a simple programming design language (PDL) to describe the internal logic of the LogIn class. PDLs are often called **pseudocode**.

The LST holds a pseudocode description of a program. Its objective is to clearly and concisely explain what the program is to do and how. Pseudocode

TABLE 11.9 EXAMPLE LOGIC SPECIFICATION TEMPLATE (LST)

Student	J. Developer	Date	10/27
Program	LogIn	Program #	
Instructor	Humphrey	Language	C++

Design References	Operational Specification – page 231
	Functional Specification – page 234
	State Specification – page 238
Parameters	n : the error counter, maximum value nMax
	ID : Boolean indicator of ID Valid and ID !Valid
	PW : Boolean indicator of PW Valid and PW !Valid
	Fail: Boolean indicator of failure condition, end session

Log a user onto the system.
Start by initializing the n error counter, set ID: = !Valid, PW := !Valid, and Fail := false.
Get user ID.
Repeat the main loop until a valid ID and password or Fail.
Check ID for validity. {CheckID state}
If no ID response in MaxTime, set Fail := true.
Get password and check for validity. {CheckPW state}
If no password response in MaxTime, set Fail := true.
If PW !Valid or ID !Valid, step the n counter.
If n exceeds nMax, set Fail := true.
Until ID and PW Valid or Fail = true.
Otherwise, repeat the main loop.
If Fail = true, cut off user, otherwise, log in the user. {End state}

should be written in ordinary human language and, to the extent practical, it should not use programming language constructs (McConnell 1993). When developers use programming expressions in their pseudocode, they often end up writing the program in pseudocode instead of the programming language. This is programming and not design.

In writing the pseudocode, don't bother with design details that would be obvious to an experienced implementer. Appropriate pseudocode statements might be "initialize the class" or "repeat main loop until ID and password valid." However, before completing the design, make sure the pseudocode is sufficiently detailed that the implementation is obvious without further design.

Pseudocode can be written in stages, much like the outline of a paper or a book. Start with an overall statement of what the program does. Then, as you refine the design, expand this initial statement to include added pseudocode detail. A common approach is to use your development environment to write the pseudocode as comments and then, during implementation, insert the code in the appropriate places to implement the pseudocode. Assuming that the pseudocode is clear and sufficiently detailed, it will provide the comments needed to produce a clear, understandable, and correct program.

11.7   A State-Machine Design Example

Although designing a state machine may seem simple, it can also be tricky. The problem is devising just the right states to completely and efficiently do the job. Because there are many possible state machines for any given problem, it is easy to produce a large and unnecessarily complex structure. Such designs are error-prone and expensive, however, so it is worthwhile taking enough time to produce a good design. A few minutes of design and design verification can save hours in implementation and testing. It will also produce a neater and higher-quality product.

LogIn State-Machine Example

A common program design approach is to think in scenarios. Although this is effective for applications, it can lead to overly complex state machines. For example, in designing the LogIn state machine in this way, you might begin with a Start state and then get and verify the ID. This implies two more states: ValidID and !ValidID. Then, starting in ValidID, the next step would be to get and verify the password. If the password were valid, the program would·end, implying an End state, but if the password were not valid, you would need a ValidID-!ValidPW-1 state for this first PW error. After another invalid password, you would have a ValidID-!ValidPW-2 state, and so forth. Similarly, starting in !ValidID, you might end up with !ValidID-1, !ValidID-2, and so forth. You might also consider the sequence: !Valid ID, Valid ID, !Valid PW, and so forth. This approach typically produces a large number of states that must be condensed into a reasonable design. However, because there is no general method for simplifying state machines, you might not end up with a very clean design.

A generally effective state-machine design strategy is as follows:

1. Think through the logical flow of the system to understand it.

2. Devise a solution strategy.

3. Define the decisions that must be made by the program to implement this strategy.

4. Identify the information required to make these decisions.

5. Identify the subset of this information that must be remembered.

6. Determine the minimum number of states required to hold all valid combinations of the remembered information.

For example, in the LogIn case, the strategy is to always request an ID and a password, whether or not the submitted ID is valid. This makes it more difficult for potential attackers to identify valid IDs and passwords. Therefore, the program must make only two determinations: after requesting an ID, it must determine whether to transition to the CheckPW state or the End state; and after requesting a password, it must determine whether to end the session or check another ID. The only information needed for the first decision is whether a timeout has occurred. For the second decision, the program must know if the most recent ID was correct, how many ID and password errors have occurred, whether the current password is correct, and if there has been a password timeout error. Because this information can be held in a few Boolean parameters, only four states are needed: Start, CheckID, CheckPW, and End.

Search State-Machine Example

For a slightly different and more complex case, consider the state machine to conduct a search. The objective is to find the value of x for which some function $F(x)$ = M, a user-specified value, where $F(x)$ is assumed to monotonically increase or decrease with x. That is, for each x, there is a unique value of $F(x)$ and the reverse. In addition, assume that you have a program that will calculate $F(x)$ for a given value of x. One solution to this problem is a simple searching procedure that makes successive trial calculations until the value of $F(x)$ is within an acceptable error range of the desired value M. An example of this search procedure is shown in Figure 11.5. For steps 1 and 2 of the state-machine design process, a possible solution strategy would be as follows:

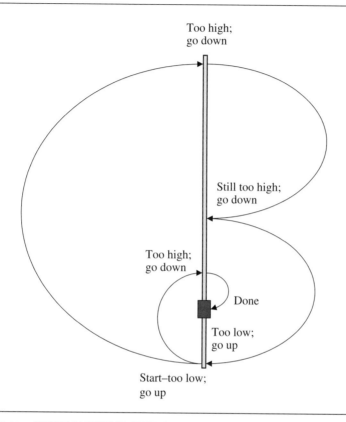

Too high;
go down

Still too high;
go down

Too high;
go down

Done

Too low;
go up

Start–too low;
go up

FIGURE 11.5 STATE-MACHINE SEARCH STRATEGY

1. Determine the desired final result M, select an arbitrary positive number for Delta, and define an acceptable error range, Range. The program should then find a value of x for which: M – Range < F(x) <= M + Range.

2. Assume an initial value of x_{init} and calculate F(x_{init}).

3. Also calculate values for F(x_{init} + Delta) and F(x_{init} – Delta).

4. Set error values e+ := F(x_{init} + Delta) – M and e- := F(x_{init} – Delta) – M.

5. If e+ >= e-, it means that the value of F(x) increases with x, so set Sign := +1. If e+ < e-, set Sign := –1.

6. Test to determine whether F(x_{init}) is within, above, or below the target range.

7. If the initial test was too low, increase x by the increment Sign*Delta and repeat.

8. Test to determine whether this value is within, above, or below the target range.

9. If, this time, the result is too high, go down, but by a smaller step. For a binary search, set Delta := –Delta/2 and $x := x +$ Sign*Delta.

10. Calculate the new F(x) value.

11. Test to determine whether this value is within, above, or below the target range.

12. Continue this procedure until the result x is within the target range.

With this design strategy, consider design step 3: List the decisions to be made by the program. The two decisions are whether to use a positive (Up) Delta or a negative (Down) one and when to divide Delta by 2. The next step in the state-machine design strategy is to identify the state-unique information needed to make these decisions. The decisions are whether to add or subtract Delta and whether the search is completed. The information needed is whether the current trial is too high, too low, or within the error range and whether the previous change in x was an increase or a decrease. The states don't need to remember the results of the current trial but they do need to remember whether the prior test increased or decreased x.

To decide whether or not to divide Delta by 2, look at Figure 11.5: Delta is halved every time the search reverses direction. If Delta > 0, the search was going up, so a high guess requires a reversal and halving Delta, giving Delta = –Delta/2. Similarly, if Delta < 0, the search was going down, so a low guess would require setting Delta = –Delta and dividing it by 2. Therefore, every reversal results in Delta = –Delta/2. Where there is no reversal, Delta is not changed. This suggests that the states only need to remember whether the prior search step was upward (Up – positive Delta) or downward (Down – negative Delta).

In the final design step, identify the possible states. The information to be remembered requires only the following two states: Up and Down. In addition, the program needs to know whether F(x) increases or decreases with increasing x. If a larger x results in a smaller F(x), the Delta should be subtracted instead of added. This requires a state for setting DeltaSign. Start and End states are also needed. With these states defined, it is relatively easy to complete the State Specification Template in Table 11.10, providing the transition conditions and functions for each state.

As part of state-machine design, it is usually a good idea to draw a state diagram. This will provide a clear and understandable picture of state-machine operation as well as a useful test of the design. Put the transition conditions and state functions on the diagram if they can be included without overcomplicating the picture. This is not essential, however, because the State Specification Template has all of the required information. If you have trouble producing the state diagram, either the state specification is incomplete or the design is too complex to represent clearly in a simple picture. Then you must use the SST to define the program's behavior. The state-machine diagram for the search example is shown in Figure 11.6.

TABLE 11.10 STATE SPECIFICATION TEMPLATE FOR SEARCH

Student   J. Developer   Date   10/30

Program   Search   Program #

Instructor   Humphrey   Language   C++

State Name	Description
Start	Start condition for program
DeltaSign	For determining if $F(x)$ increases or decreases with increasing x
Up	Last test was below the target range
Down	Last test was above the target range
End	Last test was within the target range
Function/Parameter	**Description**
x	Initial value set for calculations, later adjusted to find x for $F(x) = M$.
Target, M	The final target value = M, with $M - Range < F(x) <= M + Range$
Delta	The amount by which the search range is adjusted for each test
Sign	Indicates whether $F(x)$ increases with x ($+ 1$), or decreases with x ($- 1$)
e	Error in $F(x)$ test: $e = F(x) - M$
e+	Error for $x + Delta$: $e+ = F(x + Delta) - M$
e-	Error for $x - Delta$: $e- = F(x - Delta) - M$
x+	$x+ = x + Sign*Delta$
x-	$x- = x - Sign*Delta$
x+/2	$x+/2 = x + Sign*Delta/2$
x-/2	$x-/2 = x - Sign*Delta/2$

States/Next States		Transition Condition	Action
Start			
	DeltaSign	e+ < e-	Sign := -1, Test $F(x)$
	DeltaSign	e+ >= e-	Sign := +1, Test $F(x)$
	End	In Range, $M - Range < F(x) <= M + Range$	
DeltaSign			
	Up	$F(x)$ < Target	x := x+, Test $F(x)$
	Down	$F(x)$ > Target	x := x-, Test $F(x)$
	End	In Range, $M - Range < F(x) <= M + Range$	
Up			
	Up	$F(x)$ < Target	x := x+, Test $F(x)$
	Down	$F(x)$ > Target	x := x-/2, Test $F(x)$
	End	In Range, $M - Range < F(x) <= M + Range$	
Down			
	Up	$F(x)$ < Target	x := x+/2, Test $F(x)$
	Down	$F(x)$ > Target	x := x-, Test $F(x)$
	End	In Range, $M - Range < F(x) <= M + Range$	
End			

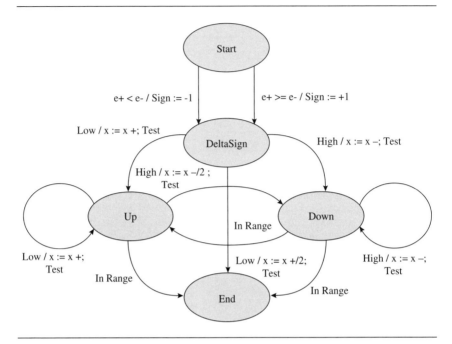

FIGURE 11.6 SEARCH STATE DIAGRAM

11.8 Using the PSP Design Templates

The principal intent of the PSP design templates is to record the design, not to aid you in producing that design. The templates precisely define what the program is to do and how it is to be implemented. Your choice of design method is particularly important because design is an intellectual process and it is hard to do good intellectual work in a language or with methods with which you are not fluent. Therefore, at least until you have used these templates for a while and are familiar with them, continue producing designs as you have in the past but record them on the templates. By completing the templates, you will often identify design problems. As you gain experience with the templates, you may also find that they help you to produce the design. The PSP2.1 exit criteria for the design phase calls for the completed templates.

The PSP design templates were made as generic as possible so they could be used with any design method. If your design method already produces the information required by one or more of the templates, you need not bother duplicating that material. Before deciding to omit one or more of these templates, however, ensure that your design method captures all of the required information in the detail specified by the templates.

Comparison with UML

Figure 11.7 compares the PSP design templates and the UML. It shows that the OST contents are provided by a combination of the UML use case diagrams, use case descriptions, activity diagrams, and sequence diagrams. The SST is covered by the UML state diagram, but only if you include the detailed specifications for the states and state transitions. FST is partially covered by the class diagram. Here again, the shortcomings concern the precision of the functional definition. The LST has no UML equivalent, although most UML tools provide a way to enter and store the pseudocode with a design.

Redesign

Most industrial software development work, and all software maintenance work, involves modifying and enhancing existing systems. Whether making modifications or adding functions to an old product, you can still use the PSP design templates. They are particularly helpful when delving deeply into an old product to make fixes or add enhancements. Because you must understand the product to have any chance of making defect-free changes, the condition of the product's design is

	External	Internal
Static	Class Diagram with Object Constraint Language descriptions	No UML equivalent to the Logic Specification Template
Dynamic	Use Case Diagram Use Case Description Activity Diagram Sequence Diagram	State Diagram

FIGURE 11.7 UML EQUIVALENTS TO THE PSP DESIGN TEMPLATES

important. If suitable design documentation is available, the job will be easier. However, software designs are rarely documented, and when they are the documentation is usually not current, correct, or understandable. Then you must either work without a design or start with the source code, if you have it, and reconstruct the design. Although the methods for doing this depend on the product, the PSP design templates can help by recording the parts of the design that you must understand.

11.9   Using the Design Templates in Large-Scale Design

You can also use the PSP design templates to specify large software products or systems. You could specify the system's external functional and operation behavior with FST and OST. Then, as you decompose the system into multiple smaller subsystems or components, you could specify their external operational and functional behavior with additional FST and OST specifications. Where needed, you could use the SST to define the state behavior of the system and its component parts. Then, at the next level, you could repeat the same steps for the lower-level parts.

One way to visualize this design process is shown in Figure 11.8. The system requirements statement describes what the users need. The functional and

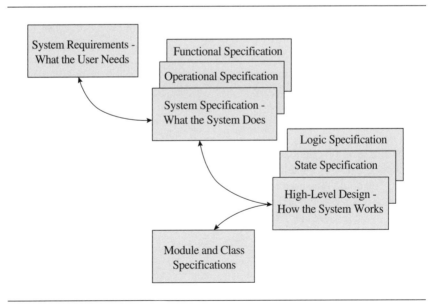

FIGURE 11.8 THE DESIGN HIERARCHY

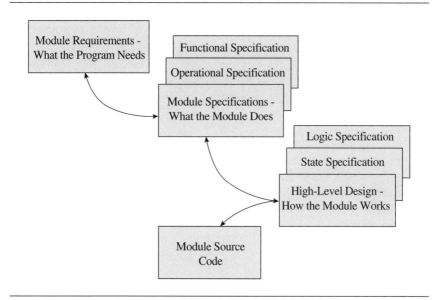

FIGURE 11.9 THE IMPLEMENTATION HIERARCHY

operational specifications then describe the system's external behavior. The system's high-level design would include an SST for its state behavior and an LST for any high-level control logic. An example of this logic would be the interrupt-control design of a real-time system. Next, postulate the services needed from the lower-level parts and capture their behavior in FST and OST specifications. For large systems, you could repeat this process several times, completing OST, FST, SST, and LST specifications at every design level. At the end, as shown in Figure 11.9, you would have the detailed design for the lowest-level modules.

This top-down strategy is only one approach. You might instead require some critical low-level function that you did not fully understand, and need to create a prototype or even complete its detailed design and code before you can count on using it. You could thus bounce from the highest design level down to implementation and back many times during design. Regardless of the strategy, do not consider any element's design complete until you have fully defined all of the logic connecting it to the higher-level program elements that use its services. You must also have specified all of the services it requires from lower-level parts. The PSP design templates can help you to do this.

11.10   Summary

In the PSP, designs are described with the aid of four templates. The Operational Specification Template describes the program's operational behavior via one or more scenarios. The Functional Specification Template describes the functions performed by a program, a class, or a procedure. The Logic Specification Template uses pseudocode to precisely describe a program's logic. Finally, the State Specification Template describes the program's state behavior.

You can use these templates to specify the internal and external behavior of both large systems and small programs, as well as the behavior of their parts. The PSP templates are designed to capture the precise content of a design and are intended to complement existing design methods. The intent is for developers to produce designs with whatever methods work best for them and then to record these designs in the PSP templates. Doing this will usually identify errors, oversights, and inconsistencies, as well as provide a useful design record.

11.11   Exercises

The assignment for this chapter is to use PSP2.1 to write one or more programs. Use the PSP design templates for these programs and, if the program has a search function, consider using a search machine like the one described in Table 11.10 (see p. 245) and Figure 11.6 (see p. 246). The PSP2.1 process and the program specifications are provided in the assignment kits, which you can get from your instructor or at **www.sei.cmu.edu/tsp/**. The kits contain the assignment specifications, an example of the required calculations, and the PSP2.1 process scripts. In completing this assignment, faithfully follow the PSP2.1 process, record all required data, and produce the program report according to the specifications given in the assignment kit.

References

Booch, G., J. Rumbaugh, and I. Jacobson. *The Unified Modeling Language User Guide.* Reading: Addison-Wesley, 1999.

de Champeaux, D., D. Lea, and P. Faure. *Object-Oriented System Development.* Reading, MA: Addison-Wesley, 1993.

Jacky, J. *The Way of Z: Practical Programming with Formal Methods.* Cambridge, UK: Cambridge University Press, 1996.

McConnell, S. *Code Complete.* Redmond, WA: Microsoft Press, 1993.

Rumbaugh, J., I. Jacobson, and G. Booch. *The Unified Modeling Language Reference Manual.* Reading, MA: Addison-Wesley, 1999.

Schneider, G., and J. P. Winters. *Applying Use Cases.* Redmond, WA: Microsoft Press, 1998.

12

Design Verification

There are many ways to verify a program's design. Some of these methods, like testing, can be automated, while others cannot. For large and complex programs, even the most time-consuming of the labor-intensive methods is much faster and more effective than testing. This chapter explains why this is true and describes some of the more effective methods for verifying the correctness of your programs.

Although it may seem pointless to verify the design of each small PSP exercise, you should use these methods as often as you can. This will give you the experience needed to use the methods on larger and more complex programs, and it will help you to build the skills required to properly use the methods when you need them.

The following five verification methods described in this chapter are relatively straightforward and can be mastered fairly quickly:

1. **Design standards:** Standards provide the basis for verifying that a design properly performs its intended functions.

2. **Execution-table verification:** The execution table provides a simple and orderly but labor-intensive way to check a program's logic.

3. **Trace-table verification:** A trace table is a general way to verify a program's logic.

4. **State-machine verification:** State-machine verification provides analytical methods for verifying that a given state machine is proper and thus correct.

5. **Analytical verification:** Analytical verification provides a mathematical way to demonstrate the validity of program logic.

This chapter works through several examples that show how to use some of these verification methods with the PSP exercises. In order to become fluent with the methods, you must use them several times on a variety of programs. Then you should be reasonably proficient and able to use them to verify larger-scale designs.

There are many verification methods, and this book covers only a few of the most effective ones. Some of the most promising verification methods that are not covered are based on mathematical proofs. Although many of these methods are very powerful, useful descriptions would take more space than is practical for this book. In addition to the many verification methods already available, new ones will almost certainly be developed, so try any methods that look promising and use your PSP data to evaluate the results. Then make a practice of using those that you find most effective.

12.1   Why Verify Programs?

The principal challenge with design verification is convincing yourself to do it. We all learned to program by writing small programs. After a few tests and fixing a few defects, we could usually get our programs to run. Although the finished programs occasionally still had defects, these were usually easy to fix. These early experiences often give the impression that a few defects are acceptable as long as the program can be made to work. Unfortunately, this belief is dangerous. One or two defects in every 100-LOC program means that there are 10 to 20 defects in a 1,000-LOC program, and 10,000 to 20,000 defects in a 1,000,000-LOC program. This is no longer just a couple of bugs. Some of these defects could cause serious problems.

For example, the Osprey aircraft was designed to transport U.S. marines under battlefield conditions. It flies like a high-speed aircraft and lands like a helicopter. Although the Osprey is a marvelous engineering achievement, it is also very complex and contains a lot of software. And, like most software, the Osprey programs have latent defects. On December 11, 2000, as one of these aircraft was carrying four marines, the hydraulic system failed just as the pilot was landing. Even though the Osprey had a built-in backup system to handle such emergencies, a software defect in the flight-control computer caused "significant pitch and thrust changes in both prop rotors." This led to a stall and a crash (Gage and McCormick 2004). All aboard were killed. Although development management told me that the Osprey software was very high quality, the quality was obviously not high enough.

To most people in the software business, improving quality means running more tests, but the Osprey software had been extensively tested. Although its quality, by today's standards, was almost certainly high, this experience demonstrates that today's generally accepted software quality standards are not good enough for life-critical systems. The problem is not that testing is wrong but that it is not enough. To find the thousands of latent defects in large software systems, we must thoroughly verify their designs, carefully review and inspect the code, and then run exhaustive tests.

Various authors have described the problems of using a test-based process to produce highly dependable programs. Littlewood cites a case in which it took over 74,000 hours of testing to determine that a software system had a mean time to failure (MTTF) of over 1,000 hours (Littlewood and Strigini 1993). Similarly, Butler shows that more than 10^5 years of testing would be needed to ensure that a software system could achieve the reliability levels now commonly specified by transportation and other life-critical systems (Butler and Finelli 1993).

To see why extensive testing alone cannot ensure software quality, consider what a comprehensive test would have to cover. Because untested software systems typically have thousands of defects, one obvious testing strategy would be to test every possible path through the software. Covering all possible paths through a program would be like threading all of the possible paths through a maze. Suppose, for example, that the program were like the maze shown in Figure 12.1, where every intersection was a branch instruction. As shown in Table 12.1, testing every possible path from point A to point B can require a lot of tests. For this simple 4-by-4 maze, there are 70 possible paths. As you can also see, the number of possible paths through larger mazes increases very rapidly. For a maze with

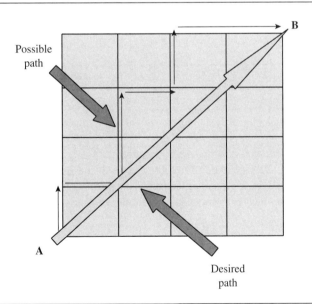

FIGURE 12.1 THE TESTING MAZE

only 400 branches, the number of possible paths is astronomical, and these are just for the numbers of paths. They do not consider loops, case statements, or multiple data values. As these numbers show, it is practically impossible to test all possible paths in any but the simplest programs. Furthermore, when you start with thousands of defects, just about any untested path could uncover a latent defect.

Since our job is to get complex systems to work, what can we do? No method will magically guarantee program quality but some verification methods are more effective than others. For example, testing is an ineffective and expensive way to find the hundreds to thousands of defects in the programs developers now typically deliver to test. However, testing is also the only practical way to find the few really complex problems that involve overall system behavior. Conversely, personal reviews and team inspections are very fast and effective for finding coding and simple design problems, but not as useful for complex performance or usability problems. When teams properly use all of these quality-management methods, quality improvements of 100 times are common.

For high-quality software work, no single method is sufficient by itself. We must use sound design methods and verify every program's design during the design review. We should write code only after we are confident that the design is sound and defect-free. We should then review, compile, inspect, and test the program to verify that it was correctly implemented. The verification methods described in this book can be cost-effective and efficient, but they are most effective when used in combination with team inspections and thorough testing. This chapter describes several ways to do design verification. It also discusses some issues to consider in deciding how to verify a program's correctness.

TABLE 12.1 NUMBER OF POSSIBLE PATHS THROUGH THE TESTING MAZE

Size of Maze	Number of Branches	Number of Possible Paths
1	1	2
2	4	6
3	9	20
4	16	70
5	25	252
6	36	924
7	49	3,432
8	64	12,870
9	81	48,620
10	100	184,756
20	400	$1.38 * 10^{11}$

12.2 Design Standards

Although design standards do not fit the common definition of a verification method, they do provide criteria against which to verify a design. A **standard** is a norm or a basis for comparison that is established by some authority or by common consent. Because the purpose of verification is to determine whether the design is correct, you must first define what constitutes correctness. Standards are an important part of this basis. Three standards to use in verification are as follows:

1. Product conventions
2. Product design standards
3. Reuse standards

Familiarize yourself with the appropriate standards before starting the design work and again when you do the verification.

Product Conventions

The value of product conventions is obvious when you use a system that did not have them. In developing IBM's early BPS/360 system, several programmers were assigned to work on the file-handling routines. Unfortunately, nothing had been standardized except the interfaces between their programs. One programmer specified that the file naming and addressing be in lowercase and another programmer called for uppercase. Because the two programs worked in tandem, the result was total user confusion. This problem forced us to withdraw and replace the entire BPS/360 operating system.

Product conventions are essential if multiple developers are to produce coherent and usable systems. These conventions should at least address the user interfaces, external naming, system error handling, installation procedures, and help facilities. A quality system must have a clear and consistent user interface, regardless of who designed each part.

Product Design Standards

Product design standards range from simple conventions to complete system architectures. These standards typically cover calling and naming conventions, header standards, test standards, and documentation formats. Although many product design standards are arbitrary, it is a good idea to establish your own personal set. It will help you to produce consistent designs and will make your designs easier to review. This will also help in your personal work and will greatly facilitate your work on a software team.

Reuse Standards

Reuse is a powerful technique but it must be properly managed. When it is, it can save time and money and improve product quality. Reuse can be at the system-design level, the component-design level, or the modular-part level. To get maximum benefit, think about reuse during design and specifically address reuse in the design reviews.

The effective reuse of component parts requires the absolute integrity of those parts. The group in IBM's German laboratory that developed standard parts for use in IBM's operating systems distributed and supported its standard parts much like a commercial parts supplier. Their catalogue listed the parts and their specifications. The parts were essentially sealed and could not be modified, but they did have adjustable parameters. This group had product representatives in several major IBM laboratories who helped in identifying parts applications, assisted in their use, and identified new parts needs. When I last visited this development group, some of their parts had been included in IBM's products for up to 10 years. The engineers were proud to report that none of their users had ever reported a defect in any of their parts.

To be widely usable, standard software parts must be precisely specified, of the highest quality, and adequately supported. Their acceptance will then depend on their quality, their price, the degree to which they meet the users' needs, the effectiveness of their marketing, and the adequacy of their technical support. Modern development environments generally come with large libraries of standard functions; and by learning to use these libraries, you can greatly improve your personal productivity, as well as the quality of your products. You should also develop a library of reusable parts tailored to your particular application domain. Familiarize yourself with the standard parts that are available, use them whenever you can, and make a regular practice of contributing new parts to your team's or organization's application-specific reuse library.

Unless you are confident that the library functions and other programs you reuse are defect-free, you must verify their correctness when you verify the correctness of the new functions you develop. Reuse is important for the PSP because if the reused parts are of high quality, their use will substantially improve your productivity. One objective of the PSP is to develop the personal discipline required to produce reuse-quality software.

12.3   Execution-Table Verification

There are many ways to verify a program's logic before it is implemented. One of the most general methods is the **execution table**. Execution tables provide an orderly way to check a program's logical flow. Although the method can be time-consuming, particularly for large and complex programs, it is reliable and simple and far faster than testing as a way to identify complex design problems. An execution table can produce a fairly general verification, but it usually requires a fairly large number of cases. To minimize the time required while maximizing effectiveness, follow an orderly verification procedure and carefully check every step. Use the following procedure:

1. Review the program's pseudocode and identify all of the loops and complex routines to verify with an execution table. If the program has already been implemented, review the source code instead.

2. Decide on the order for doing the analysis. If you believe that the higher-level design is solid, start with the lowest-level routines and work up to the higher-level ones. Otherwise, do an initial check of the highest-level structure, assuming that the lower-level routines are correct.

3. To analyze the first routine, construct a blank execution table like the one shown in Table 12.2 for the LogIn routine (from Table 11.9, p. 240). Make a column in the table for every variable that changes during program execution, and a column for true (T) and false (F) for all of the true/false test results.

4. Perform an execution-table analysis for each of the selected scenarios.

The following example walks through an execution-table analysis for the LogIn routine given in Table 12.2. The steps in the execution-table analysis are as follows:

1. In Table 12.2, the only logical structure to check is the repeat-until loop from lines 3 to 12. You can do this with multiple copies of one execution table.

2. Produce the execution table and make a sufficient number of blank copies to handle all of the verification scenarios.

3. Select a scenario to verify. For this example, we check the following three-step sequence: !Valid ID, Valid ID & !Valid PW, and Valid ID & Valid PW. To check additional cases, you would use additional copies of the execution table.

4. Label a copy of the execution table with the scenario step being tested and "Cycle 1," check the program design carefully to determine the initial conditions, and enter them at the top of the cycle 1 table. In doing so, make sure that these initial conditions are actually set by the program. Incorrectly assumed initial conditions are a common source of error.

5. Work through the program one step at a time, entering all variable changes exactly as the program would make them. As you do, consider the logical choices and satisfy yourself that the program behaves correctly in every case. When you encounter a repetitive loop structure, complete the first cycle

through the loop on the cycle 1 table and use a second copy of the table for cycle 2, and so on.

6. At the end, verify that the result is correct.

As simple as this program is, constructing and checking the execution table revealed three problems with the logic in Table 11.9 in Chapter 11 (see p. 240). First, step 6 was to both get the password and check it. This step had to be split into the current step 6 and a new step 8, so that the password would be checked only if there was a valid ID. Second, in step 9, the *n* counter should be stepped if either !Valid ID or !Valid PW. Finally, in step 12, if the loop is repeated, ID should first be set to !Valid; otherwise, the third cycle would start with Valid ID. Although these are all obvious problems that you would likely correct during coding, they are the kinds of problems that lead to logical defects that are hard to find in testing. They are precisely the kinds of problems that design verification is intended to find and fix. The three cycles of this corrected execution table are shown in Tables 12.2 through 12.4.

TABLE 12.2 LOGIN EXECUTION TABLE

Cycle 1: Invalid ID: Cycle 1			Function: LogIn			
#	Instruction	Test	ID	PW	Fail	n
1	Initialize: n := 0; ID: = !Valid; PW := !Valid; Fail := false.	F	!Valid	!Valid	F	0
2	Get user ID.					
3	Repeat the main loop until a Valid ID and password or Fail.					
4	Check ID for validity. {CheckID state}		!Valid			
5	If no ID response in MaxTime, set Fail := true.	F				
6	Get password					
7	If no password response in MaxTime, set Fail := true.	F				
8	If ID Valid, check PW for validity. {CheckPW state}	F				
9	If PW !Valid or ID !Valid, step the n counter.	T				1
10	If n exceeds nMax, set Fail := true.	F				
11	Until ID and PW valid or Fail = true.	F				
12	Otherwise, repeat the main loop; ID := !Valid	T	!Valid			
13	If Fail = true, cut off user, else, log in the user. {End state}					

TABLE 12.3 LOGIN EXECUTION TABLE

Cycle 2: Valid ID and invalid password		Function: LogIn				
#	Instruction	Test	ID	PW	Fail	n
1	Initialize: n := 0; ID: = !Valid; PW := !Valid; Fail := false.					
2	Get user ID.					
3	Repeat the main loop until a valid ID and password or Fail.		!Valid	!Valid	F	1
4	Check ID for validity. {CheckID state}		Valid			
5	If no ID response in MaxTime, set Fail := true.	F				
6	Get password					
7	If no password response in MaxTime, set Fail := true.	F				
8	If ID Valid, check PW for validity. {CheckPW state}	T		!Valid		
9	If PW !Valid or PW !Valid, step the n counter.	T				2
10	If n exceeds nMax, set Fail := true.	F				
11	Until ID and PW valid or Fail = true.	F				
12	Otherwise, repeat the main loop; ID := !Valid	T	!Valid			
13	If Fail = true, cut off user, else, log in the user. {End state}					

TABLE 12.4 LOGIN EXECUTION TABLE

Cycle 3: Valid ID and valid password		Function: LogIn				
#	Instruction	Test	ID	PW	Fail	n
1	Initialize: n := 0; ID: = !Valid; PW := !Valid; Fail := false.					
2	Get user ID.					
3	Repeat the main loop until a valid ID and password or Fail.		!Valid	!Valid	F	2
4	Check ID for validity. {CheckID state}		Valid			
5	If no ID response in MaxTime, set Fail := true.	F				
6	Get password					
7	If no password response in MaxTime, set Fail := true.	F				
8	If ID Valid, check PW for validity. {CheckPW state}	T		Valid		
9	If PW !Valid or ID !Valid, step the n counter.	F				
10	If n exceeds nMax, set Fail := true.	F				
11	Until ID and PW valid or Fail = true.	T				
12	Otherwise, repeat the main loop; ID := !Valid	F				
13	If Fail = true, cut off user, else, log in the user. {End state}	F				

12.4   Trace-Table Verification

The **trace table** is a generalized form of execution table. With an execution table, you are essentially acting like a computer and manually working through every step of a test scenario. With a trace table, you first consider all of the possible logical cases and select a test scenario for each one. For example, if you know that a function that works properly at $n = 0$ and at $n = 1,000$ would also work properly for all intermediate values, you would only need to check the $n = 0$ and $n = 1,000$ cases. You should also check one intermediate value and any possible cases with $n < 0$ and $n > 1,000$.

Where practical, do a trace-table analysis for each possible logical case. The proper selection of cases can significantly reduce the number of required scenarios. Although trace tables look just like execution tables, the method is much more efficient and provides a more general proof. The trace-table procedure is as follows:

1. Review the program's pseudocode and identify all of the loops and complex routines to verify with a trace table. If the program has already been implemented, review the source code instead.

2. Decide on the order for doing the trace-table analysis. If you believe that the higher-level design is solid, start with the lowest-level routines and work up to the higher-level ones. Otherwise, do an initial check of the highest-level structure, assuming that the lower-level routines are correct.

3. Identify all of the logical cases to check with a trace table.

4. To analyze the first routine, construct a blank trace table like the one shown in Table 12.2 for the LogIn routine. Make a column in the table for every variable that changes during program execution, and a column for true (T) and false (F) for all of the true/false test results.

5. Perform a trace-table analysis for all of the nontrivial cases.

A Trace-Table Example

As one example of the trace-table method, consider the following program to clear the leading spaces from a string. This example uses a for loop to remove the leading spaces from a string of length Length:

```
for N = 1 to Length do
        if (Input[N-1] <> ' ' or First)
                        Output := Output + Input[N - 1]
                        First := true
    end
```

Starting with the program preconditions, examine all of the cases that are established by the program inputs and prior logic. For this short program fragment, the preconditions are as follows:

1. First is false.
2. Length may be any positive integer greater than 0.
3. The input string includes q characters with a nonspace initial character, where q is an integer from 0 to Length.
4. The input string starts with p spaces, where p may be any positive integer from 0 to Length.
5. There may be spaces embedded in the input string after the first nonspace character.
6. The output string is initially empty.

In determining the possible cases, consider the number of leading spaces p and the number of message characters q, including embedded spaces. The numbers p and q could be 0, 1, or some larger number m or n, but p + q = Length. Therefore, the possible cases are as follows:

☐ A single nonspace message character with no leading spaces: p = 0, q = 1, Length = 1
☐ Several message characters and no leading spaces: p = 0, q = n, Length = n
☐ No message characters and one leading space: p = 1, q = 0, Length = 1
☐ A single message character with one leading space: p = 1, q = 1, Length = 2
☐ Several message characters with one leading space: p = 1, q = n, Length = n + 1
☐ No message characters and several leading spaces: p = m, q = 0, Length = m
☐ A single message character with several leading spaces: p = m, q = 1, Length = m + 1
☐ Several message characters with several leading spaces: p = m, q = n, Length = m + n

These eight conditions include all of the cases except those with zero message and space characters. If you can verify these eight cases and show that they are true for all possible values of p and q, you have verified all of the nonzero character cases. Note that for a complete test, you would also have to include the zero character case and cases for various numbers of embedded spaces.

These cases can be checked with a trace table, as shown in Table 12.5. To check all eight cases, you would need eight trace tables. Note, however, that you can abbreviate cycles where they merely repeat the same actions. In Table 12.5, for example, the . . . (ellipsis) on line 7 indicates multiple additional identical cycles that merely increase the value of N by 1 and add one additional character to the output. By checking all eight cases in this way, you can demonstrate that the

TABLE 12.5 CLEARLEADINGSPACES TRACE TABLE (CASE p = 1, q = n)

\#	Instruction	T/F	Input	Output	Length	First	N
Cycles 1 through N: p = 1, n characters			Function: Clear Leading Spaces				
1	for N = 1 to Length do		' a..n'	''	n+1	F	1
2	if (input[N-1] <> ' ' or First	F					
3	Output := Output + Input[N-1] First := true						
4	for N = 1 to Length do			''			2
5	if (input[N-1] <> ' ' or First	T					
6	Output := Output + Input[N-1] First: := true			'a'		T	
7	...						
8	for N = 1 to Length do			'a..n-1'			n+1
9	if (input[N-1] <> ' ' or First	T					
10	Output := Output + Input[N-1] First := true			'a...n'			
11	end			'a...n'			

design is correct. Although this may not seem very important for a simple loop like ClearLeadingSpaces, it is a quick way to comprehensively check simple cases and a very effective way to check complex ones.

Trace-Table Practices

In using the trace-table method, the fastest and most effective technique is to make a blank trace-table form like the one shown in Table 12.5. Then make enough copies for all of the cases and cycles that you plan to test. In completing these tables, work through the program one instruction at a time. For each variable change, think through precisely what the program would do. When you make these checks on every branch and every path and ensure that every part of every condition is correct, you will perform very high-yield design reviews and will usually produce programs that have no design defects.

During a trace-table analysis, consider program robustness. For example, examine all of the possible limits and confirm that the design will handle them. For input ID or password strings in particular, consider what would happen with 0, 10,

100, or even 100 million or more characters. Check for any limits on the routines that calculate string length and the system's handling of buffer space. Alternatively, you could modify the program to enforce limits on string length. Also consider any possible special characters and what would happen if they were included in an input string. Then take appropriate precautionary steps. Finally, clearly state any input limitations in the program's specifications and comments.

Using paper forms may seem like a laborious way to verify a design, particularly when a powerful computer is available to do the calculations. However, no computer can think through all of the possible cases as quickly as you can. To prove this, work out all of the possible cases for a simple program and then try using a debugger to test them all. If you measure the time and the work required, you will find that for a thorough test, you must do the equivalent of all the trace-table analyses without the aid of the trace-table forms and methods. In general, however, such intuitive analyses are both time-consuming and error-prone. With a blank trace table, it takes much less time to work through the program steps and fill in the blanks. When you are done, you will have a verified program and a detailed script for checking the verification work with a debugger. Then, for any but the simplest logic, check the more complex trace-table cases with the debugger to verify your trace-table analysis.

Complex programs often result in complex trace tables, but this is when a trace-table analysis is most important. It is almost impossible to verify a complex logical structure with test cases. Often, however, these complex structures can be greatly simplified by concentrating only on the decision points and treating all of the other instruction sequences as single pseudocode lines. If the logic is still too complex to analyze with a trace table, it is also too complex to adequately test and should be redesigned.

12.5   Verifying State Machines

When a program includes a state machine, it is important to prove that it is properly designed and used. To determine whether a program is a state machine, check its external behavior. If it can behave differently with identical inputs, it is a state machine. An example would be the behavior of the character reader for a LOC counter. While in the regular portion of the program, the character reader would pass all characters to the counter. When it detected the start of a comment, however, it would ignore all subsequent characters until it came to the end of the comment. To do this, the character reader would need two states: CommentText and ProgramText. With the identical character as input, in one case it would produce no output and in the other it would pass the input character to the output.

Completeness and Orthogonality

Although there is no general way to prove that a state machine is properly designed, there are some common design problems. Examples are overlooking possible states or having conflicting or overlapping state transition conditions. Such problems are extremely hard to find in testing but can be quickly found in a design review. You can also greatly reduce the likelihood of having state-machine design problems if you consider these issues during program design. A state machine that conforms to all generally accepted design criteria is called a **proper state machine**. To be proper, it must be possible for it to reach a return state, if there is one, from every other state; and all of the transitions from each state must be complete and orthogonal. If there is no return state, there must be a way to transition from every state to every other state, with the possible exception of the initial state.

Complete Functions

A complete function is one that includes all possible logical conditions. For example, if you were designing a poll to determine how people feel about an issue, you might consider the following four population characteristics: male or female, political party member or not, married or not, and registered voter or not. If you then produced three reports—poll A to tally the opinions of the male party members, poll B for the opinions of the registered voters, and poll C for the opinions of married people—would you have a complete set of opinions? If you didn't, who would you have left out?

This is not a complete function or set of poll reports. It leaves out female unmarried nonvoters and unmarried men who are not party members or voters. To see why, examine Table 12.6. This table is called a **Karnaugh map** and it shows all of the possible combinations of all the variables. The cells covered by each report are labeled A, B, and C, respectively, and the empty cells indicate combinations not covered by any report. A complete set of poll reports, like a complete function, would cover all of the possible combinations of the variables, with no empty cells.

TABLE 12.6 MAP OF POLL REPORTS

	Male				Female			
	Member		Nonmember		Member		Nonmember	
	Married	Single	Married	Single	Married	Single	Married	Single
Voter	ABC	AB	BC	B	BC	B	BC	B
Nonvoter	AC	A	C		BC		BC	

Orthogonal Functions

A set of functions is orthogonal if none of its members have any common conditions. In the polling example, this would mean that no groups were double-counted. From the Karnaugh map shown in Table 12.6, it is clear that the three poll reports are not orthogonal. The double- and triple-counted groups are married voters and male party members who are either married or voters. The only triple-counted group is male party members who are both married and voters.

Complete and Orthogonal Functions

An example of orthogonal reports would be D: male party members, and E: female voters, as shown in Table 12.7a. However, this is not a complete set of reports. A complete set would be polls of F: all women, G: male voters, and H: men who are not voters or are not party members, as shown in 12.7b. A complete and

TABLE 12.7 MAP OF POLL REPORTS

Table 12.7a D: male party members, E: female voters

	Male				Female			
	Member		Nonmember		Member		Nonmember	
	Married	Single	Married	Single	Married	Single	Married	Single
Voter	D	D			E	E	E	E
Nonvoter	D	D						

Table 12.7b F: women, G: male voters, H: male nonparty members or nonvoters

	Male				Female			
	Member		Nonmember		Member		Nonmember	
	Married	Single	Married	Single	Married	Single	Married	Single
Voter	G	G	GH	GH	F	F	F	F
Nonvoter	H	H	H	H	F	F	F	F

Table 12.7c I: male voters or singles, J: nonvoters who are women or married, K: women voters

	Male				Female			
	Member		Nonmember		Member		Nonmember	
	Married	Single	Married	Single	Married	Single	Married	Single
Voter	I	I	I	I	K	K	K	K
Nonvoter	J	I	J	I	J	J	J	J

orthogonal set of reports would cover all of the cells in the Karnaugh map with no duplication. For example, as shown in Table 12.7c, the following three reports would be complete and orthogonal. Report I is for men who are either voters or unmarried (or both), report J for the nonvoters who are either women or married (or both), and report K for the women who are voters.

When the state transitions of a state machine are complete and orthogonal, all of the possible next states have been specified and each is unique. This is important for software design because program loops involve state transitions. If such a state machine does not have a complete set of transitions, some possible conditions have not been defined. Similarly, a state machine with state transitions that are not orthogonal means that there is some set of conditions for which more than one next state is possible.

When either of these conditions is encountered, a program is likely to enter into an endless loop, hang up, or do something unexpected.

Verifying That a State Machine Is Proper

By taking the following steps, you can verify that a state machine is proper:

1. Draw the state diagram and check its structure to ensure that it has no hidden traps or loops.
2. Examine the design to ensure that the set of all transitions from each state is complete. That is, there is a defined transition from every state to some next state for every possible combination of conditions.
3. Verify that the set of all transitions from each state is orthogonal and that there is only one next state for every possible combination of state-machine input values and attributes.

Step 1 means that the state machine cannot get stuck in an endless loop and never reach a return state. This could happen if the transitions among a set of states can become circular. For example, if the transitions among a set of states only increased n and the exit from this set of states required that $n = 100$, an endless loop would occur whenever the state machine entered any of these states with $n > 100$.

State-Machine Verification Examples

The procedure for verifying the correctness of a state machine is illustrated with two examples. The first is for the LogIn function designed in Chapter 11 (see pp. 231–240) The second is for the Search state machine, also designed in Chapter 11 (see pp. 242–246), to find the value of x for which $F(x) = N$.

Verifying the LogIn State Machine

The State Specification Template for LogIn is shown in Table 11.7 see p. 238). The state-machine verification procedure is as follows:

1. From checking the state diagram in Figure 11.4 (see p. 237), it is clear that there are no hidden traps or loops. Because the only possible loop is between CheckID and CheckPW and because $n := n+1$ for every cycle, the $n >= nMax$ exit condition means that there will eventually be an exit.

2. The transition conditions from every state can be examined for completeness and orthogonality by examining the state template in Table 11.7 (see p. 238). From Start, the only transition is to CheckID. From CheckID, the three possible transitions are CheckPW {ValidID}, CheckPW {!ValidID}, or End {Timeout}. Although the actions where !ValidID $\land$ Timeout do not appear to be defined, they are logically included in the Timeout case. These transition cases are thus complete and orthogonal.

3. Finally, from CheckPW, the transitions are to CheckID {(!ValidID $\lor$!ValidPW) $\land$ n < nMax $\land$!Timeout)} or to End {(ValidID $\land$ ValidPW) $\lor$ (n >= nMax $\lor$ Timeout)}. Because these cases are too complex to check by inspection, the decision table in Table 12.8 is used to examine all the possibilities.

TABLE 12.8 DECISION TABLE FOR CHECKPW TRANSITION CONDITIONS

n	< nMax				= nMax				> nMax			
Password	Valid		!Valid		Valid		!Valid		Valid		!Valid	
ID	Valid	!Valid	Valid	!Valid	Valid	!Valid	Valid	!Valid	Valid	!Valid	Valid	!Valid
Next State for Each Defined Transition Condition												
A		ID	ID	ID								
B	End				End				End			
C					End	End	End	End	End	End	End	End
Resulting Values of Fail for Each Defined Transition Condition												
A												
B	F				F				F			
C					T	T	T	T	T	T	T	T

In a decision table, the variable combinations are shown in a treelike structure with all of the possible final values shown at the "leaf" end at the bottom. The three transition conditions from CheckPW are as follows:

A: (!ValidID ∨ !ValidPW) ∧ n < nMax ∧ !Timeout → CheckID / n := n + 1

B: ValidID ∧ ValidPW → End / Fail := false and LogIn user

C: n >= nMax ∨ Timeout → End / Fail := true and cut off user

The Timeout cases are not shown because Timeout always transitions to End with Fail = 1. The cases discussed therefore assume !Timeout. For the next states, all cases are defined with no conflicts. For the values of Fail, the undefined cases are left at 0, the initialized value of Fail. In two cases, however, there is a possible conflict. This indicates that the LogIn state machine has a defect because there are two different ways to get to End from CheckPW and they each result in different values of Fail. The case of a valid password with ValidID and n > nMax is impossible, so it can be ignored, but the case of a valid password with ValidID and n = nMax is possible. It could occur from the following sequence: a transition from CheckPW to CheckID where n = nMax -1 followed by a valid ID and a transition back to CheckPW with n = nMax. Then, with a valid password, this conflict condition would arise.

This problem can be fixed by changing transition condition C as follows:

C: (n >= nMax ∨ Timeout) ∧ (!ValidPW ∨ !ValidID) → End / Fail := 1

Note that this problem did not show up in the execution-table check because neither the case of nMax = 2 nor the Timeout cases were checked. In addition, the pseudocode logic stepped the *n* counter to n + 1 before the test for n > nMax. This implementation choice resolved the conflict.

Verifying the Search State Machine

Next, we verify the correctness of a slightly more complex state machine, the Search function designed in Chapter 11. This state machine finds a value of *x* for which F(*x*) = M, where F(*x*) is a monotonically increasing or decreasing function of *x*. Here, the value of M is given by the user, and you are assumed to have a program that generates F(*x*), given *x*. The State Specification Template for Search is shown in Table 11.10 (see p. 245) and the state diagram is in Figure 11.6 (see p. 246). The state-machine verification procedure is as follows:

1. From checking the state diagram in Figure 11.6, it is clear that there are no hidden traps or loops. Although this may not be immediately obvious, the loop where Down transitions to Down with the high condition progressively

reduces the value of F(x). Ultimately, F(x) must drop below M. The same argument holds for the loop where Up transitions to Up. For the loop between Up and Down, the value of F(x) is oscillating from above to below M. Because Delta is reduced for every cycle, however, F(x) must eventually fall within the error range around M.

2. The transition conditions are also complete: Start always goes to DeltaSign, and the transition conditions from DeltaSign, Up, and Down are the same: whether F(x) < Target, F(x) > Target, or F(x) within the Target. Because these are all the possibilities, the transition conditions are complete.

3. Similarly, these transition conditions are orthogonal because they do not overlap.

This test verifies that the Search state machine is proper. If you are not sure of any orthogonality or completeness checks, use a decision table to check all of the possibilities.

12.6   Loop Verification

The PSP Design Review Checklist calls for verifying that all loops are properly initiated, incremented, and terminated (see Table 9.7 on p. 184). Because it is rarely possible to verify loop correctness by merely reading over the design, it is important to follow a defined verification method. The methods described here can be very helpful in verifying the logic of an existing program before modifying or correcting it or when verifying loop logic in a design review or inspection. Mills and Dyer described these methods many years ago, but they still provide useful guidance on determining loop correctness (Dyer 1992; Mills et al. 1987). The methods that are most generally useful are for the for loop, the while loop, and the repeat-until loop.

Even if you do not follow a rigorous loop-verification process every time you use these methods, they can still be helpful. For example, in a quick review, consider the proof questions when you review a loop's design. Just thinking about these questions will help you to identify problems that you might otherwise miss.

For-Loop Verification

Before doing the for-loop verification, identify the for-loop preconditions and verify that these preconditions are always met. The for-loop verification is as follows:

Does ForLoop = FirstPart + SecondPart + . . . + LastPart?

272 Chapter 12 Design Verification

Here, ForLoop is assumed to have the following form:

```
ForLoop
        for n = First to Last
                begin
                nPart
        end
```

where nPart takes the values FirstPart, SecondPart, ThirdPart, and so on through LastPart. If you laid out the execution of this program through all the loops, it would be as follows:

```
ForLoop
begin
        FirstPart
        SecondPart
        ThirdPart
. . .      . . . . .
        LastPart
end
```

Although this test may seem obvious, the actual verification is not trivial. To verify the equality, either construct a trace table or analyze the logic for each side of the equation and show that they always produce identical results. In this case, you would determine the results produced by ForLoop and then determine the results produced by FirstPart + SecondPart + … + LastPart. If the two results are identical, the for-loop logic is verified.

While-Loop Verification

Before doing the while-loop verification, identify the while-loop preconditions and verify that they are always met. This while loop is in the following form:

```
WhileLoop
        begin
                while WhileTest
                        LoopPart
        end
```

In this loop, the WhileTest is performed first; if it fails, the LoopPart is not performed. The while-loop verification involves answering the following questions:

☐ Is loop termination guaranteed for any argument of WhileTest?

☐ When WhileTest is true, does WhileLoop = LoopPart followed by WhileLoop?

☐ When WhileTest is false, does WhileLoop = identity?

The first question is crucial: Is loop termination guaranteed for any argument of WhileTest? If loop termination is not guaranteed, this logic could possibly cause an endless loop, which is obviously to be avoided. Proving that this condition is either true or false can sometimes be difficult, but it can be demonstrated by identifying every possible case and either using a trace table or carefully examining the logic to prove that it is true. Although you will often be able to verify this condition by inspection, it is essential to consider every possible case.

The second question is somewhat trickier. To determine whether the WhileTest is true, you must find out if the function WhileLoop is identical to a function that consists of LoopPart followed by WhileLoop. If this is not true, then WhileLoop has a defect. To understand why this is true, consult the Mills or Dyer references (Mills et al. 1987; Dyer 1992). As before, you can answer the second question by constructing a trace table or studying the logic for the WhileLoop and the logic for LoopPart followed by WhileLoop and showing that they produce identical results for all cases.

The final question asks whether, when WhileTest is false, the logic continues through WhileLoop with no changes. If it does not, there is a defect. Again, this case can often be verified by inspection.

Example of While-Loop Verification
This next example illustrates the general loop-verification approach with the following pseudocode logic for a while loop:

```
NormalizeReal(Mant, Exp, NegEx)
1        while Mant > 10 do
2                Mant = Mant/10
3                if NegEx then Exp = Exp – 1
4                else Exp = Exp + 1
5        while Mant < 1 do
6                Mant = Mant*10
7                if NegEx then Exp = Exp + 1
8                else Exp = Exp – 1
```

This logic reduces a nonzero real number in the form *Mantissa*$*10^{Exponent}$ to a standard form in which the Mantissa has a single nonzero digit before the decimal point. In this problem, Mant = abs(Mantissa) and Exp = abs(Exponent). Thus, Exp is a nonnegative integer and Mant is a positive real number. Two Boolean variables, NegMant and NegEx, indicate whether the Mantissa and/or the Exponent are negative. It is assumed that the values of these numbers are within the range of the number systems for the compiler and language being used.

To verify this logic, verify both while loops. Both loops are examined for question 1, but only the first loop is used to illustrate questions 2 and 3. First examine the while tests to determine whether they terminate. The cases to examine are for Mant >10, Mant < 1, and 1 <= Mant <= 10. The first case is Mant > 10. Here, when Mant > 10, the first loop is executed and successive divisions by 10 ultimately reduce Mant to less than 10. The while test is therefore not satisfied and the first while loop terminates. Now, Mant is less than 10 and greater than 1, so the second while loop will not be invoked and the loop will terminate.

The second case is Mant < 1. The first while loop is skipped and the second is invoked. Now Mant is progressively multiplied by 10 until its absolute value exceeds 1 and the second while test fails. This also terminates the loop.

Even though these two while loops terminate in these cases, this examination raises the question of what happens when Mant = 10 or Mant = 1. In the first case, both loops fail with the incorrect result of Mant = 10. The program thus has a defect, and line 1 should be changed as follows:

```
NormalizeReal(Mant, Exp, NegEx)
1       while Mant >= 10 do
2               Mant = Mant/10
3               if NegEx then Exp = Exp - 1
4               else Exp = Exp + 1
5       while Mant < 1 do
6               Mant = Mant*10
7               if NegEx then Exp = Exp + 1
8               else Exp = Exp - 1
```

When Mant = 1, both loops are skipped and the number is unchanged. Because it is already in the correct form, this is the correct result. Both while loops in this procedure now satisfy question 1 of the while-loop verification proof. The second question is, when WhileTest is true, does WhileLoop = LoopPart followed by WhileLoop?

To answer this question, you must examine all cases of WhileTest and WhileLoop. To invoke the first while loop, the cases must all have Mant >= 10.

Because Mant must be a nonnegative number, this then involves only two conditions as follows:

1. Mant >= 10, NegExp

2. Mant >= 10, ! NegExp

For the first case, the test consists of substituting the Mant and NegExp values into the program to determine whether WhileLoop equals LoopPart followed by WhileLoop. For the first case, the WhileLoop side of the equality is as follows:

```
1        while Mant >= 10 do
2                Mant = Mant/10
3                if NegEx then Exp = Exp - 1
4                else Exp = Exp + 1
```

For the test of whether LoopPart followed by WhileLoop produces the same result, we have the following pseudocode:

```
2                Mant = Mant/10
3                if NegEx then Exp = Exp - 1
4                else Exp = Exp + 1
5        while Mant >= 10 do
6                Mant = Mant/10
7                if NegEx then Exp = Exp - 1
8                else Exp = Exp + 1
```

This equality can be easily demonstrated either with a trace table or by carefully working through the loop logic. The first part of this equality in the top table cycles through the while test until the value of Mant is less than 10. If it started with Mant >= 10 and less than 100, for example, there would be one cycle of the while loop and the final result would be Mant/10 and Exp - 1. Mant is now equal to or greater than 1 and less than 10.

Under these same conditions, with Mant between 10 and 100, the second part of the equality would take one pass through LoopPart in steps 2 through 4, leaving the result of Mant/10 and Exp - 1. In this case, the while test fails and steps 5 through 8 are not executed. In the general case, the while loop in the second part of the equality would be performed one less time than the first while loop, leaving the identical result. The equality is thus true.

The second verification case is identical, except with !NegExp. Here, the results are also identical, except that the resulting Exp values are increased to Exp + 1 when Mant starts between 10 and 100.

The cases for the second while loop, with Mant < 1, are handled the same way, so their verification is not repeated.

The third question for the while test is, when WhileTest is false, does WhileLoop = identity? This condition can be demonstrated by inspection. The first while loop is as follows:

```
1      while Mant >= 10 do
2              Mant = Mant/10
3              if NegEx then Exp = Exp - 1
4              else Exp = Exp + 1
```

Here, when Mant < 10, the entire loop is skipped and step 5 is next executed. This means that nothing is changed, and this logic is equivalent to identity. This same reasoning can be used with the second while loop. The program with the change made to correct the defect when Mant = 10 thus passes these tests and is correct.

Repeat-Until Verification

The repeat-until verification is similar to that for the while test. Before doing the repeat-until verification, identify the repeat-until preconditions and verify that they are always met. These tests assume repeat-until has the following form:

```
RepeatUntil
        begin
                LoopPart
                UntilTest
        end
```

In the repeat-until loop, the until test is performed after the LoopPart, so the LoopPart is always executed at least once, regardless of the initial conditions. The repeat-until verification questions are as follows:

1. Is loop termination guaranteed for any argument of UntilTest?

2. When UntilTest after LoopPart is false, does RepeatUntil = LoopPart followed by RepeatUntil?

3. When UntilTest after LoopPart is true, does RepeatUntil = LoopPart?

As before, answer the second question by constructing a trace table or studying the logic for RepeatUntil and the logic for LoopPart followed by RepeatUntil. The third question can be similarly answered with the aid of a trace table if needed.

12.7   Other Analytical Verification Methods

In addition to compilation and testing, both manual and automated verification methods can be helpful. Some of these methods provide more general proofs than are possible with test cases or other single-case verification practices. Analytical verification methods are particularly useful for verifying the logic of an existing program before modifying or correcting it or when verifying the logic of new programs.

Because analytical verification methods generally require some training and considerable practice, this section provides only an overview of the key topics to consider in using analytical verification. It also describes a few of the currently available automated verification methods. As previously noted, however, new methods will almost certainly be developed, so you should watch the technical literature and use your PSP data to determine which methods are most effective for you.

Analytical Verification Issues

The key issues to consider in selecting an analytical verification method concern the usefulness and effectiveness of the method. In addition, because various vendors offer tools for automated verification, it is important to consider how effective these tools are and the degree to which they can help you to economically and quickly produce quality products. In discussing verification methods, the following terms are commonly used:

□ **Soundness:** Does the verification provide misleading results? That is, can it indicate that the program is free of a defect category when it is not?

□ **Completeness:** Does the verification method find 100% of the defects of a given category or only as many as it can? An incomplete method can be "honest" and indicate areas of doubt or incompleteness or it can be silent. The "false-alarm" rate is also critical, as excessive false alarms can waste development effort.

□ **Depth:** A deep analysis covers such complex topics as buffer overflow, while a shallow analysis might address coding standards and formats. Deep analyses are rarely complete.

□ **Efficiency:** Efficiency concerns the time required for the analysis and the degree of human assistance required.

□ **Constructive or retrospective:** A constructive analysis can be run on partially completed products, whereas a retrospective analysis can be used only with finished products.

□ **Language level:** The language level concerns the types of products that can be verified. Examples would be the specification level, the design level, or the source-code level.

□ **Domain-specific or general-purpose:** Does the method work only for selected application domains or is it of more general use?

Automated Verification

Although automated verification methods can be very helpful, they can also be dangerous. The problem is not with the tools but with how they are used. For example, many programmers assume that their compiler will find all of their simple coding mistakes. Although good compilers will identify all of the cases in which the programmer produced incorrect syntax, they will miss those cases where the programmer made a mistake that accidentally produced valid syntax but incorrect logic.

A principal reason why many verification tools find such a low percentage of the logic defects is that the programs they analyze are written in imprecise languages such as C, C++, and Ada. Moreover, these tools often have no way to determine what the programmer intended to do. When programs use a precisely defined language and when the programmers precisely describe their intentions in program annotations, tools can often find 95% or more of many defect types (Barnes 2003). Programming with these methods is generally called **design-by-contract**.

PSP data show that with traditional languages, compilers generally miss about 10% of the typographical or simple coding mistakes we make. The problem is that when a tool provides around 90% or higher completeness, it is easy for programmers to fall into the habit of believing that it has found 100% of their mistakes, and not bother trying to find the rest.

Suppose you had a tool that would reliably find only 10% of all of your logical design mistakes. How would you use it? One possible strategy would be to use the tool first in hopes of fixing as many problems as you could before doing personal reviews or inspections. However, this would not reduce your workload by much and you would get limited benefit from the tool. A counterstrategy would be to do your personal reviews and possibly even your inspections before running the tool. Then, when you ran the tool, you would have a way to measure the quality of your reviews and inspections. If, for example, the tool didn't find any defects, you probably found most of them yourself. Conversely, if the tool identified 11 defects, you could assume that you probably missed over 100 defects and that you had better make a more concerted effort to clean up the program before putting it into testing.

Although this should not be an emotional issue, it often is. Many programmers who have not completed PSP training become upset when I suggest that they review their programs before compiling them. They would presumably have the same reaction to reviewing their designs before using an automated tool to find buffer overflows, for example. However, the available evidence indicates that with commonly used languages and methods, automated tools for finding complex defects such as buffer overflows are rarely more than about 25% complete.

The danger is not with tools that are 25% complete, as most developers quickly learn that they can't trust them. The problem is with tools that are 90% or 99% or even 99.9% complete. Now the key question is, how important is it to produce a defect-free product? If it is a life-or-death matter, you must do the review first and use the tool to provide the information needed to evaluate the quality of your work. Then you can logically decide on the proper quality-management steps.

To rationally make such decisions, you need the following information:

□ How sound, complete, and efficient is the tool?

□ How does the completeness and efficiency of the tool change when run before or after your personal reviews and inspections?

□ How do the completeness (yield) and cost of your reviews and inspections change when they are run before or after the tool?

□ What is the variability of these data? That is, does your personal yield or the tool's completeness vary widely or is it reasonably consistent?

□ What is the expected cost of missed defects?

After they examine their PSP data, most developers conclude that doing careful reviews before compiling or testing their programs pays off in saved time and improved program quality. Although I suspect that would also be true for any verification tool that was less than 100% complete, the only way to know is to run experiments, gather data, and make a rational fact-based decision.

Verification Methods

Considerable work has been done on automatic verification methods. This section describes some of these methods. The following is only a limited listing of the available materials.

ASTREE

The ASTREE static analysis tool was developed in 2001 and has been used on several high-dependability programs with considerable success. It uses abstract interpretation to identify possible runtime errors (Blanchet et al. 2003).

Microsoft

Microsoft has produced a number of tools both for internal use and for general availability (Larus et al. 2004). Early examples are the PREfix and PREfast tools that perform various types of static analysis. PREfix has been used on the Windows products with considerable success. PREfast performs local analysis on C and C++ programs, with a principal focus on programming mistakes. More recent Microsoft verification tools include SLAM, ESP, and Vault.

SPARK

The SPARK language and Examiner tool statically analyze programs written in the SPARK language (Barnes 2003). This approach restricts the programmer to a clearly defined and unambiguous Ada subset (the SPARK language) and then utilizes programmer-written annotations to analyze and prove program correctness.

Splint

The Splint tool performs static checking of C programs for security vulnerabilities and coding mistakes. It was produced by the Computer Science Department at the University of Virginia (Yang and Evans 2004).

Because the effectiveness of automated design verification and other formal methods depends on the clarity and precision of the design description, developers using these techniques often use a formal notation based on mathematical methods to document their designs. One widely used formal notation is Z (pronounced "zed"), for which many support tools are available (Jacky 1996). As the safety and security problems with software developed with current methods increase, more formal methods will have to be adopted. If you are serious about producing truly high-quality programs, you should become familiar with such methods.

12.8   Verification Considerations

When designing complex logic, just about everybody makes mistakes. Therefore, it is important to thoroughly verify every design; and the more complex the design, the more important it is to use proven and practiced verification methods. This, in turn, suggests that you identify and consistently use a family of verification techniques. To build verification skill, use these methods even when you write small programs. If you don't use these methods with small programs, you will not have the skill, experience, and conviction to use them when you are verifying larger programs.

Verification Strategy

For small programs like the examples in this chapter, the pseudocode logic will look like code, but more complex programs will generally have several classes and methods. You can merely name these classes and methods in the trace table, but a complete design must specify the detailed logic for every one of the main program's loop constructs. In producing the trace table, enter every program pseudocode instruction, but just name the classes and methods. If you know the behavior of these higher-level constructs, you can treat them as single trace-table steps. In the trace-table analysis, just enter the result from each class or method without tracing through its execution. This suggests a general verification strategy: design down and verify up. That is, when designing each routine, specify the functions to be provided by each class and method. Then start the design review process at the bottom and verify each class or method before verifying the high-level routines that use them. That way, you can be confident that each class or method works properly when you encounter it in a higher-level verification.

The best time to use the design verification and analysis methods described in this chapter is while you are producing the design. While doing the analysis work, make a permanent record of the results and keep this record with the program's design documentation. Then, when you do the design review, follow the Design Review Script shown in Table 12.9 and the Design Review Checklist shown in Table 12.10 to check what you did during the design work. Ensure that the design analysis covered all of the design, was updated for any subsequent design changes, is correct, and is clear and complete. If you did not complete any of the analyses, complete and document them during the design review. Note that these design review script and checklist tables are different from the PSP2 versions shown in Chapter 9 because these include use of the verification methods described in this chapter. Use this script and checklist hereafter in verifying your designs.

Verification Practice

Verification methods take time, and as programs get larger and more complex, the verification methods get more complex and take even more time. Thus, as the need for these methods increases, they become progressively harder to use. Although there is no simple solution to this problem, the key is to learn which verification methods work best for you and then to use these methods on every program you develop. If you do this consistently, your large programs will be composed of multiple small programs that you have already verified. The verification problems will then be reduced to ensuring that the small programs were properly combined. Although this might not be a trivial check, it is far simpler than checking the details of every small program.

TABLE 12.9 DESIGN REVIEW SCRIPT

Purpose	To guide you in reviewing detailed designs	
Entry Criteria	• Completed program design **documented with the PSP Design templates** • Design Review checklist • Design standard • Defect Type standard • Time and Defect Recording logs	
General	Where the design was previously verified, check that the analyses • covered all of the design and were updated for all design changes • are correct, clear, and complete Where the design is not available or was not reviewed, do a complete design review on the code and fix all defects before doing the code review.	

Step	Activities	Description
1	Preparation	• Examine the program and checklist and decide on a review strategy. • **Examine the program to identify its state machines, internal loops, and variable and system limits.** • **Use a trace table or other analytical method to verify the correctness of the design.**
2	Review	• Follow the Design Review checklist. • Review the entire program for each checklist category; do not try to review for more than one category at a time! • Check off each item as you complete it. • Complete a separate checklist for each product or product segment reviewed.
3	Fix Check	• Check each defect fix for correctness. • Re-review all changes. • Record any fix defects as new defects and, where you know the defective defect number, enter it in the fix defect space.
Exit Criteria		• A fully reviewed detailed design • One or more Design Review checklists for every design reviewed • **Documented design analysis results** • All identified defects fixed and all fixes checked • Completed Time and Defect Recording logs

In practicing verification methods, track your time and the defects you find and miss and use these data to improve your verification practices. Try whatever methods seem potentially most useful, but be guided by your data. After you have tried several methods and used them enough to build reasonable competence, your data should indicate the methods that work best for you.

TABLE 12.10 DESIGN REVIEW CHECKLIST

Student	_____	Date	_____
Program	_____	Program #	_____
Instructor	_____	Language	_____

Purpose	To guide you in conducting an effective design review
General	• Review the entire program for each checklist category; do not attempt to review for more than one category at a time! • As you complete each review step, check off that item in the box at the right. • Complete the checklist for one program or program unit before reviewing the next.

Complete	Verify that the design covers all of the applicable requirements. • All specified outputs are produced. • All needed inputs are furnished. • All required includes are stated.				
External Limits	Where the design assumes or relies upon external limits, determine if behavior is correct at nominal values, at limits, and beyond limits				

Logic	*Use a trace table, mathematical proof, or similar method to verify the logic.*
	• Verify that program sequencing is proper.
	  • Stacks, lists, and so on are in the proper order.
	  • Recursion unwinds properly.
	• Verify that all loops are properly initiated, incremented, and terminated.
	• Examine each conditional statement and verify all cases.				

State Analysis	*For each state machine, verify that the state transitions are all complete and orthogonal.*				
Internal Limits	Where the design assumes or relies upon internal limits, determine if behavior is correct at nominal values, at limits, and beyond limits.				
Special Cases	• Check all special cases. • Ensure proper operation with empty, full, minimum, maximum, negative, zero values for all variables. • Protect against out-of-limits, overflow, underflow conditions. • Ensure that "impossible" conditions are absolutely impossible. • Handle all possible incorrect or error conditions.				
Functional Use	• Verify that all functions, procedures, or methods are fully understood and properly used. • Verify that all externally referenced abstractions are precisely defined.				
System Considerations	• Verify that the program does not cause system limits to be exceeded. • Verify that all security-sensitive data are from trusted sources. • Verify that all safety conditions conform to the safety specifications.				
Names	Verify that • all special names are clear, defined, and authenticated • the scopes of all variables and parameters are self-evident or defined • all named items are used within their declared scopes				
Standards	Ensure that the design conforms to all applicable design standards.				

12.9   Summary

The objective of design verification is to determine whether a design meets its requirements and is correct. This means that the program's specifications and standards are an important part of the verification process. The standards of concern are product conventions, product design standards, and reuse standards.

There are many ways to determine the correctness of a design before you implement it. The methods described in this chapter are trace-table checking, state-machine analysis, and analytical verification. You can use various combinations of these methods on most programs and they are both relatively fast and effective. Using these methods saves time because when your designs are complete, clear, and correct, the implementation will be faster and the finished program will have few (if any) design defects.

Although trace-table verification can be time-consuming, it is much faster and more effective than verifying all possible cases with testing. Because most of the work for a trace-table analysis must be done to properly use a debugger, it is faster and more efficient to use that analysis effort to verify the program's correctness with a trace table. With a completed trace table, it is then relatively easy to run any needed tests.

When a product includes a state machine, verify that the state machine is properly designed and consistently used. The conditions for a proper state machine are twofold: all state transitions should be complete and orthogonal and the machine must be able to reach a program return state from every other state.

Verifying design correctness is simple in concept, but it takes time to build sufficient skill to do it quickly and efficiently. To build this skill, use these verification methods on every program you develop and measure and track your work to determine the verification methods that are most effective for you. Then use these data to regularly analyze and improve your design-verification skills.

12.10   Exercises

The assignment for this chapter is to use PSP2.1 to write one or more programs. For these programs, use the PSP design templates and the state-machine and trace-table verification methods. The PSP2.1 process and the program specifications are given in the assignment kits, which you can get from your instructor or at **www.sei.cmu.edu/tsp/**. The kits contain the assignment specifications, example calculations, and the PSP2.1 process scripts. In completing the assignment, faithfully follow the PSP2.1 process, record all required data, and produce the program report according to the specifications given in the assignment kits.

References

Barnes, J. *High Integrity Software: The SPARK Approach to Safety and Security.* Reading, MA: Addison-Wesley, 2003.

Blanchet, B., P. Cousot, R. Cousot, J. Feret, L. Mauborgne, A. Mine, D. Monniaux, and X. Rival. "A Static Analyzer for Large Safety-Critical Software." In *PLDI 2003—ACM SIG-PLAN SITSOFT Conference on Programming Language Design and Implementation,* 2003 Federated Computing Research Conference, San Diego, Calif., June 7–14, 2003, 196–207.

Butler, R. W., and G. B. Finelli. "The Infeasibility of Quantifying the Reliability of Life-Critical Real-Time Software." *IEEE Transactions on Software Engineering* 19, no. 1, January 1993.

Dyer, M. *The Cleanroom Approach to Quality Software Development.* New York: John Wiley & Sons, 1992.

Gage, D., and J. McCormick, "Can Software Kill?" *eWeek Enterprise News and Reviews,* March 8, 2004. www.eweek.com.

Jacky, J. *The Way of Z: Practical Programming with Formal Methods.* Cambridge, UK: Cambridge University Press, 1996.

Larus, J. R., T. Ball, M. Das, R. DeLine, M. Pahndrich, J. Pincus, S. K. Rajamani, and R. Venkatapathy. "Righting Software." *IEEE Software* (May/June 2004): 92–100.

Littlewood, B., and L. Strigini. "Validation of Ultrahigh Dependability for Software-Based Systems." *Communications of the ACM* 36, no. 11, November 1993.

Mills, H. D., V. R. Basili, J. D. Gannon, and R. G. Hamlet. *Principles of Computer Programming: A Mathematical Approach.* Newton, MA: Allyn and Bacon, 1987.

Yang, J., and D. Evans. "Dynamically Inferring Temporal Properties." *ACM SIGPLAN-SIGSOFT Workshop on Program Analysis for Software Tools and Engineering (PASTE 2004),* June 7–8, 2004.

13

Process Extensions

As developers gain experience, they usually develop a practiced and comfortable personal working style. Although this is normal, it can cause problems. The trouble is that the best style for a particular job depends on many factors that are more important than your personal preferences. The kind of application being developed, the tools used, and the practices of the other team members can all affect the best way to do a job. One factor that should have great impact on a developer's programming style is the scale of the product being developed. Methods that work well for small jobs are often inadequate for larger ones.

Although the practices that work reasonably well for small programs are often not appropriate for large programs, many of the practices that are effective for large programming jobs are equally effective for small ones. Examples are personal quality management, planning, and data gathering. As the scale of a project increases, additional practices are needed. Examples are team inspections, team planning, and team coordination. These practices are needed as soon as you switch from working alone to working with a team. These process changes are dictated by the need to do cooperative work instead of working alone.

Although some level of design coordination is usually helpful on small team projects, small-scale design problems are generally fairly simple, and rudimentary design practices are often adequate. The problem is that design work takes time, and when experienced developers write small programs, they often find that the time required to produce a documented design is largely wasted. These designs are generally small and simple enough for one person to completely understand. That is why, for example, many software developers spend very little time producing designs and much more time writing code. Because they intuitively understand the design, the first time they document the design is during the coding. However, by not using well-practiced and sound design methods when developing small programs, developers often have design problems when they work on large-scale systems.

Because we all learned to program by writing small programs, the practices we learned as students often stick with us, even when they are no longer appropriate. To appreciate the problem, consider Figure 13.1. Here, the code-intensive developers spent relatively little time in design. For every hour of coding time, they spent less than 15 minutes in design work. Conversely, the design-intensive developers spent at least as much time in design as in coding. As shown in the figure, on average, the designers took longer than the coders to develop the PSP exercise programs.

However, this is not the entire story. One of the most important lessons of the PSP is that a little time properly invested early in the process can save a great deal of time later. Code reviews are one example. Even though reviews take time, that time is generally made up almost immediately by reduced compiling and testing time. The much greater later savings in system testing and use are an added bonus. For design, the long-term savings are not as clear. One indication of the benefits of design work is shown in Figure 13.2: the designers generally produced smaller

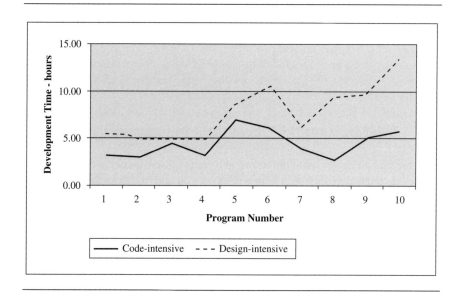

FIGURE 13.1 DEVELOPMENT TIME VERSUS DESIGN TIME (810 DEVELOPERS)

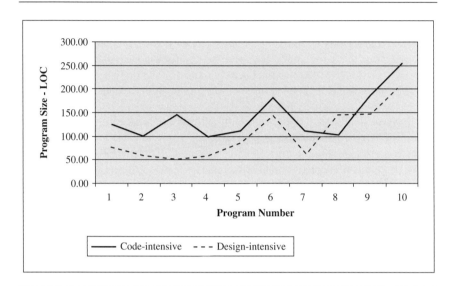

FIGURE 13.2 PROGRAM SIZE WITH AND WITHOUT DESIGN
(810 DEVELOPERS)

programs than the coders. Although design work pays, the fact that it doesn't pay off right away makes it much more difficult for developers to take the time to produce sound and precise designs. The PSP has you produce designs not because you need them for the class exercises but because you need to practice sound design methods with small programs if you are ever to use them with large programs.

13.1   Customizing the Development Process

There are many ways to write programs, and some are more effective than others. The key is to use a process that both works for you and produces the desired results. Because every process has advantages and disadvantages, you should use different processes for different situations. When you write programs in only one way, you cannot be uniformly effective with all of your work. For example, in developing applications for secure environments, you must produce designs, regardless of how long it takes. Security is a design issue and it is almost impossible to find security flaws by searching through source code. If, as with the PSP exercises, the problems are so simple that a design is not usually needed to write the code, development time will generally be less when you just bang out code. Conversely, when security or safety is important, when small program size is critical, or when you are developing large or complex systems, a design is needed, regardless of how long it takes. Therefore, you need at least two defined and practiced personal processes: one that works when you need to produce a design and another one for when you do not.

The principal challenge addressed by this chapter is how to change your processes as you work on progressively larger and more complex systems. Although there is no general answer, a well-defined and practiced personal process will enable you to answer these questions for yourself. This chapter discusses some of the principles and strategies for dealing with these process development issues, both when developing new processes and when enhancing existing ones. Starting with a discussion of the PSP process strategy, the chapter covers process development concepts and a suggested way to define personal and team processes. At the end, the chapter describes four example processes.

13.2   Why Define a Process?

There are two reasons to define a process. First, you need a process to provide the data and the framework for planning, tracking, and managing your work. Second, you need a process to guide the work while you are doing it.

To appreciate the importance of the first reason, consider the six PSP principles discussed in Chapter 8 (see p. 157). They explain why a defined process is essential for doing quality work and for planning, tracking, and managing that work. Without a defined process, you can't specify or interpret the measures needed for planning and managing the work. Once you agree with the need for a defined process, you next need to identify the processes required for both your work and that of your team. To do this, consider your personal preferences, the type of work to be done, and the working environment. In addition, because most of us work with rapidly changing technology, consider the kinds of work you expect to do in the future.

The sizes of the software products that you develop in the future will probably be much larger than those you develop today. The software in even simple products will soon be larger than individuals can intuitively master. Although individual developers will still develop software components, their work will increasingly involve large teams, and even groups of teams. A process that was optimum for your last project will probably not be the optimum one to use for a job that is five to ten times larger. As the sizes of the products you develop increase, your process should scale up as well. Although you should not use a more sophisticated process than you need, you should tailor your personal and team processes to fit your current project.

Processes are useful for guiding such personal activities as writing the PSP exercise programs in this book, and they are even more helpful for larger projects and for working on development teams. Just as in sports, development teams are most effective when all of the team members have common goals and they all understand and agree on the strategy, plan, and process for doing the work.

13.3 The PSP Process Strategy

Because software development is intellectual work and because our skills and abilities are dynamic and varied, there is no canned process that everyone will find convenient and usable. This is particularly important for complex system design. Such creative work would be seriously inhibited by an inconvenient or annoying process. The objective, therefore, is for development teams to define their own processes and to change these processes whenever they see better ways to do the work.

Conversely, it would be difficult, if not impossible, for anyone to define a usable personal process before they had actually used one. That is why this book begins by having you use the predefined PSP processes. Then, after you have used these processes and seen how they work, you will be better able to define processes for yourself and your team.

Once you have used the PSP to develop several small programs, you will want to expand and adapt it to meet your project's needs. For example, if you plan to develop a large system, you may decide that these PSP processes are not adequate and want to adapt the PSP to your particular environment. You could even develop a new process to perform totally different tasks such as writing reports, building databases, conducting tests, developing requirements, or redeveloping existing programs. Although there is no cookbook method that fits all process development situations, this chapter provides some process definition guidelines and some customized processes to guide you in your own process development work.

13.4 Defining a Process

So far in this book, you have used processes without worrying about where they came from, but processes must be developed. Even for a simple PSP process, this development can take a fair amount of work. Although process definition is relatively straightforward, a structured process-definition process can help you to do process development work properly and to be more productive.

Process Elements

A personal process contains the following items:

- ☐ Scripts that describe how the process is enacted and that refer you to pertinent standards, forms, guidelines, and measures.

- ☐ Forms that provide a convenient and consistent framework for gathering and retaining data. These forms specify the data required and where to record them. When the process is supported by the development environment, the forms will generally be included in the tool.

- ☐ Standards that guide your work and provide a basis for verifying product and process quality. The PSP provides example coding and defect type standards as well as design review and code review checklists. Although these are adequate for the example programs in this book, enhance them or develop new ones to fit your particular needs.

- ☐ Process improvement. The Process Improvement Proposal (PIP) is a process defect-reporting procedure. It is part of the process improvement process. Include a similar procedure in every process that you develop. A multiperson process should also include means for receiving, evaluating, and responding to PIPs as well as a periodic procedure for assessing and updating the process.

With the TSP, the process that you and your team use belongs to you. You and your teammates should work together to change it to best fit your evolving needs.

Process Definition

Define a software process in much the way that you develop software products: start with the users' needs and end with final testing and release. For a personal process, the normal negotiation and support activities of most software projects are unnecessary. Therefore, the steps for defining a personal process are as follows:

- ☐ Determine your needs and priorities.
- ☐ Define the process objectives, goals, and quality criteria.
- ☐ Characterize your current process.
- ☐ Characterize your target process.
- ☐ Establish a process development strategy.
- ☐ Define your initial process.
- ☐ Validate your initial process.
- ☐ Enhance your process.

Although these steps are listed in a specific order, they need not be done in that order. It is likely, for example, that the needs and goals steps will affect each other, as will many of the other steps. Do them in whatever order is most appropriate for your situation; just make sure that you address all of the steps.

Determining Process Needs and Goals

The purpose of a software development process is to produce software products. These products must, in turn, satisfy users' needs. Hence, a process definition should consider both the product and the process objectives. To do a complete job of addressing these needs, however, you should follow an orderly procedure. TSP teams start with a launch process that walks them through such a procedure for defining their processes, so this chapter focuses on defining a personal process. The process-definition principles are the same for both cases, however, so this discussion will also provide useful background for defining team processes. The TSP launch is described in Chapter 14.

For a personal process, the objective is to identify the improvements and enhancements that will help you to do better work. If you already know the changes you want to make, list them, and then make a plan for the work. If you merely know that you'd like to make some changes but don't know which ones to make or how to make them, start by using the process you already have and fill out a PIP form whenever you find something you'd like to change. For any process, the principal items to define are as follows:

- ☐ The process purpose or objective
- ☐ Entry criteria
- ☐ Any general guidelines, usage considerations, or constraints
- ☐ The process steps
- ☐ Process measures
- ☐ Quality criteria
- ☐ Exit conditions

Before defining any process, you must know the purpose of the process, how it is to be used, and the entry criteria. You should also know the exit criteria and understand the quality objectives and measures. After you have defined these items, you are ready to start the process-definition work.

13.5   Process Evolution

It is practically impossible to produce a usable process the first time you try. The problem is that the work of defining a process changes that process. This concept is best explained by considering the five processes shown in Figure 13.3. The perceived process is what you think you do. If you have not defined your process, you will have an idealized perception of it. In any complex activity, we often know what we should do. In doing it, however, we usually encounter complications. You may be rushed and skip a review, or you may defer a design update. If someone were to ask you what you did, you would probably not mention all of these "exceptions."

The perceived process is what you would like to believe you do, whereas the actual process is what you really do, with all its omissions, mistakes, and oversights. The official process is what you are supposed to do. That process may be out-of-date or totally impractical, but it is what management would describe as your process. The target process is your objective—the ideal that you would like to reach.

When you first define your process, the objective should be an initial process that both represents reality and moves you in the direction of your target process. Generally, the initial process will be fairly close to your perceived process, but when you try to use this process, the shortcuts and omissions will stand out. This realization will change what you do. You will recognize areas that lack discipline and resolve to do better the next time. When you adjust the first definition, you will again define what you should do, rather than what you actually do. After repeating this cycle several times, your process and your actions should converge on a realistic initial process.

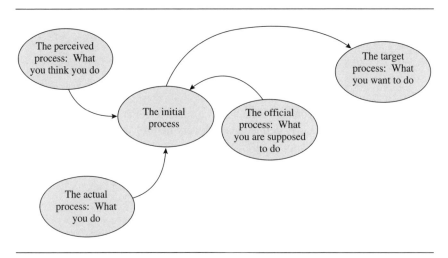

FIGURE 13.3 THE FIVE PROCESSES

Although the initial process will not likely be the same as either the original perceived or actual processes, it should be a more disciplined and stable starting point. This is one reason why defined processes are of higher quality than undefined ones. The act of defining them makes the oversights and omissions more obvious. This increases process fidelity and improves performance. The principal reason why our processes are so poor is that we often don't do what we know we should do.

Your personal process cannot usefully evolve until it reasonably represents what you actually do. When it does, you can measure your performance, identify areas for improvement, and make useful process changes. When your actual, official, and perceived processes converge on your initial process, your process improvement efforts will be most successful.

Characterizing the Current Process

"If you don't know where you are, a map won't help" (Humphrey 1989). To improve human-intensive processes, we must understand how these processes currently work. Although the PSP provides a baseline for software work, you need a picture of where you are and where you intend to go before you can establish a plan to get there.

In general, process-improvement efforts are most successful when they reflect small incremental enhancements, rather than a few large changes. Hence, you should not attempt to completely define a new process. If the task that the process is to implement is one that you currently perform, start with a simple definition of your current work and ask the following questions about it:

- ☐ How well do you understand the current process? Can you describe its principal steps, how they relate, and the time spent on each?

- ☐ What problems do you have with the current process? Make a list and determine their relative priorities.

- ☐ Do the steps in the current process have explicit entry and exit criteria? Make these as specific as you can. If they are unstated or general, the process measurements will be poorly defined and not very helpful.

- ☐ Is the current process planned and tracked? If you do not now consistently plan and track your work, this should be your first improvement priority.

- ☐ Is your current process sufficiently well measured to permit quantitative improvement? After introducing planning and defining entry and exit criteria, incorporate time and quality measures into the current process.

- ☐ Do you have a current process baseline? For the PSP, you now have productivity, quality, and planning data. These can provide a starting point for your process-improvement planning.

Even if you do not have historical data, you can often find some useful measures. You can generally estimate past performance by reconstructing the dates for prior jobs and measuring the sizes of the products produced. Such rough numbers will not be very accurate, but they will provide a crude baseline. Although these approximations are a poor substitute for precise data, they are better than nothing.

Characterizing the Target Process

"If you don't know where you're going, any road will do" (Humphrey 1989). The target process is the ideal. It is the goal you seek to reach. The reason to characterize the target process is to set improvement priorities. You can then relate the process goals and objectives to this target. If minimum cycle time is the highest priority, for example, you might establish parallel process activities, even at additional cost. To minimize late requirements changes, define early steps to validate the requirements, as well as a rigorous change-management procedure.

Next, postulate the target process structure and establish measurable criteria for the major process elements. At the outset, establish only general criteria. An example might be fully defining the target process, including that it predictably produce quality products, and that every process phase be characterized and measured. When some of these measurements are available for your current process, they will help you to decide on an improvement strategy, set achievable goals, and track against these goals.

Don't be too concerned if you have trouble defining a target process. You are likely to find that the only way to learn how to define a process is to define it. Start by examining other processes or copy what I did for the PSP. When you have defined an initial process, use it, measure it, and analyze its behavior. Then you will have the data and experience to make further improvements. Once you have defined the target process, ask the following questions about it:

- □ Which steps are new and which do you currently perform?
- □ Which steps do you understand and which are ill-defined?
- □ Which steps will you frequently repeat and which will be single shot?
- □ Which steps will consume the most time?
- □ Where do you expect the most problems?

Use the answers to guide your process-improvement priorities.

The Process Development Strategy

Now that you know where you are and where you want to go, establish the route. Even simple processes have many steps, and they are not all equally important.

Start by briefly defining those steps that you know how to do. If some are vague or confusing, observe how you do them or talk to people who might better understand them. One approach is to pick steps that someone else has performed successfully. If you have no one to learn from, observe someone doing the process, or find the most knowledgeable people on the subject and hold a technical review. You can, of course, even produce a simple process definition and observe yourself. Remember, however, that defining a general conceptual process that no one understands will not be of much help when you are doing the work. To set improvement priorities, ask some new questions and repeat some of the same questions you asked about the target process:

☐ Which steps do you understand and which are ill-defined?

☐ Which steps are frequently repeated and which are single shot?

☐ Which steps take the most time?

☐ Which steps are the source of the most quality problems?

☐ Which steps are the source of the most planning and tracking problems?

☐ Which steps are the source of the most technical problems?

To get the data that you need for continuing process improvement, include the following initial priorities in the process development strategy:

☐ Start with a project planning phase. This is an essential first step because it helps to make your process predictable. You cannot consistently manage or improve an unpredictable process.

☐ Include basic resource and product measures, such as time spent by phase, LOC or database elements produced, pages of documentation produced, and so on.

☐ If practical, include quality measures such as defects by phase or user-reported problems.

☐ Include estimates for all measured items.

☐ Define planning and reporting forms for all measured items.

☐ Define a final report to summarize project results, report key process findings, and suggest process improvements.

☐ Define a postmortem phase for recording and analyzing the data, producing a final report, and submitting process improvement proposals.

Defining the Initial Process

Now that you have characterized the current and target processes and established objectives, goals, and a strategy, produce the scripts, standards, and forms for the initial process. This initial process should be relatively close to your current process, but include a few changes that move you towards the target process. Although you should establish aggressive improvement plans, it is almost impossible to make more than a very few changes at any time.

In defining the initial process, start by considering the entire process as a single phase that includes multiple steps. Next, treat each step as a phase and define its steps. Continue this refinement procedure until you reach a refinement level that is reasonably consistent with your current process knowledge and needs.

There is little point in defining process steps that are not current problems. Conversely, when you do not understand a process area, you cannot define it in much detail. The appropriate definition level is as deep as you can knowledgeably go in the areas that cause you the most trouble. Define what you know and then carry the definition a little further. This helps you to learn about this step when you next perform it. It will also give you ideas about how to further refine it the next time.

For example, with the PSP, you started with only general planning, development, and postmortem steps. The first enhancements focused on planning. Measures were introduced to ensure that the appropriate data were gathered, and measurement and estimating techniques were introduced. The postmortem step then ensured that you retained and analyzed the data.

The next PSP improvement refined the design, design review, code, and code review steps. Although the PSP evolution stopped at this point, you could further refine any or all of these steps as you learn more about them. You could, for example, extend the design process to cover a particular design method. This could help you to match the design templates to your design methods, and to provide data on how you spend your time or where you make errors.

Validating the Initial Process

Now it's time to test the process. First, walk through a simulated enactment using data from a project that you have recently completed. If you do not have the needed data, assume some and do a walk-through. Next, try the process on a small project or a prototype. The better the test, the more likely you are to flush out any problems.

13.6   Example Processes

The following sections describe the process scripts for four example processes: the Process Development Process (PDP), the PSP3.0 Process, the Prototype Experimental Process (PEP), and the Product Maintenance Process (PMP). Although none of these are likely to precisely fit your needs, they should give you some ideas about how to define similar processes for yourself or for your team.

The Process Development Process (PDP)

An example process development script is shown in Table 13.1. Although this process is not for developing code, it is similar to the PSP and should use all of the PSP methods, including PROBE. For a complete PDP process, also produce a plan form and a review checklist.

The PSP process also calls for the Process Improvement Proposal (PIP) form that was introduced with PSP0.1 for recording process problems and improvement suggestions (PIP forms are available at **www.sei.cmu.edu/tsp/** and are included in the assignment kits.). Many process problems concern minor details. Such details, however, make the difference between an inconvenient process and an efficient one. Although you may remember that some form or step was a problem, you are likely to forget the details pretty quickly if you do not record them. Keep blank PIP forms at hand and record each of your process improvement ideas as they occur to you. Surprisingly, if you wait even a few minutes, the idea will often be hard to remember. With a personal process, details are important. To fix the details, religiously complete PIPs. They provide an invaluable source of improvement ideas, even for a personal process.

TABLE 13.1 THE PROCESS DEVELOPMENT PROCESS SCRIPT (PDP)

Purpose	• To guide process development or enhancement	
Entry Criteria	• A new or updated process is needed. • Requirements or PIPs are available describing the process needs. • The PDP forms, scripts, standards, and review checklist are on hand.	
General	• The PDP process may be followed by one developer or an entire team. • When used by teams, PDP is incorporated into the team process. • Develop the scripts, forms, standards, and other elements in that order. • Break larger processes into sections and use PDP to develop each section.	
Step	Activities	Description
1	Produce the Process Plan	• Inventory the existing process (if any). • Produce the new or modified process conceptual design. • Estimate the new, reused, modified, and deleted process elements. • Separately estimate the development effort for the scripts, forms, standards, support materials, and other process elements. • Estimate the total time required for each process element type. • Estimate the total time required for each process phase. • Complete the PDP Plan Summary. *(continued)*

TABLE 13.1 (continued)

Step	Activities	Description
2	Process Requirements	• Analyze the PIPs or other requirements documents. • Define the requirements for the new or modified process.
3	High-level Design	For new or modified processes • Define any process constraints such as training, special tools, or support. • Define the process flow and principal phases.
4	Process Scripts	• Produce or modify each process script. • Using the review checklist, review and correct each process script.
5	Process Forms	• Produce or modify each process form. • Using the review checklist, review and correct each process form.
6	Process Standards	• Produce or modify each process standard. • Using the review checklist, review and correct each process standard.
7	Other Process Elements	• Produce or modify the other process elements. • Using the review checklist, review and correct the other process elements.
8	Process Notebook	• Produce or modify the process notebook, if required. • Using the review checklist, review and correct the process notebook.
9	Process Test	• Test the process by following the script to complete all of the forms. • Where possible, use the process on a real project. • Record all problems and improvement suggestions on PIPs. • Adjust the process to address all of the PIPs.
10	Peer Review	• Where possible, have peers review the process to identify errors, and suggest modifications. • Update the process based on the review results.
11	Process Packaging	• Package the finished process in a form suitable for distribution and use. • Check the final package for errors and make needed corrections.
12	Postmortem	• Record the process data on the Plan Summary. • Calculate the element and phase times and rates. • Record these data in the process database for use in future planning. • Note any PDP process improvements on form PIP.
Exit Criteria		• A completed high-quality process ready for distribution and use • A Project Summary report • Planning data for future use

The PSP3.0 Process

The PSP3.0 process was originally introduced with the first PSP text (Humphrey 1995). It is the cyclic process that I have found helpful for developing programs of several thousand lines of code. Although only the Development Script is shown in Table 13.2, the rest of the PSP3.0 process is described on pages 641 to 649 and pages 725 to 740 of *A Discipline for Software Engineering* (Humphrey 1995).

TABLE 13.2 PSP3.0 DEVELOPMENT SCRIPT

Purpose	To guide development of component-level programs
Entry Criteria	• Problem description or component specifications • Process forms and standards • Historical estimated and actual size and time data
General	• Where the forms and templates are in a support tool, print and retain completed copies in a personal file or notebook. • Where suitable tool support is not available, complete and retain paper copies of all required PSP3 forms. • Record the time spent in each process step. • Record all defects found.

Step	Activities	Description

1	Requirements and Planning	• Obtain the requirements and produce the development plan.
		  • requirements document
		  • design concept
		  • size, quality, resource, and schedule plans
		• Produce a master Issue Tracking log.

2	High-level Design (HLD)	Produce the design and implementation strategy. • Functional Specifications • State Specifications • Operational Specifications • development strategy • test strategy and plan
3	High-level Design Review (HLDR)	• Review the high-level design. • Review the development and test strategy. • Fix and log all defects found. • Note outstanding issues on the Issue Tracking log. • Log all defects found.
4	Development (PSP 2.1)	• Design the program and document the design in the PSP Design templates. • Review the design and fix and log all defects. • Implement the design. • Review the code and fix and log all defects. • Compile the program and fix and log all defects. • Test the program and fix and log all defects. • Complete the Time Recording log. • Reassess and recycle as needed.
5	Postmortem	Complete the Project Plan Summary form with the actual time, defect, and size data.

Exit Criteria	• A thoroughly tested program • Completed Project Plan Summary with estimated and actual data • Completed Estimating and Planning templates • Completed Design templates • Completed Design Review checklist and Code Review checklist • Completed Test Report template • Completed Issue Tracking log • Completed PIP forms • Completed Time and Defect Recording logs

The PSP3.0 process is cyclic and it builds a large program in a sequence of small incremental steps. Depending on your development style, you could make each step anywhere from about 10 LOC up to hundreds or even thousands of LOC. I found that increments of 30 to about 100 LOC were best, but this is a matter of individual preference; I do not believe that any increment size is generally optimum. What I found most interesting about the PSP3.0 process was that, with high-quality increments, this cyclic strategy actually improved my productivity above what I had achieved with small programs.

Prototype Experimental Process (PEP)

The Prototype Experimental Process (PEP) script shown in Table 13.3 is the one I found most helpful when I first started programming with the .NET environment. Because I was unfamiliar with many of the available functions, I had to experiment before I could use them. Rather than waste time designing something I didn't understand, I devised this hybrid process to help me learn the new environment. The general approach was to get a function to work and then to design it. Initially, I had to write entire programs this way, but I soon learned enough that I could experiment with only one or two new functions before producing the design. Once I had learned the .NET functions needed for the programs I was writing, I switched to the PSP2.1 process.

When you work with an unfamiliar environment, consider using a PEP-like process for your personal work. Then, when a prototype meets one or more of the product's requirements, there is no need to throw away the code you have produced and start over. However, if the prototype is to be used in a delivered product, you must document its design, review it, and have your team inspect it. Even when the prototype will not be part of a delivered product, it is a good idea to document its design, if only to build the design skills needed for working on a TSP team.

The Product Maintenance Process (PMP)

A common challenge that many TSP teams face is making small modifications to large legacy systems. Although the PSP methods will help you to produce nearly defect-free enhancements, these base systems are often highly defective and can have many test defects. A common question is, "How can I use the PSP to fix the quality problems of these large existing systems?" The Product Maintenance Process (PMP) script shown in Table 13.4 is one approach to this problem. Even if this personal process does not precisely meet your needs, it should give you ideas about how to handle such maintenance problems.

The principle behind the PMP is that defects tend to cluster. I like to think of programs as gardens with occasional weeds. Although just picking these lone

TABLE 13.3 PROTOTYPE EXPERIMENTAL PROCESS SCRIPT (PEP)

Purpose	To guide PSP experimental program development
Entry Criteria	• Requirements statement or a problem description • All PEP process scripts, forms, standards, templates, and logs • Historical data for estimated and actual size, time, and quality
General	• Where the forms and templates are in a support tool, print and retain completed copies in a personal file or notebook. • Where suitable tool support is not available, complete and retain paper copies of all required PSP forms. • Record time spent, defects found, and product size produced at each process step.

Step	Activities	Description
1	Planning	• Base development planning on the best available requirements information. • Produce the program's conceptual design. • Use the PROBE method and Size Estimating template to estimate the program size, development time, and prediction intervals. • For projects of more than a few days duration, complete Task and Schedule Planning templates. • Enter the plan data in the Project Plan and Quality Summaries.
2	Requirements and Strategy	• Assess the plan and conceptual design to identify risks and uncertainties. • Where the risks are significant, start with a prototype development phase.
3	Prototype Development	Develop one or more working prototypes to resolve the identified risks and uncertainties.
4	Development (PSP2.1)	• Produce and document the product's design in State, Operational, Functional, and Logic Specification templates. • Provide designs for all the prototype elements that will be used in the final product. • Review, analyze, and correct the design. • Plan and develop tests to verify correct program operation. • Where required, implement the program's design. • Review and correct the implementation. • Compile, build, test, and fix the program until all tests run without error.
5	Postmortem	• Complete the Project Plan and Quality Summaries with actual time, defect, size, and quality data. • Update the Design and Code Review checklists to reflect new defect data. • Produce PIPs for any process improvement ideas.

| **Exit Criteria** | • A documented, analyzed, reviewed, tested, and corrected program
• Project Plan and Quality Summaries with estimated and actual data
• Completed Estimating, Planning, Design, and Test Report templates
• Updated Design and Code Review checklists.
• Completed Defect Recording, Time Recording, and Issue Tracking logs
• A personal project notebook with plan and actual data
• Completed PIP forms |

TABLE 13.4 PRODUCT MAINTENANCE PROCESS SCRIPT (PMP)

Purpose	To guide PSP enhancement and repair of legacy systems

Entry Criteria	• Requirements statement or a problem description
	• All PSP and PMP process scripts, forms, standards, templates, and logs
	• Historical data for estimated and actual project size, time, and quality
	• Historical data for legacy system test defects and customer-reported defects
	  • defect data for every system component
	  • for defective components, defect data by module

General	• Rank the replacement modules by level of user impact. • Where the forms and templates are in a support tool, print and retain completed copies in a personal file or notebook. • Where suitable tool support is not available, complete and retain paper copies of all required PSP and PMP forms. • Record time spent, defects found, and product size produced at each process step.

Step	Activities	Description
1	Planning	• Base development planning on the enhancement requirements and the resources allocated for cleaning up (remediating) the legacy system. • Produce and document the enhancements' conceptual designs. • Use the PROBE method and Size Estimating template to estimate the size of each enhancement, the development time, and the prediction intervals. • Include the allocated remediation effort in the Task and Schedule plans. • Enter the plan data in the Project Plan and Quality Summaries.
2	Requirements Review	Review and inspect the enhancement requirements and resolve any open issues or questions.
3	Maintenance Strategy	• From the enhancement requirements and conceptual design, identify the legacy components and modules to be modified. • Review the legacy-system defect data and classify components and component modules as defect-free, defective, and replacement. • Rank the replacement modules in priority order, based on user impact. • Identify all of the defective and replacement modules that are to be changed by the enhancements.
4	Enhancement–Defect-free Modules	Follow a personal PSP process to develop, review, inspect, and test the required enhancements for each defect-free module.
5	Enhancement–Defective Modules	For each defective module with one or more planned enhancements • Review the unmodified module and correct any defects found. • If any module has more than one defect found or has design problems, hold a team inspection and fix all defects found. • If the module's design problems are serious, reclassify the module for replacement and proceed to script step 6. • Test and regression test the fixed module before making the enhancements. • Follow a PSP2.1-like process to develop, review, inspect, and test the module's enhancements.

TABLE 13.4 (continued)

6	Enhancement of Replacement Modules	For each replacement module with one or more planned enhancements • Document the unmodified module's design with the PSP Design templates. • If the design has serious defects or is overly complex, produce a new design and implementation, and review and inspect the design and implementation. • If the design appears sound, review and fix the design and code, hold a team inspection and fix all of the defects found. • Test and regression test the fixed module before making the enhancements. • Follow a personal PSP process to develop, review, inspect, and test the module's enhancements.
7	Module Remediation	If remediation resources are available, start with the highest-ranked replacement module that has no planned enhancements. • Document the unmodified module's design with the PSP Design templates. • If the design has serious defects or is overly complex, follow a PSP2.1-like process to produce a new design and implementation and to review and inspect the design and implementation. • If the design appears sound, review and fix the design and code, hold a team inspection and fix all defects found. • Test and regression test the replacement module.

8	Postmortem	• Complete the Project Plan and Quality Summaries with actual time, defect, size, and quality data.
		• Update the Design and Code Review checklists to reflect new defect data.
		• Produce a remediation report, identifying the replaced components and modules.
		  • Summarize the time, size, and defect data for each module repair and replacement.
		  • Update the historical database with the remediation data for use in planning future maintenance efforts.
		• Produce PIPs for any process improvement ideas.

Exit Criteria		• Documented, analyzed, reviewed, tested, and enhanced legacy program • Project Plan and Quality Summaries with estimated and actual data • Completed Estimating, Planning, Design, and Test Report templates • Updated Design and Code Review checklists • Completed Defect Recording, Time Recording, and Issue Tracking logs • Personal project notebook with plan and actual data • Maintenance report and updated database of remediation data • Completed PIP forms

weeds is usually adequate, occasionally you will come across a patch of jungle. Such junglelike parts of programs can be caused by overly complex designs, multiple erroneous fixes, several different developers, defective enhancements, or other similar causes. To fix them, you will usually need to completely rip out and replace that junglelike part of the program.

The PMP strategy uses system-test and user-reported defect data to identify the junglelike patches of code to be replaced. Although the PMP script criteria for defect-free, defective, and replacement modules should be suitable as a starting point, gather data for your products and use these data to set your own classification criteria.

13.7   Process Development Considerations

There is nothing more annoying than a process that prescribes some complex procedure that you can't understand or remember. At the time you wrote it, you may have known exactly what you intended, but if you did not explain it in terms that would be clear later, it is not a fit process. You can also go too far in the other direction. There is no value in defining steps in great detail if a simple summary provides all of the information that you need to perform the task.

Design the process at just the level you need to guide the work. If it provides helpful reminders and useful guidance, you are more likely to use it. People get careless when they follow routine procedures. They need simple directions and checklists to remind them of all of the steps. Remember that *you* are defining a script that will help *you* to faithfully follow the process *you* have chosen to use. You thus must decide where you will need guidance, where reminders are adequate, and where you need no help. You will quickly become proficient at any repetitive process, so make sure that it is convenient during intensive use but also helpful when you need guidance and reminders. The key point to remember is that the process is *not* a tutorial. It is a guideline to help knowledgeable people follow a process that they know how to follow.

Start with a simple process and gradually enhance it. If you make the process too comprehensive, you will do a lot of unnecessary work. When you first use the process, you may find that it is overly detailed where you don't need it and that it doesn't help where it should. In defining processes, you will unconsciously tend to describe the steps that you understand and skip over those that you do not. Your needs, however, are the reverse. Until you make trial definitions, you will not know enough to provide detail where it will help the most.

One example is the Code Review Checklist. Without historical data, you would not know what to include. Although you could start with the checklist in the textbook, it might not fit your needs. From reviewing your PSP data, you could set preliminary review priorities and make a first-draft checklist. After using the checklist, you could then see where to refine it. For example, you could initially call for a general punctuation review and then later list specific punctuation marks.

Forms are more difficult to design than you might expect. To be convenient, a form must capture the essence of the task being performed. If you do not understand the task, you cannot design a good form. Form design takes time, and your first pass will rarely be complete or convenient. The best advice is to produce a simplified form and then elaborate, revise, and enhance it as you use it.

This evolutionary principle applies to the entire process. Produce a simple initial process, and then elaborate, revise, and enhance it as you gain experience using it. View every process enactment as a test. Record all of your improvement ideas in PIPs and use these PIPs to guide your next process update.

You define a process to help you both understand and use it. Process definition is an experiment in which you almost know the answer. In other words, you generally know how the job should be done but have not defined the precise steps. Start with an experimental definition that extends the process in a direction you think would improve it. When you next perform it, you may find that some ideas worked as expected and that others need to be changed. Such learning is an inherent part of process definition. As you evolve the process, focus on your current needs. When your knowledge and skills improve, your process needs will change, and you should improve the process.

13.8   Summary

Software process development is much like software development. It has similar artifacts and requires many of the same disciplines and methods. The steps for designing a process are to define the needs, establish goals, and define quality criteria. Next, characterize the current and target processes and establish a development strategy. Finally, define and validate the initial process and establish means for its enhancement.

It is practically impossible to produce a usable process the first time you try. The problem is that the work of defining a process changes that process. This concept is best explained by considering the following four processes: The perceived process is what you think you do, the actual process is what you actually do, the official process is what management thinks you do, and the target process is the process to which you are evolving. A principal reason why the quality of our processes is so poor is that we often don't do what we know we should. However, you cannot evolve your process until it reasonably represents what you are doing.

Process development should be planned, measured, tracked, and improved. Guidelines for an effective process development process include planning and measuring the work, tracking the products produced, and recording the time spent by each major product type and development category. To plan process development, you must define the important measures for your work, use these measures to plan the work, and keep a development record. Finally, produce a summary report for each process development.

13.9   Exercises

The assignment for this chapter is to produce a final report on the programs that you wrote while learning the PSP. This work includes three tasks: updating the process that you developed for the midterm report R4, planning the effort to produce the final report, and producing the report. For the details of the assignment, consult the specifications for report R5 in the assignment kit. For the R5 assignment kit, see your instructor or get it at **www.sei.cmu.edu/tsp/**. The kit contains the R5 report specifications. In completing this assignment, produce the R5 report according to the specifications given in the assignment kit.

References

Humphrey, W. S. *Managing the Software Process.* Reading, MA: Addison-Wesley, 1989.

———. *A Discipline for Software Engineering.* Reading, MA: Addison-Wesley, 1995.

14

Using the Personal Software Process

Now that you have learned the PSP, the next step is to apply it on a real development project under real schedule pressures. This turns out to be a significant challenge and it is the principal reason why the SEI developed the Team Software Process (TSP). It is also why most PSP developers work on TSP teams. The TSP shows you how to use the PSP on a development project and how you and your teammates can develop your own best practices to augment and enhance what you learned with the PSP. TSP teams also learn teamwork, how to support each other, and how to control and direct their own projects.

This chapter describes the principal challenges that software professionals face and how the PSP and TSP can help you to address them. It describes the TSP's objectives, structure, and methods, and it explains how these methods help you to be a disciplined professional software engineer. Finally, it covers the responsibilities we all face as software professionals.

14.1 Development Challenges

Although modern development work poses many technical challenges, the problems that seem to cause the most trouble are not technical at all. They concern negotiating commitments, maintaining control of our projects, delivering quality products, and sustaining effective teamwork. To have a successful project, we must handle all of these challenges. Falling short on any of these aspects will seriously damage and possibly destroy our projects, almost regardless of how well we handle the other challenges or how fine a technical job we do in designing and building the product.

Few software development teams can simultaneously handle all four of these challenges, which is why so many software projects are troubled. The Standish Group reports that only 26% of all the software projects it has studied are considered successful. Of the remaining 74%, a full 28% either were cancelled or failed in other ways. The remaining 46% were late and seriously over budget (Standish Group 1999). For the late projects, the average delay was over 100%. Table 14.1 shows the Standish data on project success as a function of project size.

Although it is common knowledge that large software projects are almost always troubled, the key question is why. The reason is that current software practices do not scale up, and the reasons for this are related to the four challenges we face on development teams.

First, the larger the project, the less the team has to say about the project's commitments. It seems that, at least with current practices, as projects get larger, management pays less and less attention to what we developers have to say. They tell us how our projects are to be initiated, planned, and run. Though no one is picking on us, if we don't have anything to say, nobody will listen to us.

Second, project control is challenging for small software jobs; and as job scale increases, it is progressively more difficult to understand job status and to keep all the parts of the work synchronized and on schedule. Although this is a management problem, its roots are in the developers' personal practices. If we don't know where we are on a job, there is no way management can know where the overall job stands.

Third, in scaling up a process, the quality of all of the system's parts becomes progressively more important. Without high-quality parts, it is impossible to build high-quality systems. This is where the practices of the individual developers come in. Every developer is important, and with large software systems, any poor-quality

TABLE 14.1 PROJECT SUCCESS VERSUS PROJECT SIZE (STANDISH GROUP 1999)

Project Size	People	Time - Months	Success Rate
Less than $750K	6	6	55%
$750K to $1.5M	12	9	33%
$1.5M to $3M	25	12	25%
$3M to $6M	40	18	15%
$6M to $10M	+250	+24	8%
Over $10M	+500	+36	0%

part will eventually cause problems. With large or small software projects, the personal practices of every developer are critically important to the success of the overall job. This is where the PSP comes in.

Fourth, as teams grow larger, it becomes progressively more difficult to build cohesive and motivated teams and it is much more challenging to maintain team energy and commitment. This is why the TSP is so important.

Although it would be unfair to blame every software problem on the software developers, there are things we can do to ensure that our projects regularly deliver quality products on time and for their committed costs. The PSP teaches you how to do this with your personal work and the TSP shows you and your team how to do it, even with large complex projects.

Negotiating Commitments

In almost any development organization, the developers are often pressured into making schedule commitments that they think are unrealistic. The problem is that the managers are also pressured by their executives and customers to meet aggressive commitments. Unfortunately, these managers typically think that the only way to manage development work is to give their projects a sense of urgency. Unless their staff are striving to meet an aggressive challenge, managers intuitively feel that their projects will not likely be successful. Therefore, managers will push until they are convinced that you and your teammates are striving to meet an aggressive plan. The problem we face as professionals is figuring out how to get management to accept a realistic plan. With the PSP skills and the TSP process, you will be able to do this.

Although most managers are reasonable, few have a sound basis for deciding what is a good plan. They may ask for a few expert opinions, but they will primarily depend on how you react when pressed. The proper way to deal with such requests is to *always* make a plan, even if management doesn't ask for one. Say that you will do your best to meet management's goals but that you won't make a commitment without a plan. Don't say how hard the job is, that you think that a bigger team is needed, or anything else that might imply that you will not do your utmost to meet their requested date. Management has told you what is needed and you will do your best to do it, but you need a plan before you can commit to a schedule.

Only the dumbest managers want a flimsy plan that you can't meet. Managers have business commitments, and timely delivery is important. Product schedules are the foundation for revenue and expense projections. The managers may blame you for the current fiasco, but if they have too many fiascoes, they will lose their jobs. The most successful course for you and your team is to produce the best plan that you can, regardless of the pressure. Then defend it. In defending the plan, a generally successful approach is to stress the following points:

□ This is the best plan we can make to meet the requirements you gave us. We can show you the plan assumptions and the historical data on which the plan is based and we can show you comparisons with similar projects. We think you will then agree that this is a tight but realistic plan.

□ If you want to change the requirements or other assumptions, we will reexamine the plan to see how that will affect the schedule.

□ This is a minimum-cost plan. If you are more concerned about the schedule, we could save time, but at added cost. We could also develop some schedule options if you can tell us what alternatives you would like us to consider.

You might even have alternative plans prepared in advance. The key points are to be responsive, to do a thorough job, and to make a plan before making *any* commitments. Examine any alternatives and do whatever you can to meet management's objectives, but resist any schedule or resource cuts that are not backed up with a plan.

This strategy works for individuals and for teams. With PSP training, you have learned how to make a personal plan, collect data, and use data to manage and improve your performance. On a TSP team, the TSP coach will walk you through the TSP launch process and guide you and your team in developing the plan and defending it to management. This may sound risky and counter to your organization's culture, but it isn't hard when you use the TSP. Surprisingly, based on the experiences of TSP teams to date, it is *always* successful.

Maintaining Project Control

Having a sound and detailed plan is an important first step in maintaining project control. To maintain project control, however, you must follow the plan and keep it up to date. You must also keep management informed of your progress. Keeping the plan up to date is crucial because software development is a continuously changing business and every surprise usually means more work for you and your team. Although some of this change is a natural consequence of development work, the changes that are the hardest to manage are the ones that impact requirements scope and development resources. The key to managing such change requests is to take the time to update the plan and to explain to management what the change will cost. Then you must get management's approval for the cost, schedule, resource, and product impact before agreeing to the change.

This is not a question of blame but an objective way to explain the consequences of a proposed change. You had not planned to do whatever is now requested and it will take additional time and effort. Unless management and the customer are willing to accept the cost and schedule consequences, you cannot make the change and meet the original commitment. When you and your team follow this strategy, you will be surprised at how many changes turn out to be either unnecessary or deferrable.

Following the plan and keeping management informed are two aspects of the same issue. If you don't follow the plan, you won't know where you are in the project. Then you can't inform management of your status. If you can't keep management informed of project status, they will not trust you to run the project. Then you will face all kinds of uncontrollable pressures, such as scope changes, resource cuts, or special team-member assignments. Even worse, you won't have the plan to help you negotiate these changes with management. There are many ways that management can help but they all require trust and understanding. If you know where you are and if you keep management regularly informed, they will trust you and support you in maintaining control of your project.

Delivering Quality Products

Quality management is a major focus of the PSP and TSP because without effective quality management, the inevitable quality problems will impact your project's cost and schedule, and sharply reduce the value of your products. Although you may not be too concerned with the business value of your products, you should be. Management hires and pays software developers because the value of our products is substantially more than it costs to develop them. If your projects cost too much then your products will cost too much and your customers could start looking elsewhere. If that happens too often, you could lose your job.

Sustaining Effective Teamwork

Teams are the most effective means humans have devised for doing complex creative work. Teams can be enormously effective when they work properly; without adequate guidance and support, however, they can fail miserably. Team performance depends largely on the capability of the team members to work together. To be fully effective, teams must be properly formed, guided, and led. Unfortunately, in the development world, team formation, guidance, and leadership is largely a matter of chance. There is no teambuilding process, team leaders are rarely trained in effective leadership methods, and there is little or no team coaching. As a result, software teams are rarely as effective as they could be.

14.2 The Team Software Process (TSP)

The TSP was developed to address the commitment, control, quality, and teamwork problems faced by most software development teams. It has proven to be effective at showing software teams how to capitalize on the skills of their members and how to produce high-quality products on predictable schedules and for their committed costs. The following TSP topics are described in the next few sections:

☐ The logic of the TSP

☐ Teambuilding

☐ The TSP launch process

☐ The TSP coach

☐ Managing your own project

☐ TSP results

14.3   The Logic of the TSP

Although the TSP is not magic, it will help you to address the key issues that have continued to plague software teams. Thousands of developers have now been trained in the PSP, and many TSP teams are now consistently meeting cost and schedule targets with high-quality products (Davis and Mullaney 2003). By following a defined, planned, measured, and managed personal process, you can plan your own work, make commitments that you consistently meet, and be more productive. You will also have a more rational family life, be proud of the products that you produce, and enjoy working on a cohesive and productive team.

A basic TSP principle is that the only group that can determine the best way to run a project is the team that will do the job. This is the only group that understands the technical details of the job and can effectively map the work to the team members' skills and knowledge. After the team members figure out this "best way," the next challenge is for them to actually work that way, even when in a crisis.

The purpose of the TSP is to build and guide teams in defining their own strategies, processes, and plans, and then to guide and support them in following these strategies, processes, and plans. The PSP provides the skills that developers need in order to make personal and team plans, to track their work, and to build quality products. These skills are required to be fully effective TSP team members.

14.4   Teambuilding

A team is a group of at least two people who are working toward a common goal for which each person has a specific role and the team members must all contribute and support each other to be successful (Dyer 1984). Many studies have shown that successful teams share the following characteristics (Humphrey 2002):

1. The team members are all skilled and capable of doing their job.

2. The team has an aggressive and important goal that the members must cooperatively accomplish.

3. The team members believe that the goal is achievable, and they each have a defined role in achieving that goal.

4. The team members have a common process and plan that guides them in doing the work and in tracking their progress.

5. The team leader supports and protects the team and keeps the members informed of management issues and team progress.

These five characteristics are all essential for a group to become a high-performing team. Though the TSP launch process helps groups develop these characteristics, team motivation is crucial. Most professionals want to perform, and motivated professionals strive for superior performance. As Martin says, "Improved performance comes from motivation, from arousing and maintaining the will to work effectively, not because the individual is coerced, but because he is committed" (Martin 1993).

Team motivation is the single most important aspect of the TSP. To appreciate how the TSP addresses this need, consider what motivates you. How important is it to be working on an exciting product? Does it matter who you work with? How about the way you do the job? Do you like to be told how to work or would you rather make these decisions for yourself? Most developers want to work on important products with a great team, and do the job in the way and according to the plan that they believe is best. The TSP methods enable teams to work this way. The TSP calls these **self-directed teams**. They provide as near to an ideal software development environment as I have ever seen.

A principal purpose of TSP management training is to explain what self-directed teams are, why they are desirable, and how they should be guided and supported. This training generally convinces management to allow their TSP teams to direct their own work. They do this in return for an implicit promise that the teams will plan and manage their own work, keep management and the customer regularly informed of their progress, and produce high-quality products. Therefore, to work on a self-directed TSP team, the team members must all be trained and the team must be built. The training is done in the PSP course and the teambuilding is started with the TSP launch process. Teambuilding, however, must continue as long as the team works as a group.

14.5   The TSP Launch Process

Shortly after PSP training, TSP teams are guided through the TSP launch process by a trained and qualified TSP coach. In this launch, management and the team hold a series of ten team and management meetings during which they work through the following activities:

1. In meeting 1, management and a user representative (or the customer) meet with the team to explain why the project is needed, what management expects from this team, and what the customer or user wants. During this meeting, management outlines their goals for the team and explains why the project is important. They also describe their critical needs and any trade-off opportunities. This and meeting 9 may be attended by visitors and observers. The other eight meetings are for the team, the team leader, and the coach, with no outside observers.

2. In meeting 2, the team defines its goals and the members select their personal team roles. The goals are of two kinds: the explicit goals stated by management and the implicit goals the team members define for their own work. Although the team leader is usually selected by management, the TSP suggests eight team-member roles to provide oversight for planning, process, support, quality, requirements, design, implementation, and testing. Teams may add or delete roles depending on their project's needs. By agreeing on the team's goals and selecting their personal roles, the team members start the TSP teambuilding process.

3. During meeting 3, the team produces its initial product concept, decides on a development strategy, and defines the process needed to support the goals and strategy. A key part of building an effective team is having the team develop a common understanding of the right way to do the job.

4. In meeting 4, the team produces an overall plan for the job. In this step, the team reviews the overall job and produces a high-level plan that covers all project phases and will produce all of the required deliverables.

5. In meeting 5, the team produces a quality plan. Here, the team members use the PSP quality measures to set numerical goals and agree on how to achieve them.

6. During meeting 6, the team members make detailed personal plans for the next several weeks. Here, each team member takes responsibility for a portion of the team's plan. Also during meeting 6, the team reviews every team member's workload and produces a balanced plan. Where one member has an excessive workload, others agree to take some tasks or to otherwise provide help.

7. In meeting 7, the team produces a project risk assessment and assigns team members to monitor and mitigate the key risks. The team thoughtfully

reviews the plan and identifies known and likely problems, quantifies their likelihood and impact, and agrees on the highest-priority mitigation efforts.

8. During meeting 8, the team prepares a plan presentation for management. If the plan does not meet management's desired goals, the team also produces one or more alternative plans. Although the team leader usually presents the plan, it is the entire team's plan and all of the members participate in its preparation and presentation.

9. In meeting 9, the team, team leader, and coach meet with the management group that attended meeting 1. Typically, the team leader presents the team's plan, and the team members help explain and defend it.

10. The final meeting is the postmortem during which the team reviews the launch process, records improvement suggestions, ensures that all important decisions and data are recorded, and assigns responsibility for any outstanding follow-up items.

With only one exception that I know of, management has always accepted the team's plan or one of its alternative plans. Out of many TSP team launches, the only exception was one in which management had asked for a one-year schedule and the team found that the work would take five years. Management then killed the project. This was really a success. Without the TSP, no one would have understood the magnitude of the job until after the team had spent a year or more trying to accomplish the impossible. The TSP saved the team a lot of frustration, and it saved management a lot of money.

14.6 The TSP Coach

Performing artists and competitive athletes know the value of coaching. Coaches help professionals to maximize their talents. Coaches in sports and the performing arts observe and study each practice and each performance. They are constantly looking for improvement opportunities. They push you to your known limits and then a little beyond. They can even drive you past what you thought was possible. They make the practice sessions so tough that the performance seems easy. Your coach is your greatest fan and your most demanding audience.

Accomplished coaches recognize talent and see the possibilities for excellence. As long as their charges start with the essential skills and a commitment to excellence, the coach will help them produce superior results. The objective is to make their occasional achievements seem normal and natural. Superior coaches also experiment. They watch each session and seek new ways to train and to motivate. They strive to help you improve while viewing every training session as a practice coaching session. It is unlikely that truly superior software development performance will be achieved without the help of skilled coaches. The software coach has three objectives:

1. Motivate superior performance

2. Insist on a dedication to excellence

3. Support and guide individual and team development

With the TSP, coaches are first taught PSP skills and practices, and then trained in coaching. Organizations are urged to have at least one TSP coach for every four or five teams that they support. This gives the coaches enough time to both launch and support their teams and to spend time with each team and team member.

After an initial launch, new teams need full-time coaching support for at least two weeks. The members invariably have questions and are confused about how to handle common problems. Although experienced TSP teams usually need less coaching support, they do need periodic help and guidance to maintain their process discipline. Because the TSP represents a substantial change in working practice for most software developers, it is easy for them to get discouraged and to revert to their prior methods. Although many teams have been able to work through these issues by themselves, full-time coaching support can smooth TSP introduction and help to ensure team success.

14.7   Managing Your Own Project

Following the team launch and management's decision regarding the team's plan, the team follows its plan to do the work. In addition to the development work, the principal activities are managing the plan, tracking and reporting progress, managing change, and managing quality.

Maintaining the Plan

When new TSP teams first use the detailed plans they produced during the TSP launch, they invariably find that they have left out some important steps, included activities that are not essential, improperly defined some tasks, or made some significant estimating errors. Although this is normal, it can make the plan hard to follow. To handle these problems, teams must generally make many plan adjustments almost immediately after they start the job. Although these changes are usually relatively small and easy to make, it is important to keep the plan consistent with the way you work. If you don't, you will not be able to track your progress or see when you are falling behind. This makes it very difficult, if not impossible, to make credible management status reports or to get sufficient warning of problems to take corrective action.

Another important part of maintaining the team plan is the team relaunch. Even though the overall team plan may extend for several years, the TSP's detailed plans extend for only a few months. Teams must therefore hold a relaunch every two to four months. A relaunch usually takes only two or three days, and it enables teams to update their plans based on what they have learned, to alert management and the customer to any problems, and to integrate any new members into the team.

Tracking and Reporting Progress

The role of development projects is to solve problems. We spend our lives dealing with unknowns and we frequently encounter unexpected problems and opportunities. Unfortunately, it seems to be a law of product development that every surprise involves more work. This means that our projects will always run late unless we recognize the problems in time to do something about them. For example, on a 26-week project, if you discover in week 5 that the work is taking longer than planned, you have time to replan the work, to get help, or to renegotiate the product's content. However, if you cannot precisely measure job status, you will not know that you are in trouble until it is too late to recover.

The TSP uses earned value (EV) to measure your status against the plan. With the help of this measure, you will always know job status to within a few hours. However, EV works only when the plan accurately represents what you are doing and when all team members regularly measure their work. Figure 14.1 shows an example of the status information that TSP teams get every week. This team had completed 7 weeks of a 17-week project and was falling behind. To understand the problem, the team planning manager made the following calculations:

1. The team members had spent 493.4 hours so far compared to a plan of 467 hours, so they had spent 5% more hours on the job than planned.

2. The team had accomplished 22.3 EV of work to date, compared to a planned 28.2 PV. This was a 26% slip in the schedule.

3. For the tasks the team had completed, the members had spent 458 hours compared to a planned 354.3 hours, or a 23% underestimate.

4. At the rate of 22.3 EV in 7 weeks, the team was earning 3.186 EV per week.

5. At this rate, the team would reach 100 EV in $(100 - 22.3)/3.186 = 24.39$ weeks.

6. Therefore, at the average EV rate the team had earned so far, it would take $24.39 + 7 = 31.39$ weeks to complete the 17-week project, putting them 14.39 weeks behind schedule.

Weekly Data	Plan	Actual	Plan/ Actual
Schedule hours for this week	121.0	126.7	0.95
Schedule hours this cycle to date	467.0	493.4	0.95
Earned value for this week	7.6	6.4	1.19
Earned value this cycle to date	28.2	22.3	1.26
To-date hours for tasks completed	354.3	458.0	0.77
To-date average hours per week			

FIGURE 14.1 TSP TEAM WEEKLY STATUS (WEEK 7 OF A 17-WEEK JOB)

This summary form represents a real TSP team, and the members initially detected their schedule problem in week 3. They decided to concentrate on their task hours and to defer or stop any nonessential activities. Doing this increased their total task hours from an average of 70.5 per week to 126.7 hours in the latest week. If they could maintain this rate, they would be only 2.6 weeks late. To determine this, they made the following calculations:

1. At 458.0 hours for 22.3 EV, each EV point has been taking 20.54 hours.
2. At this rate, the hours required to reach 100 EV were 77.7 * 20.54 = 1,596 hours.
3. At the rate of 126.7 hours per week, they would reach 100 EV in 12.6 more weeks.
4. Because they had already spent 7 weeks on the job, they would finish in 19.6 weeks instead of the 17-week commitment, or 2.6 weeks late.

With this information, the team could monitor their work every day. In fact, the members continued to manage and even slightly increase their task hours and finished on exactly the day they had committed to management. With the TSP, teams can identify their problems early enough to handle them. That is why these teams generally deliver on or very close to their committed schedules.

Managing Change

It is "common knowledge" that the best way to develop software is to start with firm, clear, and complete requirements. However, experience shows that even when we get what is purported to be a firm requirement, it will change. The one exception I remember was when I was director of IBM's software development operations. I was so convinced that we should start with firm requirements that I threatened to cancel a big project if either the team or the marketing group changed the requirements after we had agreed on them. The product was then produced on schedule and within costs, but it did not meet the customers' true needs. We then had to withdraw it and start over to develop the "right" product. This product failure was more expensive than the likely schedule delays that would have resulted from requirements changes.

Software developers soon learn that there is no such thing as a "firm requirement." Conversely, requirements changes can be very expensive. The key is to ensure that management understands the costs of every change as well as the cost of evaluating every proposed change. Then they will ask you to evaluate only the most critical changes. The TSP guidelines for handling the requirements-stability problem are as follows:

□ Focus on quality from the beginning of the job. After the initial launch, the TSP process recommends that teams thoroughly review their requirements and resolve any questions, issues, or problems. This early focus on quality reviews, quality management, and quality planning will help you to identify requirements problems early, when they are least expensive to fix. Although most teams readily agree to doing this, they almost always seriously underestimate the time it will take to do it.

□ Analyze the cost of every change, particularly the smallest ones. The big changes are generally easy to manage, but many small changes can nibble you to death. The PSP's detailed planning methods help you to quickly determine the impact of even the smallest change.

□ Before accepting a change, make sure that the customer and management understand and agree to its benefits and expected impact. Again, the PSP planning process helps here.

□ Because there is often disagreement about the meaning of a requirements statement, focus on the costs of the work and how your new understanding of the requirements impacts the plan. If the customer's interpretation is correct, as it often is, and if your plan was based on different assumptions, make sure that everyone understands the change's impact on the plan. Even if your project will have to "eat" the added costs, get the issue on the table as soon as you understand it and let management handle the cost and schedule problems with the customer. Again, the PSP planning methods will help you with this strategy.

TSP Quality Management

If the product didn't have to work, we could build it really quickly. Although it may not appear that the customers and managers care as much about quality as they do about cost and schedule, they do want our products to work. However, because quality is the key to both schedule management and product performance, quality is really our job. In fact, before they learn the PSP, most software developers spend 20% to 30% of their time finding and fixing defects. Then their teams spend nearly half of the project schedule finding and fixing more defects in testing. Finally, after delivery, many organizations spend as much money fixing defective products as they did originally developing them. By using the quality methods you learn with the PSP, you can cut these personal, team, and organizational costs by five to ten times. Furthermore, while you are doing this, you will produce more competitive products on shorter schedules and at less cost.

14.8   TSP Results

Although the PSP and TSP are relatively new, enough teams have used them to demonstrate their effectiveness. When the members are all trained, the team is professionally coached, and management provides proper leadership and support, TSP teams have been remarkably successful. In a study of 20 TSP projects in 13 organizations, schedule performance ranged from 20% ahead of schedule to 27% late. The average delay was 6% (Davis and Mullaney 2003). Although this is not perfect, it is far better than typical industry performance, where most projects are either cancelled or over 100% late.

The quality of these TSP teams' products ranged from 10 to 100 times better than previously, with an average of 60 defects per million lines of code. Over one-third of these products have had no customer-reported defects. These teams accomplished all of this while achieving an average 78% productivity improvement.

Although the business benefits of the TSP are impressive, the most significant improvement is in the developers' working environment. TSP team members find that their work is more rewarding and that they truly enjoy being on a cohesive and supportive team. With the TSP, team members typically report that software development is the fun that it ought to be.

14.9   The Rewards of Teamwork

After PSP training, quality work will seem normal and natural. In fact, TSP teams typically find that they don't want to revert to developing software the old way; it's much less fun and not nearly as satisfying. Learning and using the PSP will change your life. To understand why this is true, consider the factors that developers consider most important for project success. Linberg (Linberg 1999) has published a study of software developers' views of project success and failure, and he concludes that the following four points are most important:

1. A sense of being involved and making a significant contribution

2. An enjoyable and fun environment where even the little successes are recognized and celebrated with your managers and peers

3. Positive feedback from management and the customer on the product and the way you developed it

4. The autonomy to do the job in the way you think best

This is exactly the environment the TSP provides, and the following reactions of developers on TSP teams reflects their positive feelings:

- □ This really feels like a tight team.
- □ The TSP forces you to design, to think the whole thing out.
- □ Design time is way up but code time decreased to compensate.
- □ Tracking your time is an eye-opener.
- □ Really good teamwork on this project—no duplication of effort.
- □ I'm more productive.
- □ Gives you incredible insight into project performance.
- □ Wonderful to have team members assigned to specific roles.
- □ Team really came together to make the plan.
- □ I feel included and empowered.

14.10   The TSP Team of One

Whether you work on a TSP team or on a project by yourself, the PSP can help you to do more professional work and have a more rewarding career. To do so, however, you must consistently act like a professional software developer. Although this is demanding, it is also a much more enjoyable way to work. The key is to do the following:

- □ Plan and manage your personal work.
- □ Use effective personal methods.
- □ Recognize your strengths and weaknesses.
- □ Practice, practice, practice.
- □ Learn from history.
- □ Find and learn new methods.

Plan and Manage Your Personal Work

Whether you work alone or on a team, continue to use the PSP methods to plan your work, track your performance, and measure and manage the quality of the products you produce. When you are asked to do a job, take the time to make a plan before agreeing to a schedule. Next, keep your management informed of your progress at least every week. Then, whether or not you are on a self-directed team, you can be a self-directed software developer.

After PSP training, one developer was given a one-week assignment by his manager. Instead of accepting the job on the spot, he asked for a little time to make a plan. When the manager agreed, the developer estimated the size of the product and, from his PSP data, estimated that the work would take two weeks. When he showed his boss the detailed plan and explained why he needed more time, the manager agreed to the two-week schedule. This had never happened to the developer before and he was so excited that he called his coach to tell him. If you want to manage your own work, make plans for every job and negotiate these plans with your management. Be sure to base your plans on careful estimates, and base your estimates on your own historical data. Then, when management agrees to your plan, regularly track and report on your work.

Use Effective Personal Methods

The tragedy of modern software engineering is that almost all disasters are avoidable. Good software practices are straightforward, but few people consistently use them. Often, in fact, the appropriate methods were known and even planned for but not used. When the schedule pressures grow, as they always do, software developers often panic and throw out all of their good intentions in a mad scramble to meet the schedule. Unfortunately, this causes most software developers to immediately start coding and testing. Until they have used sound methods and seen the benefits, many professionals will claim that there is no evidence that these methods would really help them. In fact, there is plenty of evidence. As a dedicated professional, you must find the methods that work best for you and then use them. Finding them can take a little effort, but the really challenging part is using them once you find them.

Recognize Your Strengths and Weaknesses

Recognizing your strengths and weaknesses is the role of the postmortem. As you better understand your abilities, you will find tasks that you are good at and areas for improvement. Strengths and weaknesses are relative. Balance your capabilities with those of your associates. Capitalize on your strengths and seek support where you are weak, and don't forget to ask for help. That is what teams are for. Teambuilding requires that you help your teammates as well as rely on them when you need help.

Treat every part of every project as a chance to learn. Measure your work, analyze the data, and see what works. Learn from variation. When things go well, figure out why. Practice what you did and attempt to repeat it. Perhaps you will develop a new trick or technique. Above all, focus on small improvements. If you can regularly make small improvements, the major changes will take care of themselves.

Practice, Practice, Practice

To improve your skills, get in the habit of practicing. Try new methods and work on personal problem areas. There may not be time for practice projects, but there are practice opportunities on most projects. You may need a prototype to prove a design or to resolve an interface. Prototypes are not always needed, but experiment when you can. Although you should use proven methods on product code, learn from your prototypes.

You can also practice on your projects, particularly those parts that are not on critical schedules. When learning a new method, practice it to build skill. Using new measurements, new process forms, or new analyses or verification methods is acceptable, as long as it does not jeopardize the project's quality and schedule performance. Practice is an essential part of personal improvement, so make practicing a normal part of your daily work.

Learn from History

The difference between a tragedy and a fiasco is that in a tragedy, you have not learned from the fiasco. We do few things for the first time. Invariably, somebody has produced a program just like the one you are now developing. They have made the mistakes you will make, and they know the traps and pitfalls. A little exploration can save you a lot of grief. Look for relevant experience and check the literature. You will often find pertinent books and articles.

As Santayana once observed, "Those who cannot remember the past are condemned to repeat it" (Santayana 1905). Observe and learn from others and, as you build your knowledge, make it known to others. You can then be part of building a more effective software engineering discipline. The power of science comes from the accumulating wealth of knowledge. Take advantage of what you find and contribute what you have learned.

Find and Learn New Methods

This book has introduced a number of methods and techniques, but they are only examples. Many tools and methods are now available and new ones are constantly being developed. You cannot learn everything, but you can watch for innovations that are pertinent to your personal needs. Keep a list and select those that are most important to you now. Allocate time for skill-building and spend a few hours each week learning something new. If you do this consistently, you will learn the equivalent of one graduate course per year. With the current pace of technology, this is the bare minimum needed to keep up.

The rate of technical change is accelerating and new tools and methods are being developed faster than ever before. Although there is a vast amount of literature to monitor, many tools are available to help us. Most libraries will run keyword searches and provide lists of pertinent articles. The Internet is a vast storehouse of potentially useful information. Think of it this way: Suppose you had a serious medical problem and wanted a competent doctor. Would you pick one who never cracked a journal or attended a conference? Or would you seek a skilled person who regularly updates his or her skills? When you trust your life to someone, you want them to behave professionally.

Your professional life is no different. Should you entrust it to someone who is out-of-date? If you were looking for career guidance, would you ask someone who had not studied a technical book since college? Probably not. The skill, knowledge, and ability you bring to your job will determine your future. Your future is in your hands.

14.11   Your Future in Software Engineering

As you look to the future, you will face many questions. How will your field evolve and what can you do to meet the mounting challenges? Although no one can know the future, your progress will likely be limited by your ability to build personal skill. Make practice a part of every project, and measure and observe your own work. Since you cannot stand still, treat every project as a way to build talent, rather than merely treating your talent as a way to build projects.

Deciding what you want from your chosen field is like asking what you want from life. Surprisingly often, people achieve their objectives, but in ways they did not expect. Life rarely turns out the way we plan. Although our carefully developed strategies may go down in flames, a new and more rewarding opportunity often shows up in the ashes. The key is to keep an open mind and to keep looking. In life, we all reach the same end, so we need to concentrate on the trip. Just as with a process, once you decide how you want to live, the rest will follow. Devote yourself to excellence and you just might achieve it. That would be worth the trip.

References

Davis, N., and J. Mullaney. "Team Software Process (TSP) in Practice." SEI Technical Report CMU/SEI-2003-TR-014, September 2003.

Dyer, J. L. "Team Research and Team Training: A State-of-the-Art Review." *Human Factors Review* (1984): 286, 309.

Humphrey, W. S. *Winning with Software: An Executive Strategy.* Boston: Addison-Wesley, 2002.

Linberg, K. R. "Software Developer Perceptions about Software Project Failure: A Case Study." *Journal of Systems and Software* 49 (1999): 177–192.

Martin, D. *Team Think: Using the Sports Connection to Develop, Motivate and Manage a Winning Business Team.* New York: Dutton, 1993.

Santayana, G. *The Life of Reason.* (1905). (Reprinted by Dover Publications, 1982, p. 284.)

Standish Group. "CHAOS: A Recipe for Success." Dennis, MA: The Standish Group International, Inc., 1999. www.standishgroup.com.

INDEX

After PSP,^{SM} there's TSP^{SM}

Your next step in software process improvement

The Team Software Process (TSP) provides software engineers and project managers with a proven framework designed to help your organization build and maintain more effective teams. This book, particularly useful for those trained in the PSP, introduces the TSP and the concrete steps needed to improve software teamwork.

ISBN 020147719X • Hardcover • 496 Pages

The SEI Series in Software Engineering

ISBN 0-321-18613-3

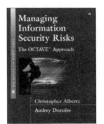

ISBN 0-321-11886-3

ISBN 0-201-73723-X

ISBN 0-321-15495-9

ISBN 0-201-54664-7

ISBN 0-321-15496-7

ISBN 0-201-70372-6

ISBN 0-201-70482-X

ISBN 0-201-70332-7

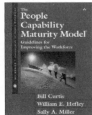

ISBN 0-201-60445-0

ISBN 0-201-60444-2

ISBN 0-201-52577-1

ISBN 0-201-25592-8

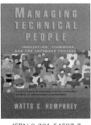

ISBN 0-201-54597-7

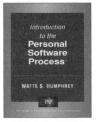

ISBN 0-201-54809-7

ISBN 0-201-18095-2

ISBN 0-201-54610-8

ISBN 0-201-47719-X

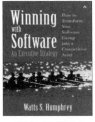

ISBN 0-201-77639-1

ISBN 0-201-61626-2

ISBN 0-201-70454-4

ISBN 0-201-73409-5

ISBN 0-201-85480-5

ISBN 0-321-11884-7

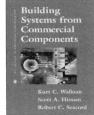

ISBN 0-201-70064-6

Please see our Web site at http://www.awprofessional.com for more information on these titles.

Terms Introduced with PSP1 (continued)

Linear Regression	
Linear Regression Parameters	$$\beta_1 = \frac{\sum_{i=1}^{n} x_i y_i - n x_{avg} y_{avg}}{\sum_{i=1}^{n} x_i^2 - n\left(x_{avg}\right)^2}$$ $$\beta_0 = y_{avg} - \beta_1 x_{avg}$$
x_i, x_{avg}	For size and time estimates, the estimated proxy size (E) for each previously developed program and the average of these values
y_i, y_{avg}	For size estimates, the actual size (A&M) of each previously developed program and the average of these values; for time estimates, the actual total time spent developing each previously developed program and the average of these values
Range	$$Range = t(p, n-2)\sigma \sqrt{1 + \frac{1}{n} + \frac{\left(x_k - x_{avg}\right)^2}{\sum_{i=1}^{n}\left(x_i - x_{avg}\right)^2}}$$
Variance	$$Variance = \sigma^2 = \left(\frac{1}{n-2}\right)\sum_{i=1}^{n}\left(y_i - \beta_0 - \beta_1 x_i\right)^2$$
x_k	For size and time estimates, the estimated proxy size (E) for the new program
$t(p, n-2)$	The value of t that, with $d = n-2$ degrees of freedom, gives a value of p for the integral of the t distribution from ∞ to t
p	The probability value of the t distribution. For the range calculations, p is typically 0.7 (for 70%) or 0.9 (for 90%).
d, n	The degrees of freedom (d) is a measure of the number of independent variables in a relationship. For the range calculations, $d = n-2$, where n is the number of values in the data set used for the β calculations.
Standard Deviation	$Standard\ Deviation = \sqrt{Variance} = \sigma$

Terms Introduced with PSP1.1

PSP1.1 Project Plan Summary	
Cost Performance Index	CPI = planned total development time to date divided by Time in Phase, Total To Date
% Reused	The percentage of total program size taken from the reuse library
% New Reusable	The percentage of the added and modified size planned for addition to the reuse library

Task and Schedule Planning Templates	
Planned Value	The percentage of total planned project time that the planned task represents
Cumulative Planned Value	The running cumulative sum of the planned values
Earned Value	The planned value of a task is earned when the task is completed. There is no partial credit for partially completed tasks.

(continued)